Contents

DANMARK

Målestok 1 : 1.500.000

0 10 20 30 40 50 km

1

Legend

- Over 1.000.000 indb.
- 100.000-1.000.000 indb.
- 50.000-100.000 indb.
- 25.000-50.000 indb.
- 10.000-25.000 indb.
- 5.000-10.000 indb.
- Under 5.000 indb.

- Hovedvej
- Motorvej
- Personjernbane
- Færgerute
- Bro
- Fyr og fyrskib
- +126 Højde over havet i meter
- Rigsgrænse
- Lufthavn

8°   9°   10° ø.f. Greenwich   11°   12°

Skagerrak
Skagens Rev
Grenen
Skagen
GÖTEBORG
BORÅS

Råbjerg Mile
Tannis Bugt   41°   Ålbæk
Hirtshals   Bugt
Hirsholmene

Simdal
Lønstrup
Hjørring   Tårs
Løkken   Frederikshavn
Nordre Rønner
Sæby

Vendsyssel
Jammerbugt
Blokhus   Brønderslev
Store   Læsø   Læsø
Vildmose   Rende
136°   Knesen
Kobbergrund
Varberg

SVERIGE

Skarreklit
Svinkløv   63
Bulbjerg
Hanstholm
Klitmøller   Fjerritslev
ÅLBORG
Nibe   Limfjorden
Thisted   Lim-   Aggersund   Løgstør
Thy   fjorden   Lille   Muldbjerge
Livø   Vildmose 48
Bredning
Fur
Nykøbing M.   Års   Rebild
Mors   114
Hadsund
Thyborøn Kanal   Thyborøn
Nissum   Salling   Mariager Fjord
Bredning   Hobro   Manager
Odde sund   Vena   Skals Å   Randers Fjord
Lemvig   41   Skive
Bovbjerg   Skive Å   Randers   Fornæs
Struer   Grenå
Nissum   Viborg   Djursland
Fjord   Holstebro   Bjerringbro   Gudenå
Store   Karup   Skelhøje   Testrup
Jylland   Hadsten   Kalø   Mols
Ringkøbing   Herning   Ikast   Silkeborg   137   Ebeltoft
Himmelbjerget   147   Hjelm
Strøm   95   162   Mossø   Skanderborg
Hvide Sande   Momhøj   ÅRHUS
Holmsland   Fjord   Skjern   Silken Å   Brande   Yding Skovhøj   Odder   Helgenæs
Klit   172   Em Bavnehøj   Tuno
Tippere   Tarm   Omme Å   Ejstrupholm   Horsens   Hou   Samsø
Blåbjerg   64   Grindsted   Skive   Jelling   Horsens
Varde   Billund   Fjord   Hjelmsminde   Endelave
Blåvands   Skallingen   Varde Å   Vejle   Helnæs
Huk   Bramming   Kolding   Munkebjerg Vejle Fjord   Æbelø
Horns Rev   Esbjerg   Vejen   113   Bogense
Fanø   Kongeå   Middelfart   Fredericia
Ribe   Ribe Å   Gram   Skamlingsbanke
Mandø   Vojens   Haderslev   Assens

Kattegat

Halland
Falkenberg

Anholt
Halmstad

Hallands
Vaderø
Skälderviken
Kullen
Høganäs
Angelho

Lysegrund
Hessela
Gilleleje   Hornbæk
HELSINGBOR
Helsinge   Esrum Sø
Helsingør
Frederiksværk   Aresø   Hillerød
Hundested   Nykøbing S.   Slangerup   Hørsholm
Sjællands   Isefjord   Frederiks-   Birkerød
Odde   Ods-   sund   Ølstykke
Sejerø Bugt   herred   Farum   Øresund
Sejerø   Holbæk   Horns-   Landskrona
Rosnæs   Nekselø   herred
Kalundborg   Roskilde   KØBENHAVN
Asnæs   Saltholm
Tisso   Halleb Å   Gyldenløves   Dragør   MALMÖ
Hong   Ramsø   Køge   Amager
Sjælland   Køge
Slagelse   Ringsted   Bugt
Storebælt   Sorø   Hasley   Stevns
Korsør   Tystrup   Store   Stevns
Sprogø   Sø   Heddinge   Klint
Nyborg   Agersø   Skælskør   Næstved   Fakse
ODENSE   Omø   Glæno   123   Fakse Ladeplads
Ringe   Gavno   Fakse Bugt
Fyn   Svinninge Bakker   120   Præstø
120   Lohals   Vordingborg
Fåborg   Smålandsfarvandet
Svendborg   Vejrø   Aborrebjerg   Mons
Fynshav   Thurø   Femø   143   Klint
Dreja   Budkøbing   Stubbekøbing   Stege   Møn
Lye   Avernakø   Askø   Grønsund
Ærøskøbing   Marstal   Nakskov   Sakskøbing
Langeland   Lolland   Maribo   Nykøbing F.
Bagenkop   Rødby   Nysted   Falster
Guldborg
Gedser   Sund

Schleswig-Holstein
Angeln
Flensborg
Gelting
Føhr
Amrum
Nordfriesland
Pellworm   Nordstrand
Husum
TYSKLAND
Eiderstedt   Friedrichstadt
Tönning   Eiderstedt
Rendsburg   KIEL
Eckernførde   Eckernførde Bugt
Schleswig   Idstedt (Isted)
Kieler Bugt
Fehmarn
 Femer Bælt
Rødbyhavn
Puttgarden

Øster   Søen

Erthofmene
Allinge-   Christiansø
Sandvig
Hammeren   Gudhjem
Rytterknægten   Svaneke
162   Åkirkeby
Rønne   Neksø
Bornholm   Dueodde
55°
Østersøen   15°

Nordsøen

Havdybde -30 -10 0   0 10 40 80 120 meter Højde
Tørt ved lavvande   Land under havets overflade
© WN Atlas Productions

Preface

"Greater than Lesser"
Glimpses of Life in Denmark

With just 43,100 km² of land and a population of just over 5 million, Denmark definitely qualifies for a place in the league of small nations of the world - and the EC.

The Danes can look back at a very chequered past. The country has had much wider borders, to the north and south as well as east and west. England was part of Denmark 1000 years ago, Estonia in the 13th century, Norway and Denmark were a dual monarchy for nearly 500 years until 1814, and in the south the duchies of Schleswig and Holstein belonged to Denmark until 1864. Iceland was linked to Denmark by Act of Union until 1944.

With the surrender of Schleswig Holstein to Prussia in 1864 a third of Danish territory was lost. Along with the inferiority complex this engendered, the will to "win inwardly, that which outwardly is lost" was born. This will has become a quintessential trait of the Danes, who now occupy a small, homogenous nation state.

The physical location of Denmark, between the North Sea and the Baltic and between the European continent and the Scandinavian peninsula, has meant that the country has always been at the heart of a busy crossroads, dependent on the world around it and open to external influences.

Between 1864 and 1940 the country sought to retain its neutrality. But since 1945, Denmark has made an active commitment to international cooperation, in organisations such as NATO, The European Council, The European Community etc. At the same time the Scandinavian connection has been maintained through the Nordic Council and other bodies.

Most foreign visitors will find a lot of things in Denmark quite familiar. Things 'typically Danish' may have developed in the course of interaction with other countries, but the practical form they have assumed is Danish.

Which is why we believe that it is worthwhile exploring a small country, which is different without being completely strange. Which is "Greater than it is Lesser" as the poet Piet Hein put it.

This book provides an opportunity for people from the world around us to embark on an exploration of our compact little Danish society. We invite you to identify areas of similarity and contrast.

This is not a systematic handbook or textbook. The book will provide you with some glimpses of how the Danes organise their society and their lives. The bibliography at the end of the book provides further references for those who wish to explore a subject in greater detail.

The Danish way of life harbours a sense of respect for the individual. The Danish democratic social system is based on liberty, equality, care and responsibility. The Danes are regarded as informal, unpretentious, ironic and anti-authoritarian. They are individualists, but united by a multiplicity of fellowships. They are regarded both as conformists and as 'anarchists'.

We wish to extend our grateful thanks to the Foundation for International Understanding, without whose economic support it would not have been possible to fulfil the many requests for this publication, providing broad and basic, if not elementary, information about Danish society. And we also extend thanks to the many Danes who have advised us on the selection of the themes for this book.

Per Himmelstrup
Secretary-General
The Danish Cultural Institute

Denmark and the Danes

by Helle Askgaard

As Denmark Sees Herself and is Seen by Others

"One day all Nordic lands were in your power
And England too - no longer your domains
A tiny land, but in the world you tower -
There ring the song and chisel of the Danes."
(trans. Paula Hostrup-Jessen. 1988)

A declaration of love to his native land, written by the fairy-tale writer Hans Christian Andersen over one hundred years ago.

A tiny country - and yet so big. Denmark has left its mark on the world stage. We are proud of our own Hans Christian Andersen, of the writer Karen Blixen, of the Danish engineers who helped to con-

You can still see half-timbered houses in Danmark. Front of a house in Ærøskøbing. Photo: Ærøskøbing Turistforening.

struct the Chinese telegraph system, of the nuclear physicist Niels Bohr and of Johan Otto von Spreckelsen, the architect of the cube-like modern counterpart to the Arc de Triomphe, called Tête Défense, in Paris.

But bragging loudly about our achievements is not a Danish characteristic. The Norwegian-Danish writer Aksel Sandemose captured the Danish mores in his notorious "Jantelov" (Jante's Law) of which the first principle is "Du skal ikke tro, du er noget" (Thou shalt not believe that thou art something). H.M. Queen Margrethe II described this trait in one of her New Year's speeches to the nation: "We are very proud of our modesty. It is our inverted megalomania. It is highly sophisticated".

On the other hand, our foreign visitors remark on our incredible delight at all things Danish. We sing about them: the Danish language, the Danish coast, the Danish forest. Even mineral water is called "dansk vand"(Danish water) here. Christmas is also very Danish. We hang our national flag (the Dannebrog) on our Christmas trees, and on festive occasions we eat almond cakes decorated with these flags.

Tourists regard the Danes as an obliging and helpful people, but very few get a chance to meet the Danes in their homes. Foreigners feel that it is difficult to penetrate the smiling facade of the Danes.

The image presented to the tourist who studies the colourful promotional brochures is one of a fairy-tale country:

We are the oldest kingdom in the world, a peaceful country, where the farmers still live in half-timbered houses, and the fishermen haul their boats onto the beaches. The water is clean, and white sand covers miles and miles of beaches. Many of our towns are old and full of atmosphere and interesting experiences, and the forests are quiet and peaceful.

There *are* half-timbered houses in Denmark, and there *are* still some fishermen, who haul their boats onto the beaches. But the majority of farmers live in modern houses and most of the fish are netted by a modern fleet of trawlers. In Denmark the majority of people are employed in the service sector, and the manufacturing industries comprise the second largest economic sector.

Location

Denmark is located on the periphery of the European continent, but also provides a bridging link to the rest of Scandinavia. The Danish economy, politics and culture are affiliated to both regions, but linguistically we still find it easiest to communicate with the Scandinavian countries.

Denmark's current borders date back to 1920, when part of Southern Jutland was returned to the Kingdom from Germany as a result of a referendum in the area. The country covers 43,100 square

kms and there are 5.1 million inhabitants.

Greenland, the largest island in the world, and the Faroes, a small group of North Atlantic islands, are also part of Denmark.

The Geography

Denmark consists of the peninsula of Jutland and 527 islands. The visitor will come across a variety of scenery when crossing the country from west to east. Even though mankind has put considerable effort into harnessing nature to his own ends over the last 5,000 years, the main geographical features left by the receding ice-age are still evident.

Sandy beaches and dunes extend along most of the west coast of Jutland. But the dunes soon give way to the flat, sandy countryside of western Jutland. By contrast, eastern Jutland and many of the islands are characterised by more fertile soil and undulating countryside formed

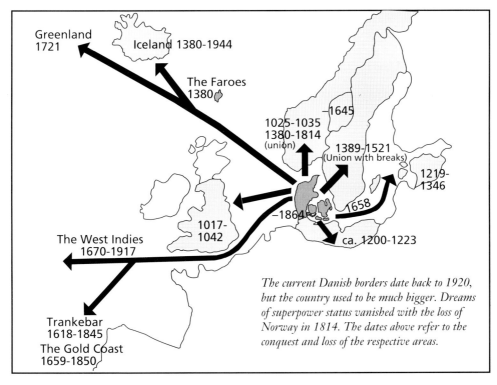

Greenland
1721

Iceland 1380-1944

The Faroes
1380

1025-1035
1380-1814
(union)

1645

1389-1521
(Union with breaks)

1219-
1346

1658

The West Indies
1670-1917

1017-
1042

1864

ca. 1200-1223

Trankebar
1618-1845

The Gold Coast
1659-1850

The current Danish borders date back to 1920, but the country used to be much bigger. Dreams of superpower status vanished with the loss of Norway in 1814. The dates above refer to the conquest and loss of the respective areas.

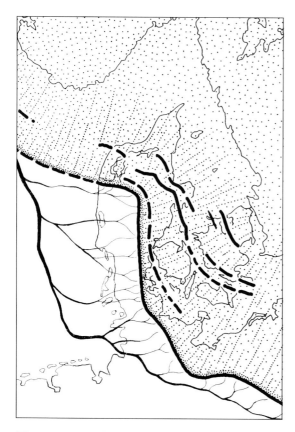

The maximum ice limit. The countryside to the north-east of the line is quite undulating, whilst west of the line it is flatter and sandier.

morainic hills, deposited when the ice receded. These hills seem strenuous enough if the traveller is on a bicycle, but foreigners tend to smile disparagingly when they are told that Denmark's highest hill, the "Ejer Baunehøj", is only 173 m above sea level.

The coastal areas are largely flat plains, where the sea bed has risen, or sandy stretches and dunes formed by marine deposits and the ravages of wind and water. In the south-western part of Jutland there are marshlands, similar to those in The Netherlands and Germany.

The sea continues to eat away at the west coast of Jutland, and the coastline is constantly changing.

Transportation

Denmark is thus a typical morainic archipelago. Its long coastline and its 527 islands, of which 86 are currently inhabited, have always been ideal for the development of sea transportation and fishing. Even though the construction of the railway network at the end of the 19th century reduced transportation times across the country, it was still necessary to sail across the Storebælt (The Great Belt) and the Lillebælt (The Little Belt) on a journey from Copenhagen to Esbjerg or another town in Jutland. Major bridge-building projects were not initiated until after the First World War, when motor cars became increasingly important. The bridge over the Little Belt was completed in 1935.

An 8 km long suspension bridge, the longest in Europe, is currently under construction as part of the land link across the Great Belt. A complementary tunnel is being constructed for rail traffic. A combined road and rail bridge will cover the rest of the route, giving a total combined bridge length of 18 km. It is hoped that this link will be completed by 1996.

by glacial deposits.

West Jutland is the oldest land mass. It consists of glacial deposits from the last but one ice-age and of moorland plains left by the last ice-age. The ice extended as far as central Jutland (the maximum ice limit) and during the last ice-age the soil in West Jutland bore no vegetation, which resulted in some leaching. The ice reached its maximum extension about 18,000 years ago. And when it started to recede the lowest lying areas were flooded by vast glacial rivers, and the moorland outwash plains were formed by the glacial deposits from these rivers.

The countryside to the north and east of the maximum ice limit is notable for its

The sandy beach on the west coast of Jutland (left). Hill island and heathland plains in West Jutland (right). Beechwood in Central Jutland (below).

Land Use

Were it not for human intervention, the country would be covered by woodland. But it is several hundred years since the last primeval forest vanished. The forests were cleared to provide land for cultivation or grazing, or as a source of fuel and building materials. By the beginning of the 19th century only 3% of the land was still woodland. The introduction of a forest preservation order secured the preservation of the last remaining woodland areas. There have been numerous new afforestation projects, which frequently assumed the fervour of a national cause. 12% of the land area in Denmark is now covered by forest, of which two-thirds is coniferous.

Agricultural land dominates the countryside, and nearly all of it is intensively cultivated. The great stretches of heathland, coastal meadows, commons and bogs, which still dominated the scenery in the early 19th century, have all but disappeared, due to extensive drainage and soil improvement projects. These areas were chiefly in Jutland, where they have now been replaced by homogenous fields or intensive animal husbandry. This intensive cultivation, which includes the incorporation of riverside meadows, the use of artificial fertilisers and pesticides as well as huge quantities of animal manures, is creating environmental problems in these areas of light sandy soil.

In the old days it was the prevailing west wind, the distribution of rainfall and the composition of the soil which largely determined what the farmers could cultivate, but nowadays their production is based on the application of technology, ownership, global market prices and the EC agricultural policy!

The Population

Denmark was one of the first European

Constitution and Administration

Denmark is a constitutional monarchy, with the right of succession secured by the Constitution, last revised in 1953. Constitution Day is celebrated on 5th June when political speeches are held all over the country. To enable the public to attend these rallies, the afternoon is a public holiday.

The legislative authority is vested in the sovereign and the Folketing (the Danish Parliament) conjointly. Denmark has had a female monarch since 1972; Her Majesty Queen Margrethe II.

The Executive authority is formally vested with the sovereign, but it is exercised through her ministers in the Folketing. Judicial authority is vested solely with the Judiciary.

The Danish political system is a multi-party system based on proportional representation. At the last elections in 1990, eight parties passed the 2% threshhold and thus qualified for seats in the Folketing. Minority coalition governments tend to be the rule in Denmark. The Folketing is elected for a period of four years, and has 179 members, including two for each of the Faroes and Greenland. There is universal suffrage for all Danish nationals over the age of 18, who are permanently resident in Denmark and have not been disfranchised.

The country is administratively subdivided into 14 counties. The metropolitan municipalities of Copenhagen and Frederiksberg also have county status. The counties are further subdivided into 275 municipalities, to which a considerable degree of self-government has been devolved.

countries to take a census (1769), and the result was regarded as a military secret. When the archives were opened some decades later, it was revealed that 797,584 people had resided within the modern boundaries of Denmark. Further censuses were taken in 1787 and 1801, and after 1834 the population was counted every 5th or 10th year until 1970, since when this form of registration has been considered obsolete. Registration on computer databases now ensures that up-to-date figures can always be produced.

The evolution of society from an agricultural to an industrial society started around 1840. Although the death rate had already started dropping at the end of the 18th century, the birth rate did not start to fall until a century later.

Many immigrants have opened ethnic restaurants or greengrocer shops. "Little Istanbul" on Vesterbro in Copenhagen. Photo: Søren Rud/ Alfa Foto.

In the 19th century the vast majority of the population lived in rural areas, but only a few of these were able to support the growing population. For instance the region of Lolland-Falster was dominated by large estates, so there were few prospects for young men who dreamed of owning their own farm. Some migrated into the cities to try their luck in the newly emerging industrial sector, whilst others emigrated to America.

The migratory balance was negative until 1958, except during the First World War and the 1930s. But since 1958 increased immigration has effectively stabilised the Danish population at 5.1 million.

The debates on television, in the newspapers and the Folketing sometimes create the impression that foreign nationals constitute a large proportion of the inhabitants of Denmark. But this is not so.

Even though some districts of Copenhagen and a few other municipalities have large foreign communities, the total number of resident immigrants, guest workers and refugees only constitutes 2.9% of the population. The highest concentration of foreigners is found in the Copenhagen suburb of Ishøj, where they constitute 12% of the residents. The largest single group of foreigners are the Turks, followed by Norwegians, Brits, Yugoslavs, Germans and Swedes.

Foreign Nationals living in Denmark, according to nationality

Nationality	1972	1980	1990
Turkey	6,252	14,086	27,929
Norway	*	10,030	10,175
Great Britain	4,691	9,361	9,983
Yugoslavia	5,500	7,126	9,535
West Germany	9,436	8,700	8,092
Sweden	*	7,726	8,047
Iran	–	215	8,362
Total Foreign Nationals	54,119**	99,796	150,644

* n/a. ** Not including Scandinavian countries

For the last ten years the total number of foreign nationals from other Scandinavian and EC countries has remained constant

13

at about 47,000. Denmark's entry into the EC in 1973 was thus not followed by any notable increase in numbers from EC countries.

The Age Structure of the Population

Prams are almost a rare sight nowadays. Women give birth to an average of 1.4 children. But nearly all babies are planned, and this trend towards fewer children has been growing for the last hundred years, starting in the towns and then spreading to the rural areas.

Abortion has been freely available since 1973. The number of abortions peaked at nearly 28,000 in 1975 and then started to drop. Since 1983 the number has been fairly constant at around 20,000. In the 1980s the number of live births averaged between 50,000 and 61,000 per year,

rising to 64,000 in 1991.

Many women postpone their first pregnancy and have two children at the most. An increasing number of women choose to remain childless.

There are several reasons for this low birth rate. The female labour market participation is the highest in Europe. The majority of women complete some form of further or higher education and wish to use their qualifications, even after they are married and have children.

But what about the children? Granny is usually at work herself, or otherwise too old to look after children. And Granddad never learned how to. By international standards, the provision of child-care facilities in Denmark is excellent, but the cost is a major burden on the budget of a young family.

Denmark has become a country of

Denmark is becoming a nation of pensioners. Elderly couple on the ferry to Sweden. Photo: Søren Madsen/ Alfa Foto.

middle-aged people, heading for retirement. Men can look forward to a life expectancy of 71 years, women some six years more.

The Geographical Distribution of the Population

The population density in Denmark is much higher than in the other Scandinavian countries. In Denmark there are 119 people per km², whereas there are only 15 people per km² in Finland, 2 in Iceland, 13 in Norway and 19 in Sweden.

But the distribution of the population is uneven. One third of the total live in the Greater Copenhagen area.

The Danish population has never been evenly distributed. For several centuries the most densely populated areas have been the eastern parts of Jutland and the islands, which were the regions with the best agricultural conditions. The density is particularly high in East and North Zealand. On the other hand, the Jutland interior was practically uninhabited until about 100 years ago, when the reclamation of the large heathland areas began, in an attempt to provide new areas for cultivation to feed the growing population.

The expansion of the transport network, with road improvements and the construction of the railways, also encouraged a population spread.

Two hundred years ago 80% of the population lived in the country; one hundred years ago it was down to two thirds; but today it is only about 15%. However only 6% of the population are actively engaged in agriculture.

The Danish Level of Education

All children in Denmark can read and write. Compulsory education was introduced as early as 1814. Education has always been free, and even private schools run along special ideological or religious lines are eligible for state subsidies. Nowadays the length of compulsory primary education is 9 years. In the 19th century the ideas of the poet-priest N.F.S. Grundtvig (1783-1872) for "folkeoplysning" (a translation of this word as 'informal liberal education, enlightenment and cultural activities' provides only an approximate interpretation of a national concept which is impossible to translate!) caught on all over the land, and numerous folk high schools offering these courses were established. No examinations were held here and each one had its own particular flavour; religious or ideological. These schools still exist and still cater for all ages and social groups.

City workers were offered further education through the journals and courses provided by their trade unions. The level of union participation in Denmark is one of the highest in the world and the trade union movement has always been closely affiliated to social democracy. The Grundtvigian philosophy of "folkeoplysning" and the social democratic policies of equal access to education continue to dominate the educational system.

The educational level of the population has provided an excellent foundation for the creation of the modern welfare society.

Urbanisation

Before the country became industrialised, the borderline between town and country was very distinct.

The towns were market towns with a monopoly on commerce and the trades. Outside the towns agriculture was practically the sole occupation, and the people lived in small villages or isolated in the countryside.

The main destination for people leaving farming after 1840 was the market town. Many harbour towns were able to expand

15

their capacity when the introduction of steamships made greater harbour depth and longer quaysides necessary.

Copenhagen also experienced some growth, but its development accelerated sharply in the twenty year period following 1870, when the population grew by 3% per annum. The city of Copenhagen and the market towns continued to grow after the turn of the century.

With the development of the railway network and the concentration of agricultural production on bacon and butter which began in the 1880s, a new type of town, called 'Station Town' sprung up along the railway lines. Even though the railway may now have been discontinued and the station building put to some other use, the name still sticks.

Copenhagen is by far the largest town and between 1/4 and 1/3 of the population (depending on the administrative breakdown used) live in the Greater Copenhagen area. The regional centres of Århus, Odense and Aalborg are towns with approximately 200,000 inhabitants each.

The type of town which has experienced the most growth in the last 15 years is the small town with populations of between 1,000 and 9,999.

Decentralisation of industry continued during the 1970s, and the level of public services improved considerably throughout the country. This increase in public sector investment helped to deter further migration from the small rural communities, even though job losses in the agricultural sector continued. The coastal areas and the small islands have had the least success in maintaining their communities.

Copenhagen

Not many people who stroll through the Tivoli Gardens in Copenhagen are aware of the fact that this remarkable ambiance has been created on an erstwhile military site. The Tivoli lake was originally part of the moat in the city's fortifications. The military requirements for the defence of the city meant that the town was locked in within the ramparts until 1852.

When the go-ahead was given for the expansion of the city beyond these limits, construction began all along the main exit roads without much deference to the concerns of town planning or quality. Many of the building projects at the end of the 19th century were purely speculative, and have largely been demolished in recent years. The densely packed residential blocks have been replaced by more open and airy projects, but there is still a shortage of green areas in many parts of the municipality of Copenhagen.

It was not until the 1940s that the need for a town plan became so pressing that it was possible to raise political support for one. The plan, called "The Finger Plan", was presented in 1947 (see fig. p.57).

A number of assumptions on which the plan was based proved to be mistaken. The population of the municipality of Copenhagen was beginning to shrink. More and more people wanted to live outside the city in green surroundings, and an emerging affluence made this dream possible for many of them. Two prerequisites for this move were car ownership, which became widespread after 1958, and cheap oil prices. Commuting to work by car became popular, and the population in the city fell, whilst it rose in the suburban municipalities.

Today the suburban municipalities are shrinking too. The population base is being undermined by the break-up of households due to divorces, to the many single households, young people leaving home at an early age, and the falling birth rate. People also now expect more living

Copenhagen is still the town of the beautiful spires. Photo: Søren Rud/Alfa Foto.

space per person. Today the municipalities experiencing growth are those some 30 km from the centre of Copenhagen.

But "The City with the beautiful Spires", as it is described in the tourist brochures, is still there. And even though a few concrete skyscrapers have been built, the city's skyline is largely the same as fifty years ago.

Agriculture in Denmark

"Horses, pigs, cows and sheep, on our farm we do keep". These are the words of a Danish nursery rhyme - but this is all ancient history now.

In Denmark, unlike many other western countries, agriculture used to be one the country's most important industries, both from an employment and an economic point of view. Then in the 1930s employment in the secondary industries overtook that of the primary industries. By the 1950s the manufacturing industries' proportion of the GNP was larger than that of agriculture, and finally in the 1960s Danish agricultural exports were overtaken by industrial exports.

The agricultural acreage and the number of farms in Denmark peaked around 1930. Since then the number of farms has fallen from 210,000 to 77,000 in 1990. But the various categories of farms have experienced differents rates of decline.

The number of smallholdings (under 5 hectares) began to drop in the 1930s, whilst the number of farms between 5 to 30 hectares remained constant until the 1960s.

For most of the 20th century, agricultural legislation sought to safeguard as many independent farms as possible, and it was not until the 1960s that the amalgamation of farms was allowed. A compulsory residential order was imposed on owners, who were also required to demonstrate a degree of practical agricultural

17

expertise. Both these measures were designed to prevent speculative purchases. After 1973 the EC directives on amalgamations were incorporated into Danish agricultural legislation.

Farms of 30 to 60 hectares and over 60 hectares are now the most popular sizes. In 1970 the average farm size was 21 hectares. By 1990 it was 36 hectares. Nearly all farms are owner-occupied.

As the farming population is becoming older, the average age of farmers now being 52 years, and the number of properties on the market is increasing, the regulations regarding the purchase of agricultural land have recently been relaxed.

A consequence of the drop in the number of working farms and the increasing specialisation and modernisation of farming is a further drop in the number of people employed in agriculture. Hired hands are few and far between and nearly all farms are family enterprises.

Whereas a family-run farm in the 1930s implied the work of the husband, wife, children, farm-hand and maid, nowadays the farm may not even provide a full-time job for its owner, who may be forced to supplement his income by taking paid employment in town.

Mixed farming is too labour intensive for the small work force left in the industry. Apart from which, the introduction of technology has encouraged increased specialisation. Economies of scale must be exploited in order to make the acquisition of modern production facilities such as modern pig pens and automatic muck-clearing equipment financially viable. In other cases the technical requirements for product processing may necessitate a concentration of effort.

Agricultural Specialisation

Animal husbandry, both cattle and pigs, has moved to the west of the country.

Farms with no livestock are now concentrated on the islands.

The cattle stock has remained fairly constant, but there are now more calves and fewer dairy cows. Exports to the EC countries ran into problems during the 1960s and the consequent reduction of cattle herds was particularly drastic on the islands.

Milk yields per cow have improved dramatically, so overall milk production levels have increased despite the reduction in the number of cows. Dairy cows now yield an average of 6,200 kilos of milk per yield, and premium cows produce up to 10,000 kilos, so further reductions in the herds will not necessarily mean less milk.

The pig population has increased tenfold since the 1940s, and slaughter-house activity has increased by 1500%.

The increase in pig production is partially due to the many restrictions imposed on dairy production and cattle breeding, which encouraged young farmers to concentrate on pig breeding.

Refined breeding techniques, including closed herds and the use of SPF pigs, have produced a race which is more fertile and resistant to disease.

Nowadays pig production is concentrated in fewer but larger farms. Production has been redistributed to those areas of the country where the most modern slaughterhouses are located. There is now an increasing awareness of the dangers of the pollution of the ground water if there is an imbalance between the size of the pig production and the size of the overall acreage of the farm.

Grain crops are still the most common kind of crop grown, but compared to one hundred years ago, the distribution of crops has been radically altered.

Increased awareness of ecological problems has forced stricter supervision of individual farms by the authorities. All

Over the last decades there has been a dramatic increase in pig production, largely due to improved breeding techniques and operational rationalisation. Photo: Sonja Ilskov / 2. maj.

farms over 10 hectares in size have to submit their annual seed rotation and fertilisation plans to the Ministry of Agriculture for approval.

The plans have to demonstrate that at least 65% of the acreage will be planted with "green fields".

These green fields contribute to the reduction of soil erosion by the wind as well as the leaching of nutrient ions. The sandy soil in West Jutland is most prone to nitrate pollution, which has become an increasing risk as a result of the 'migration' of livestock to the west.

The fertilisation plan must therefore seek to maintain a balance between the quantity of animal manure produced and the land acreage of the farm.

Barley is grown all over the country, but wheat is concentrated in the undulating morainic regions. Wheat is increasingly being used as animal fodder.

Pulses and other seed crops have become more widespread since the EC began to encourage the cultivation of more protein-rich products in 1978. Seed crops and pulses are also on the 'approved' list of green crops.

Consumer taste at home and overseas has also influenced agricultural production. The modern pig is leaner, and butter production has fallen whilst cheese production has increased four-fold. This last development is partially due to the massive demand for Feta cheese from the Middle East.

There are still horses, pigs, cows and sheep on the Danish farms, but only one kind of animal on each! And the horse is no longer a working animal, but most probably a riding horse for the farmer's daughter. Agricultural specialisation has also altered the scenery of the countryside. Where previously a wealth of col- **19** ours from the variety of crops would meet the eye, the pattern nowadays tends to produce a more uniform picture.

Fisheries

A Danish lunch always starts with a herring dish. On festive occasions at least three different kinds are served, and a good housewife will have her own special recipe.

For centuries fishing was the main industry along the west coast of Jutland. Where the villages had no natural harbours, the boats were launched from the beaches, though from the end of the last century winches were used to heave the boats back and forth from the water.

Around the turn of the century special installations for the fishing industry were constructed in many ports. But with the advent of larger boats and increased technical specifications for the processing of the catch (cold-storage capacity, auction halls, fast onward transportation etc) the fishing industry has become concentrated on a few centres. The advanced safety facilities provided by the modern fishing ports has also contributed to the depopulation of some of the old fishing villages. The main centres of the fishing industry today are Esbjerg, Hirtshals, Thyborøn, Skagen and Hanstholm. 85% of the Danish catch is landed in these ports, corresponding to 55% of the total value. Many foreign cutters also land their catches here.

Before 1950 the fishing industry was geared towards seine-fishing for plaice, although herring comprised the largest quantities until the 1960s. But overfishing and environmental problems have depleted the stocks, and cod is now the number one catch, both in terms of quantity and income.

The tonnage rose dramatically in the 1960s and 1970s, due to the increased efficiency of the modern cutters. However since 1984 the industry has been restricted by the EEC quotas, and the tonnages have been subject to a downward trend. Nevertheless the Danish fishing industry still accounts for over 50% of the total EC fishing of the North Sea.

Most of the fish landed are destined for industrial use (80%) whilst the rest is marketed for human consumption. Fishmeal and fish oil are the main products in terms of quantity, whilst fillets of fish are the most profitable.

In 1988 approx. 7,000 people were employed in the fishing industry, roughly 50% less than 30 years ago. The number of registered cutters has also dropped, especially the number of small boats under 50 G.R.T. But there has been an increase in large fishing vessels, both in terms of numbers and tonnage.

For a country the size of Denmark, the quantities of fish exported are quite considerable. 5% of Danish exports are fish products, making up over 25% of the total agricultural exports.

Danish Industry

Children and young people are often called "Denmark's raw materials". Whatever one thinks of this description of children, it may be attributed to the fact that Denmark is extremely poorly endowed with the traditional mineral 'raw materials'. The fruitful soil may help to produce agricultural goods for industrial processing, but otherwise there is only some chalk for the production of cement, clay for bricks, and granite for curbstones and gravel. During the harsh years of the two world wars we had to turn to the exploitation of our own peat and lignite for fuel, and since the global energy crisis of 1973 politicians have been pressing for an increase in the production of North Sea oil. But apart from these resources it has been

The food and beverage industry is one of the most important sectors of Danish industry. Interior view of the Tuborg brewery in Hellerup, in the northern suburbs of Copenhagen. Photo: Tuborg.

our education, imagination and commercial talent which has created the Danish manufacturing industry.

The Composition and Structure of Industry

In 1950 there were approx. 300,000 people employed in the manufacturing industries. The sector expanded slowly during the first years of the decade and then very rapidly at the end of the 1950s, after which it continued to grow until 1973, when it peaked at 428,000 employees. These were the years when the products of the 1940s 'Baby Boom' were growing up, bringing an additional 300,000 people into the labour force. The manufacturing industries and the public sector managed to absorb both this new generation as well as the increasing numbers leaving agriculture. But as there was still a shortage of labour the country welcomed immigrants from other Scandinavian countries, from the EC, Yugoslavia, Turkey and Pakistan. The average unemployment rate in the period 1958-72 was 4%, the lowest in the 20th century.

Since 1973 employment in the industrial sector has fallen off slightly, but in recent years it has levelled off at about 390,000 people. The reasons for the drop are complex. One of the causes could be that companies have sought to make traditional products more cheaply rather than develop new ones.

The decline has particularly affected some of the older, established major

21

industries such as factories making paper and cardboard, radios and televisions, cement, tobacco and shipyards. On the other hand smaller enterprises in electronics and engineering, with products such as regulators and automation equipment, have experienced growth. Productivity has increased across the board.

Throughout this century the two most important industrial sectors have been the iron and metals sector and the food and beverages sector. The food industry based its production on Danish raw materials and some of the machinery used to process these was manufactured in Denmark. The development of the metal sector was largely based on the manufacture of machinery for agriculture and the food industry. In the 1980s most growth has been experienced in the chemicals and plastics sector, as well as sub-sectors such as iron and metal constructions, metal packaging, fittings, the electrical industries and measuring equipment. The iron and metals sector is still an absolute as well as a relative growth area.

The employment structure has undergone few changes over the last thirty years. There are a few more management and fewer subordinate jobs. Women do most of the less qualified work.

The structure of industry is characterised by many small and medium-sized enterprises. In Denmark a large company is one with over 500 employees. The average company has 55 employees.

Companies and employees according to size 1989

	No. of companies	No. of employees
6-49 employees	77%	26.8%
50-499 employees	22%	51.8%
500 employees and over	1%	21.4%
Total: average for the year	7,133	384,206

The small and medium-sized companies are able to adapt their production to new circumstances quickly and with the minimum of bureaucracy, but small companies find it difficult to penetrate the large overseas markets. One of the ways to overcome this difficulty is to amalgamate. Surveys of the last six years show that there has been a slight upward trend in mergers and takeovers across the entire industrial sector.

The Location of Industry

Copenhagen was the leading industrial town from the very start of the industrial era. By the end of the 19th century many provincial towns had also developed a lot of industrial activity. Significant levels of activity could not however be maintained in rural areas, despite the fact that for a short period the availability of water power had managed to attract industrial plants.

After the Second World War there was a considerable amount of relocation. Many plants moved from the centre of Copenhagen to the outskirts of the city. Some of them relocated to the so-called "Fingers", and employees found it easy to commute to work once the S-train network was extended along these routes.

Relocation activity accelerated after 1958. Some companies abandoned the Copenhagen area altogether and moved to Jutland, whilst others just moved their labour-intensive departments out of the metropolitan area, leaving some management functions at head office.

Nearly half the country's industry used to be located in the Greater Copenhagen area, but today it is down to roughly 20%.

Industry has moved to the west, and there are only a few smokestacks left in Copenhagen. Most of the centres of modern industry are now in Jutland. The new factories enjoy easy access routes and are not confined by multi-storeyed buildings which make internal transportation difficult. Provincial municipalities have been eager to win a share of this industrial relocation, and have made industrial sites available at cheap rates. The national 'regional development scheme' has also provided assistance by making loans available to established companies wishing to relocate as well as offering loans at favourable rates in the development areas. The relocated and newly established companies have benefited from a plentiful supply of unskilled labour, and these workers have not been 'inhibited' by the trade union traditions, which characterised the Copenhagen and established provincial labour force.

The relocation trend has not significantly affected the total number of jobs in this sector. The importance of industrial production is however far greater than is evident from its percentage share of the work force, which is currently 16%. Many functions which were previously carried out in-house are now contracted from service companies.

The Relationship between Industry and the State

There is no tradition for public ownership of industrial enterprises in Denmark, and there are but very few examples of this practice. Neither is there any tradition for central government or local authorities to bail companies out in cases where whole sectors are in decline. Regardless of whether the government has been right or left wing, the general policy has been to follow the traditional liberal maxim "Let it fall if it cannot stand".

However the state does support industry in a number of ways. The country has an excellent infrastructure, and the local authorities usually react positively to requests for further industrial development sites. In a number of municipalities the observation of environmental regulations is not always controlled strictly

The service sector is the largest economic sector in Denmark. View of the Danske Bank arbitration room. Photo: Kim Agersten/ Polfoto.

23

according to the letter of the law.

Of more concrete benefit are the state provision of interest subsidies and credits in connection with exports, support for technical innovations and regional development aid. Of prime importance however, are the special tax regulations governing investments.

The shipyards are an exception to the rule of non-intervention. The shipbuilding crisis which has hit all the western countries and which is partly due to competition from Japan, has also affected the industry in Denmark. The government has not saved the yards in Aalborg, Nakskov and Helsingør from closure. But ships are still being built in Danish yards, including the Lindøværft, in Frederikshavn and at B&W in Copenhagen, and shipbuilding is being subsidised by the state.

Service Denmark

The service sector is the largest economic sector today, accounting for 66% of the labour market (1988). Denmark does not differ significantly from other western countries in this respect, but what is remarkable is the size of the public sector and its dramatic expansion since 1970.

Employment in the Tertiary Sector, 1970-1990

			1,000s
	1970	1980	1990
Commerce	326	294	278
Transport	158	169	182
Finance, service	125	193	258
Other private services	225	206	227
Public services	384	691	780
Total	1,218	1,553	1,725
Share of labour market	53.3%	63.6%	66.5%

Some of the public sector growth can be explained by the high female labour market participation. Infant day-care, kindergartens and care of the elderly are major local authority functions.

The type of service industry which prevails in any town depends on its size. Financial services, business services and wholesalers predominate in the major urban areas. But the growth in the public sector in the 1960s and 1970s has contributed to a more even geographical distribution of service enterprises. "Solhjem" (Sunshine Home), and "Grønnegården" (The Green Court), are typical of the cheerful names given to the bright and beautiful new nursing homes built in practically every single municipality. And the council home help or nurse regularly visits the elderly who prefer to stay in their own homes but who need help, perhaps even on a round-the-clock basis.

Children and young people have also benefited from the growth in public investments. On the educational front centralisation and decentralisation have both been implemented, at two different levels. Small village schools have been closed, and children have been sent to larger, central schools which are able to offer more educational facilities. School buses provide transportation in rural areas. On the other hand young people in the 16 to 19 year age bracket no longer have to leave home in order to attend a Gymnasium (upper secondary school). More of these have been established around the country, as well as more technical and commercial colleges.

Nearly all these institutions and educational establishments for children, young people and the elderly, are run by the public sector, and nearly all the schools are free of charge. But even though the school capacity readily adapts to fluctuating demand, there will often be waiting lists for facilities for young people and the elderly.

Energy Supplies in Denmark

The composition of energy supplies used in Denmark has changed several times this century. As the country possesses few

The renewable energy sources attract considerable state and public interest. Tip of a windmill and solar installation at the "Nordisk Folkecenter" for renewable energy, Sønder Ydby. Photo: Ulla Koustrup / biofoto.

natural resources we have had to import practically all energy requirements. With the exception of the two world war periods, imported coal was the most popular fuel until the 1950s, when it lost ground to imported oil.

The 1973 oil crisis provided the springboard for a new energy policy. Major campaigns successfully persuaded people to save on energy consumption, whilst at the same time the country began to develop alternatives to imported sources of energy.

"Dansk Olie og Naturgas" (Danish Oil and Natural Gas) was founded in 1972 and in 1979 the Folketing voted to include natural gas as part of the national supply of energy. Danish natural gas pro-

duction started in 1984, the same year that the Folketing, after much public debate, finally passed a resolution rejecting any further consideration of nuclear power as a source of energy on Danish territory.

The renewable sources of energy attract a certain amount of public and official attention, but there is a conflict of interest between the viability of natural gas and the widespread use of renewable energy.

In order to safeguard energy supplies during the First World War, Denmark entered into a collaboration with Sweden for the supply and exchange of electricity. Since then the electricity network has also been linked to the German grid in Flens- 25 burg, and to the Norwegian grid via an underwater cable. The natural gas network was linked to the West German system in 1982, so that gas supplies could be started before Danish production had begun.

Since the publication of the Brundt-land Report "Our Common Future", strenuous efforts are being made by the local authorities such as Århus, to halve, or at least to reduce, their energy consumption by the year 2020.

The Danish Export Trade

Denmark does still sell butter and bacon to Great Britain, but there is now a far greater range of export products on offer. Great Britain is still a significant trading partner, but nowadays Germany and Sweden are more important. Trade with other Scandinavian countries, whilst still important, has diminished slightly since Denmark became a member of the EC.

Export %	1970	1980	1990*
Scandinavia	27.0	21.9	21.1
EEC	43.8	52.6	51.9

Import %	1970	1980	1990*
Scandinavia	23.1	21.0	19.3
EEC	48.7	50.3	51.9

*Estimate

During the first hundred years of the industrial age, production was almost exclusively destined for the domestic market. It was not until after the Second World War that industrial exports became significant - and not before industry had undergone a harsh period of adjustment in the early 1950s following the liberalisations introduced by membership of OECD.

However, since the mid Sixties, industrial goods have dominated Danish exports, and the categories of exports roughly reflect the overall industrial picture. "Machinery and instruments" top the list, followed by animal agricultural products.

Industrial and consumer goods make up over half the Danish imports. Fuel only accounts for 7% of imports (1990).

The Future

Denmark enjoys a high standard of living, but part of this affluence has been financed by overseas loans. The most important tasks facing Danish society in the coming years are the reduction of the massive balance of payments deficit and the reduction of unemployment in cooperation with other countries, without running down the welfare state.

A Europe based on increased cooperation will be able to benefit from Denmark's modern and high-tech agricultural and fisheries sector. The high level of veterinary care and supervision may increase export potential to critical markets. Exports of consumer goods with the hallmark of Danish Design are well established. But there is also ample potential for the rapidly expanding service sector: for instance in the environmental field, from waste treatment plants to nature restoration and windmill technology. And the health sector also has much to offer. In the long run, the often much criticised welfare state may prove to be a considerable marketable asset!

Shipping – a Historical Cross-section

by Anders Monrad Møller

SUPPLY SHIP APPROACHING NORTH SEA OIL PLATFORM. PHOTO: SØREN SVENDSEN

It is often said that the Danes have always loved "mucking about on the water". Most people now find it easy to forget why this should be so because it is difficult to disregard modern railways and motorways, bridges and air traffic. But one glance at a map of Denmark shows clearly how essential shipping used to be. To get from one end of the country to the other it was often easiest to take a short cut across the water. This intensive coastal navigation also provided the best basis for steering the ships further afield. And before leaving the map of Denmark it is worth pointing out that the maritime link between Western Europe and the Baltic runs through the Danish belts. This fact was responsible for the important role which The Sound, the old main arterial route, has played in the history of Denmark.

Some of the Vikings were Danes

The history of shipping in Denmark does not strictly begin with the Vikings, but it must be admitted that it did cause quite a stir when, around 800 A.D., Danish, Norwegian and Swedish sailors started heading both east and west. The wild Vikings are remembered, and not to their credit, as those barbarians who turned up in their long ships along the British and French coasts set to plunder churches and monasteries. Archaeologists and historians have spent much energy on reminding us that the Vikings also carried out much more peaceful trade and were quite willing to exchange the sword for the ploughshare, which they did both in Russia, Britain and Normandy.

Generations have admired the navigational skills of the Vikings, which around 1000 A.D. were used to bring the oceanic sailors right across the Atlantic to North America - not to mention back again. And their advanced shipbuilding techniques have been no less enthralling and have proved to be even more differentiated than previously assumed. They had different types of vessels, designed for different purposes. The evidence for this was discovered in Denmark with the find of the Skuldelev ships, now on display in the Viking Ship Museum in Roskilde.

Peaceful Maritime Trade and Salted Herring from the Sound

As the Viking expeditions tailed off in the middle of the 11th century there was a corresponding loss of interest in the sailors who ploughed the waters between the North Sea and the Baltic. Peaceful activities are just not recorded that much.

The success of the Vikings, both as warriors and traders, was based on their fast ships. Motif from a 9th century stone engraving from Gotland.

There is however evidence of Danish ships on a regular route to the Netherlands from the 12th century. At that time most of the traffic came from Ribe, the only really old Danish harbour town on the west coast, at the foot of the northern part of Jutland. Ribe Cathedral and many of the village churches of the area are permanent reminders of this age. They were built of Rhineland tufa stone, shipped out of Utrecht and Deventer and loaded in exchange for the agricultural products which the Danish skippers sold in the merchant towns at the mouth of the Rhine.

13th century English customs accounts contain records of Ribe skippers or Ribe merchants - the terms were more or less synonomous and meant a merchant who brought his goods over in his own ship. But this century also witnessed an increase of traffic to the north, around the peninsula of Jutland, keeping a respectful distance from the treacherous west coast of Jutland, then round the Skagen and down through the inner coastal waters of Denmark. One of the most important meeting points in the steadily growing maritime exchange between east and west was the annual herring market in Skanør and Falsterbo in southern Skåne - which at that time belonged to Denmark. Every year thousands of Danish fishermen landed their catches of herring here for salting, and buyers came from far and wide. The first on the scene had been sea-borne merchants from Lübeck, to be followed by increasing numbers of English and Flemish vessels. In the light of this considerable foreign activity in the Sound, Danish shipping would appear to have been fairly passive in nature. The foreigners came anyway to fetch the highly sought-after herring in their own vessels, so why bother to strain themselves when others were more than willing to take on all the problems of transportation? In any

case the Danish fishermen made a good living, and the king gained a handsome income in the form of customs and duties at the market at Skanør and Falsterbo.

Nevertheless there must have been a significant level of Danish sea traffic and maritime trade at that time. Otherwise there would be no explanation for the establishment and growth of the Danish seaports, which in most cases date back to the first couple of centuries after the Viking Age. And it is possible to trace the existence of both ships and seamen, however indirectly. Right up to the 16th century the king's navy consisted largely of vessels requisitioned from towns all over the country. In 1501, when the country prepared for a naval battle against Sweden, there were 21 ships from Jutland, 7 from Funen, 21 from Zealand and another 10 from the islands to the south.

The King's Tolls

By the year 1500 the herring market at Skanør and Falsterbo was finally on the decline, and interest had for some time been concentrated on the narrow passage between Helsingør (Elsinore) and Helsingborg. In 1429 the king had started a strict levying of the Sound Tolls, and over the next century this proved to be an increasingly lucrative source of income. We still benefit from this stream of gold into the royal coffers, since some of the proceeds were used to finance the construction of the magnificent castle of Kronborg. In the last decades of the 16th century the salaries for the master builder and his craftsmen were actually collected from the Customs House in Helsingør, a few hundred metres away.

The accounts which the officers at the Sound Customs House kept are famous amongst trade and maritime historians, for they represent an almost unbroken record of 300 years of activity, right up to

29

The construction of Kronborg was financed by the Sound Tolls. Ships near Kronborg Castle at Helsingør. The toll-booth is on the left of the picture. Coloured engraving, ca. 1580. Det kongelige Bibliotek, København.

the abolition of the Tolls in 1857. They reveal an enormous amount about shipping in Northern Europe and its development over this long period. In the 16th century the Danish share of this was however very small. In 1557 customs officials registered a total of 1194 ships sailing west. More than half of these came from the Netherlands, and only 10 vessels belonged to the regions belonging to modern Denmark.

Even though there was but modest participation in the international shipping which passed through the king's own waters, the Sound, it must be assumed that there was considerable traffic of small craft, which were of no interest to the customs officials in Helsingør. It was possible to sail to the Baltic or to Norway, the other royal kingdom, from most Danish seaports, without having to pass through the Sound, and there is no doubt that this was done. Of course not so much is known about that, since His Majesty could not benefit from large excises on other routes - or perhaps there was no reason to bother his own subjects unnecessarily?

Shipping on the Seven Seas

It was obvious to anyone who witnessed the stream of ships passing through the Sound that the Netherlands was the leading European maritime nation around the year 1600. The enterprising Danish king, Christian IV, who was also quite a naval expert, was in no doubt where to look for examples of great seafaring. After the establishment of the Dutch and English East Indian Companies at the turn of the century, it was not long before a Danish company was founded. It was started in 1616 with considerable royal support, and the first expedition was sent round the Cape of Good Hope. This resulted in the taking of the town of Trankebar on the Coromandel coast. This enterprise was not exactly a money spinner for Christian IV but it was the start of the small Danish colonial empire. Later that century acquisitions were made on the Gold Coast of

Africa and in the West Indies, thereby securing Denmark a modest place in European expansionism and in the overseas merchant shipping, both to the east and to the west.

These few overseas possessions were not insignificant, but the great increase in overseas trading under the Danish flag was primarily due to the favourable foreign relations enjoyed by Denmark. Its neutral position in the war between the great European powers during the last decade of the 17th century provided a foretaste of what could be achieved. And in the long period between 1720 and 1801 the Danish king managed to keep out of all the conflicts between the leading seafaring nations. His subjects, the Danes and the Norwegians, protected by the neutral Dannebrog, could earn small fortunes whilst the Dutch or French ships were imprisoned in their own harbours,

or when the British wanted to bring home capital whilst by-passing the British East India Company. At times Copenhagen became the entrepôt for the whole Baltic area, with rich cargoes on the Danish ships sailing down the Sound to be unloaded and stored in the warehouses along the quayside of the old port of Copenhagen, many of which have been preserved. And the men of this big business, the merchants and ship owners, built themselves mansions, which still feature prominently in a number of streets in the capital city of Denmark.

Sailing Ships from the Danish Provinces

Denmark's involvement in the Napoleonic wars - unfortunately on the French side - put an end to traffic to China, and the West Indian Trade was never again to

Sailing on the Seven Seas. The Asiatic Company's frigate "Christianshaun" outside Capetown on the southern tip of Africa. Tinted drawing, 1805. Museum of Trade and Shipping, Helsingør.

31

reach the same proportions. In 1814 Denmark ceded Norway, and this alone produced a drastic reduction of the number of ships under the Danish flag. When the peace came, the merchants of Copenhagen believed that the good times would return and they invested heavily in ships to renew trading. But the results were disappointing. It was difficult to compete in international freight shipping when the sea routes were open to all. Ships laid up in the port of Copenhagen began to rot, and one by one the merchant companies went bankrupt.

It was in the provinces that shipping began to revive some years later. Ships from the many small seaports had always engaged in an exchange of goods with Norway and a number of Baltic seaports.

Grain and meat products were shipped north and exchanged for Norwegian logs and iron, but the erstwhile monopoly on supplies to Norway had been lost, and it was necessary to compete on the free world market. But enterprising provincial merchants overcame this problem and successfully sold Danish grain in the Netherlands and England.

And at the same time they invested in new ships, built in those areas where there was a long tradition for ship-building. Southern Funen and Fanø on the coast of West Jutland were major centres from whence schooners were launched to play their part in the European freight trade. And both shipbuilders and ships were exported to the other provincial towns from the maritime centres of Svendborg, Tro-

Shipping in the Danish provinces began to flourish in the middle of the 19th century, especially in Southern Funen and on Fanø. 1883 painting by I.E.C. Rasmussen. The pilot boat is moored off the stern of the schooner in the foreground, whilst the small boat in front is attempting to pull it into deeper water. The stern of a typical Marstal ship is seen sailing towards Svendborg in the background. The Shipping Collection in Troense.

ense and Fåborg on Southern Funen, as well as Nordby and Sønderho on Fanø. Soon even the smallest town boasted at least a handful of new schooners. By the middle of the 19th century there were large numbers of Danish ships sailing through the Sound, which is documented by the weighty records of the Customs officials. The merchants' houses and warehouses in Danish provincial towns also bear witness to the success of the provincial merchants and shipowners in the middle of the 19th century.

Steamships from the Danish Capital

Copenhagen did not begin to catch up until about 1850. In the second half of the 19th century the Copenhagen sailing fleet began to grow again. And then there were the steamships, which had been on the scene for some time.

The first Danish steamship was bought in England in 1819 and put into service on the route between Copenhagen and Kiel in the Duchy of Holstein, which was still under Danish rule. The range of these early steamships was not very great, the sailing season was short; thus they were primarily used for the transportation of post, packages and passengers. The transition from sail to steam was to last more than 100 years. In the 1920s a few 'pure' sailing ships were still being built in the old sailing ship centres, but then the era of the sail was finally over.

The number of steamships increased steadily during the 19th century. Many of the internal routes were established locally in the provinces, but around 1870 most of them merged into one big company, "Det forenede Dampskibs Selskab" (DFDS), and this company also went on to dominate the export of agricultural products to the west, especially to the British market. Sailing ships were being ousted by the tramp traders on the Euro-

The East Asiatic Company, established in 1897, took the initiative to build up the major long distance routes. 1924 advert featuring the offices in Copenhagen and the Far East. At the top, the Fionia, one of the world's first ocean-going diesel motor vessels.

pean routes. At the close of the century many provincial merchants moved to Copenhagen, and the steam ship owners followed suite. The area around Amaliegade both to the north and south of the Royal Palaces became the home to a number of the most important Danish shipping companies, as it still is today, with the Mærsk Shipping Company in the lead.

Veteran Sails

The sailing ships lost ground all over the country. They were only still in use in the

33

The modern Danish shipyards are founded on a long tradition. Veteran ships decorated with flags in Svendborg harbour, on the occasion of the 125th anniversary of the Ring-Andersen Wooden Ship Yard, March 1992. Photo: Henrik M. Jansen.

most traditional centres. The most famous of these were the small schooners from the shipping town of Marstal on the island of Ærø south of Funen, which continued to sail the tough route across the North Atlantic to Newfoundland. By the 1920s the sail alone was no longer viable anywhere, so countless schooners and ketches were derigged, had engines installed and continued their lives for a while in coastal traffic, as stone dredgers etc. Most of these ships have now disappeared, but a small number of these old Danish sailing vessels survived and in recent decades they have been restored. They can be seen sailing during the summertime or docked in Nyhavn in Copenhagen, where some of the old wooden ships are based. The long phasing out period for sailing vessels has also meant that Svendborg can boast of a yard for

wooden boats which has been able to continue an uninterrupted tradition from previous centuries.

Danish Shipping in the 20th Century

Modern Danish shipping has its real origins in the steam tramp trade which concentrated on European routes. But with the establishment of the East Asiatic Company in 1897, renewed efforts were made on the long distance routes. The company developed a global route network in connection with its trading and plantation management activities, and in 1912 it caused an international sensation when it put the first ocean-going diesel-driven ship into service. This was built in Copenhagen in the Burmeister and Wain shipyard, and marked the beginning of that company's heyday as a supplier of diesel motors for Danish as well as foreign ships.

During the First World War Danish shipping again benefited from Denmark's neutral status. This led partly to handsome earnings and partly to hectic speculation in shipping companies and shipyards. The years following the war were thus characterised by a lot of rationalisation in the industry. There were of course some totally sound and healthy organisations which survived. Amongst these were the Mærsk shipping companies, who during the Twenties and Thirties diversified from the traditional tramp trade to include liners and tankers largely supplied by their own shipyard, Odense Staalskibsværft. At the outbreak of the Second World War, Mærsk was undisputedly the largest shipping company in Denmark, and still is.

After the German occupation in 1940 the merchant navy was split into two: the overseas fleet, most of which went into Allied service, and the home fleet, which was taken over by the Germans. The loss of lives and ships was inevitable, and thus the years after the Second World War were characterised by reconstruction. But since then Lady Luck has been with the Danish merchant fleet sailing on the seven seas - despite all the recessions. Much emphasis has been placed on the continual upgrading of tonnage in order to remain competitive on a global basis, with the acquisition of supertankers, bulk carriers and supply ships for the oil extraction industry, and thus we now have an extremely large tonnage for the size of the country. Another strong feature is the traditional emphasis placed by the shipping companies on an 'open sea' policy, by which is meant competition on equal terms, unimpeded by state subsidies or other discrimination of flags. This kind of liberal attitude is usually the sign of a strong position.

Today and Yesterday

Danish shipping today is thus thoroughly modern, but its roots in the past are clearly visible. The maritime and navigation schools are still located in the old sailing ship centres - Svendborg, Marstal and Fanø - as it is chiefly from these areas that the merchant navy is recruited, even though much of the fleet hardly ever or never sees a Danish port. However there is still plenty of activity in the Danish waters. The Great Belt is still a very important international waterway. Many of the Danish islands are still only accessible by ferry. And even though the old coastal trade to the small ports has been failing for a long time , the sport of sailing is booming. Thus countless Danes enjoy mucking about on the water, in spite of railways and motorways, bridges and aeroplanes.

Mærsk is undeniably the largest shipping company in Denmark. Modern Danish merchant tanker: "Eleo Mærsk", constructed by Odense Stålskibsværft in 1979. Polfoto.

35

6000 Years
of Danish Agriculture

by Torben Hansgaard

The Myth of Denmark

The myth of Denmark as a largely agricultural country is still thriving in many foreign countries. Of course it is true that Denmark has a large processed food production industry, two thirds of which is exported. Danish food products can be found on supermarket shelves all over the world, though more often in the delicatessen rather than the basic foods departments. The 48 billion Danish kroner in foreign currency earnings also constitute a welcome contribution to the maintenance of the high standard of living in Denmark.

Until 1960 the myth of Denmark as an agricultural country was also widespread amongst most Danes. This is because their own roots in the country were only one or two generations removed. Back in the mid Thirties the numbers of people employed in agriculture, industry and service industries were more or less equal, and even in the Fifties most town dwellers had relatives in farming, and most of the foreign earnings stemmed from agricultural exports.

And the modern traveller, passing through the open, intensely cultivated countryside with farms everywhere, dotted around the fields or gathered in the villages, will also get the impression that Denmark is still a predominantly agricultural country.

The Stone-Age Farmer

Denmark was almost completely covered by woodland when the farming culture from 'the fertile mediterranean halfmoon' reached Scandinavia about 4000 years B.C. The climatic conditions were about the same as today: a temperate climate with deciduous forests, and summer and winter temperatures ranging from 16 to 0 degrees (July/Jan), permitting only one crop yield per year. The soil conditions are generally good. In the eastern regions of Denmark, (East Jutland and the islands) it is a loamy mixture of sand and clay (ice-age deposits) covered by a thick layer of topsoil formed by nearly 7000 years of continuous forest growth. In western Jutland the soil is sandier (deposits from the melted ice) and thus less fertile. As the landscape everywhere is either completely flat or gently undulating, the natural conditions for agriculture are particularly favourable in Denmark.

It was the increasing density of population which provoked the transition from the hunter-gatherer civilisation to primitive farming, the slash-and-burn method, which was the first kind of settled occupation in Denmark. The first farmers had to clear the forest with flint axes and burn off the brushwood and branches. They sowed their corn (wheat and barley) in the layer of ash, and harvested it with a sickle. Since the yield diminished drastically after a few years, the farmers were forced to move on to another area and start all over again. Because of the continuous moves, this kind of farming culture is also known as shifting cultivation. It is still practised today in the tropical rain forest areas.

Despite its considerable space requirements, the farming culture could sustain far greater numbers than the hunter-gatherer culture. It is estimated that the population in the farming stone age (neolithic 4000 - 1800 B.C.) rose from a few thousand to about 200,000. The first farmers also had to learn how to domesticate cattle, pigs, sheep and goats. The pig was the most common animal; it lived mostly in the forests, whilst the cattle grazed in the clearings or on forest edges. To begin with the ecological balance was maintained with this woodland farming, but with the population growth the number of animals increased so much that

Stone-age farmer's dwelling place as visualised in the early 20th century. These pictures were used in Danish schools to enable children to discuss what they could see.

forest's own growth conditions were drastically reduced. The animals were exploited for more and more uses; their meat was the most important, but milk, butter and cheese were gained from the females, and the males (bulls) were castrated (bullocks) and harnessed to the plough and the first wagons. The earliest buildings in Denmark were long wooden houses with room for both people and their domestic animals at either end. Even though the existence of larger groups of dwellings in the Stone Age or Bronze Age (1800-500 B.C.) has not been established, the large number of burial mounds provide evidence of an established social organisation led by chieftain clans.

The Iron-Age Village

The first villages appear in the Iron Age (500 B.C. - 700 A.D.), most of which were located in West Jutland. The animals were now accommodated in stables with pens. This facilitated the collection of manure, which was driven out to the surrounding fields. On the other hand it was more difficult to obtain fodder in these areas with little woodland. Near the village of Vorbasse in Southern Jutland, archaeologists have found evidence of a settlement which lasted 1000 years. But every few generations the village moved a couple of hundred metres. In Vorbasse evidence has been found of a total of 8 removals, and thus the 'wandering village' has been established as a characteristic of this period. The villages demonstrate an orderly plan: all the houses were sited on an east- west orientation (to exploit sun and wind conditions), and built with enough space for a family of 5-6 people

39

and 10-12 animals. The houses were surrounded by a private area, "the croft",
which was fenced in. Gradually a number
of smaller buildings were added (barns,
stores, workshops) to the village, which
was largely self-sufficient. One farm
differed from all the others both in its size
and furbishment, and was thus obviously
the home of the largest farmer or the
village chieftain. He presumably had a
surplus production (either due to the size
of his farm or from taxes collected), which
he could sell outside the village. Perhaps
this was in nearby Ribe, where large
quantities of manure in the earth reveal
the existence of gathering places for cattle
destined for export, probably by sea.
Finds of fine burial gifts (weapons, jewellery) bear witness of close contacts with
the rest of Europe, and the Danish exchange goods could very well have been
agricultural products or fine handicraft
work. The reason for the frequent removal of the villages must have been the
problems caused by the seepage of manure. Ploughing methods were not
efficient either, as the primitive ard only
loosened the soil and did not turn it.
These problems could be overcome by
simply moving to new ground.

Mediaeval Peasant Society

In around 1000 A.D. Denmark became a
single nation under one king. The formation of the Kingdom happened at around
the same time as the serious penetration
of Christianity into Scandinavia, thus
heralding the start of the Middle Ages
(1000 -1536 A.D.). The military and civil
sovereignty of the Crown as well as the
administrative structure of the Church,
which included a large number of parish
churches, encouraged a permanent
affiliation to the land. It both provided
one's livelihood and formed the basis for
taxation. But it was hardly the ruling class

need for order and clear accounts which
was solely responsible for the permanent
settlement of the villages after the year
1000 A.D., but also the introduction of
the wheel plough, which made proper
preparation of the soil possible. In 1000
A.D. the population was around 800,000
and it continued to increase until the year
1200, when it culminated at approx. 1
million. The increased demand for food
supplies necessitated both better exploitation of the existing village fields as well as
the clearance of further areas of forest and
the cultivation of new village fields. The
plough was well-suited to both tasks,
especially when mounted with iron
shares, but it was heavy to pull (especially
in clay soil) and difficult to turn. To solve
this problem the village fields were divided up into a number of long strips, and
each farmer received an equal number of
good and bad quality strips in proportion
to the size of his 'croft' in the village.
Despite the continuation of cattle breeding, quantities of manure were still
insufficient. This problem could only be
solved by leaving some of the fields fallow
or as a common where the cattle could
graze and leave their manure. Gradually,
and particularly in eastern Denmark, a
pattern of three course rotation became
general. One third of the land was sown
with rye, one third with barley and the
rest lay fallow. The following year the
crops were rotated, so the rye field was
sown with barley etc. The extensive partitioning of land into strips meant that the
farmers had to cooperate very closely,
particularly when they had to decide on
the choice of grain, working methods etc,
which they did at the "byting" or village
assembly. Other local affairs were also
discussed and settled at these assemblies,
and mostly harmoniously.

This cooperative cultivation system
functioned successfully and survived until
it was abolished at the turn of the 19th

During the Middle Ages many freeholders sought the protection of the local squire. The Gisselfeld manor house with surrounding villages. Section of a 17th century map.

century. The only new domestic animal was the horse. Originally harnessed for military use, it gradually came to replace the bullock as the instrument of haulage. With the right harnesses, the pulling power of one horse was equal to that of 2 bullocks. As for the crops, oats now made their appearance as the fourth and last type of cereal. Oats were cultivated alongside barley, whilst wheat production gradually receded. The livestock on a typical farm would probably have consisted of 2 horses, 2 oxen, 2 cows and some pigs and sheep. That was all. The animals were small of stature, and the milk yield would be equivalent to that of an Indian cow today. Between 80% and 90% of the population lived in self-sufficent units, which normally gave them a reasonable livelihood and enabled them to pay taxes to the king, a tithe to the church and manorial dues to the squire, if they were tenant farmers, which most of them were. The

townsfolk also purchased agricultural products, and old accounts show that there was a small surplus of grain and cattle for export, which were mostly sent to nearby markets in northern Germany (Lübeck, Hamburg).

Denmark was ravaged by the "Black Death" in the years 1348-50, and about one third of the population perished. The surplus work force which had existed since around 1200, and which had enabled landowners to employ smallholders and labourers on their farms, disappeared abruptly, and many farms were abandoned. The situation slowly returned to normal in the course of the 15th century, when medium-sized tenant farms became the norm, and the former class barriers were partially dismantled. A system had developed during the Middle Ages whereby many freeholders had sought the protection of their local squire, often linked with favourable transfer terms.

41

Spring work on the farm. Illustration from Danish-German textbook, 1774.

There was probably a good deal of tax speculation connected with this trend. The squires were exempted from paying tax to the king (in return for fulfilling military duties) and the squires or nobles, as they were called after 1536, then made deals with the king to exempt their own tenants from tax liabilities. In return they had to supply a farm hand or maid to labour on the manorial estate for one day a week.

Noblemen and Tenant Farmers

At the beginning of the 16th century the nobility began to withdraw their own fields from the system of collective cultivation. They sought to gather as much land as possible around their own manors either by additional purchases or exchang-

es, and in some cases this meant that whole villages became derelict. The tenant farms were located close to the manor to make efficient use of the villeinage system. These reorganisations were motivated by the population increase in Europe and the associated growth markets for cattle in Northern Germany and The Netherlands. By concentrating production on cattle breeding many of the noblemen hoped to benefit from the economies of scale. The usual method was to buy up 3 to 4 year-old bullocks from the tenant farmers and to stall-feed them over the winter before they were driven down the Jutland "Ox Roads" to Hamburg the following Spring. This trade flourished until 1580 when war broke out between Spain and The Netherlands. An annual total of 40,000 bullocks crossed the customs point at Schleswig, as well as many more who by-passed it! Many landowners earned huge sums, and often invested their gains in the construction of splendid manor houses on their estates. Denmark enjoyed a healthy economy in this period, but a number of abortive foreign policy escapades, in particular Denmark's participation in the Thirty Years' War (1625-29) followed by the wars with Sweden (1643-45 and 1657-60) led to national ruin by 1660. On the political front this provoked the introduction of absolute monarchy in Denmark, but in the countryside it also meant that the nobility's monopoly of the agricultural estates and all important offices was broken, and it allowed the entry of both new nobility (including German families) and the burghers. But the peasant class had to endure higher taxes and duties, and no better conditions. Despite a number of favourable measures for estate management, they were still largely rental based estates (Germ. Grundherrschaft) whereby a significant element of income stemmed from the appertaining tenant farms. At no time did the Danish estate system adopt the latifundium (Germ. Gutswirtschaft), which was common in eastern Germany, Poland and southern Europe, and even though the peasant class was subjected to a number of duties and restrictions regarding mobility etc, there was never any actual serfdom in Denmark.

The Great Agrarian Reforms

By 1750 the population had again risen so much that the existing production apparatus could not manage food production demands. An increasing number of smallholders found themselves unable to take over the family farms; in other cases several families lived on one single farm, and finally some people were forced to seek poor relief or become casual labourers or

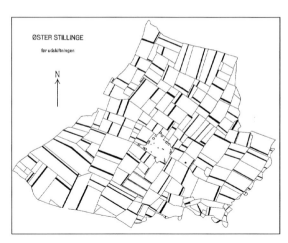

The major agrarian reforms included the abolition of communal farming by exchanges and relocations. The village fields at Øster Stillinge in the 18th century. The land is divided into 3 fields, which are again subdivided into a number of furlongs. Each furlong is again divided into strips corresponding to the number of farms in the village, in this case 16. The farm furthest to the south thus had 122 strips of land. One field was sown with rye, the second with barley/oats whilst the third lay fallow.

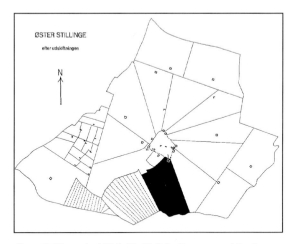

Øster Stillinge in 1805. Half of the farms stayed in the village, whilst the rest were relocated on their land. The small plots to the west are "smallholdings" for families who did not own a farm. With only a few acres of land, they were forced to take on additional work. The strips south of the village are meadow plots for digging up peat etc. From Viggo Hansen: Kulturgeografi. Gyldendal 1973.

43

beggars. Approximately 20% of the population now lived in the towns.

When the recession of the early 18th century eased and conditions began to improve again, a number of landowners acknowledged the fact that it was no longer possible to achieve growth via manorial dues and villein services. Only the latter could be increased, and this naturally met with resistance from the peasant farmers, who had to do without that manpower for one or more days a week. If however the labour services were converted into cash payments, then production could be reorganised and rationalised, possibly by leasing arrangements.

For the tenant farmers this meant that they could now ensure that any improvements they made would also benefit their children, which had previously been a major problem. In fact the security of tenure proved to be the main motivational factor for changing the system, but it also meant that the copyhold tenancy had to be converted to either a freehold or at least to an hereditary leasehold. Of course capital had to be raised to purchase a farm, but this became feasible for many during the boom years of the last decades of the 18th century, even if they had to borrow from relatives, the landowner, or latterly from the mortgage societies.

Another point of criticism was the widespread method of communal cultivation, which was now regarded as a barrier to progress. In the early Middle Ages this system had been viewed from a life insurance angle, but now attention focused on the poor crop yields.

The time was therefore ripe for change, and the spirit of the age was conducive to reform. All over Europe ideas on human rights and free speech were being formulated . Economic theory produced "physiocracy" (Quesnay: Tableau economique,1758) and "liberalism"

(Smith: Wealth of Nations, 1776). Both theories were based on the philosophy of economic growth. There were a number of government leaders who, albeit members of the landed aristocracy, nevertheless clearly recognised the significance of the peasant class as the backbone of Danish society. The problem could be boiled down to the following alternatives: whether to go for the top end of Danish agriculture in the form of more large estates (as happened in Great Britain) or for the broad base in the form of improvements for peasant farming?

The government opted for the second option, and the ensuing body of legislation provided the framework for "The Great Agrarian Reforms in Denmark". The main points were: 1) abolition of common cultivation by enclosure and relocation, 2) improvements to the legal status of the peasantry in relation to the large landowners, 3) the replacement of labour service villeinage by cash payments and 4) the transition from copyhold tenancy to freehold.

The economic boom in Europe during the Napoleonic wars facilitated the rapid introduction of these reforms, but they ground to a halt when the depression set in in 1813.

Economic Growth and Political Liberties

The reorganisation of agriculture facilitated tremendous growth in the 19th century. Production doubled between 1820 and 1870, and the export quota gradually rose to 35%, despite the large population increase, from 1 million in 1800 to 2.5 million in 1900. The main beneficiaries of the reforms were the peasant farmers and large estate owners.

The establishment of freehold farming also paved the way for the economic, social, political and cultural development of the peasant class on its own premisses.

The Education Act of 1814 introduced 7 years' compulsory schooling, and in the 1830s the peasants began to participate at public meetings. Demands for political liberty and equality resulted in the "Constitution of 5th June 1849", and the peasants began to support political parties such as "The Friends of the Peasants" and "The Liberals". Their economic and social status was consolidated by a wide range of organisational initiatives including insurance societies and savings banks. On the cultural front the peasants supported the "Folk High School Movement", whose main task was to 'awaken' the young farm hands and maids by educating them in general subjects such as literature and history.

The 19th century also offered opportunities for estate management. With smallholders and labourers as a source of cheap labour they introduced new farming methods (crop rotation), and crops (fodder plants), and they improved the utility of their property by land reclamation projects (dyking and draining). Thus the large estate farms were often regarded as agrarian pioneers by the peasant farmers, who were more interested in evaluating the practical results than in the agrochemical theories, which were worked out later.

The 19th century did not however bring any great improvements to those at the bottom end of rural society, the smallholders and farm workers. They could not subsist on their own small plots or allotments, but had to work as day labourers on farms or estates, as and when required. Conditions improved somewhat after 1870, when industrial growth began to attract workers into the towns. But nevertheless in the following decades a relatively large proportion of those in service (10-15% of each generation) emigrated to North America to fulfil their dreams of getting their own home.

After 1870 Danish farmers concentrated on the production of butter, eggs and bacon, mostly destined for the British market. Poster with the "Lur" logo, to mark the 25th anniversary of the Danish Cooperation Butter Export Association, 1920.

The Cooperative Movement

Conditions for Danish agricultural production changed dramatically after 1870, when the expansion of the railway networks enabled both the United States and Russia to flood the European grain market. The increased emphasis on animal husbandry now proved its worth, and the agricultural industry chose to concentrate on the production and sale of processed foods, mainly butter, eggs and bacon to the British market. It is interesting to note that this reorganisation was initiated

45

by the peasant farmers themselves, with their own money, and on their own terms. Decades of organisational experience combined with cultural awareness provided the foundations from which the "Danish Cooperative Movement" could be created and developed. It started in the 1880s with the construction of numerous dairies, then came the slaughter houses, and in the space of a few decades, the movement had spread to all parts of the country. The principles of the cooperative movement were:

1) all members had to put up capital/security,
2) obligation to supply all production, and payment according to the extent and quality of the supplies, and
3) an equal say for all members regardless of turnover - one vote for each member at the AGM.

This last rule was distinctly democratic and partially directed against the "capitalists" in the towns (share-issuing compa-nies), as well as the ongoing political struggle between the "Left" and the "Right", who were in power. The cooperative movement was a great success, and gradually it expanded to include the marketing functions. But also on the purchasing side many consumer cooperatives were established.

The years preceding the First World War were a Golden Age for Danish agriculture. Production doubled in relation to 1870, and nearly 80% of production went to export. However, due to urban industrial development, the percentage of the population employed in agriculture dropped to 50%.

Wars and Crises

The First World War brought an end to free trade. Whilst agriculture profited temporarily from its supply deals with the warring nations (especially Germany), Denmark's neutral position required the

Mechanisation was gradually introduced during the 1950s. Grain harvesting in 1957.

maintenance of a delicate balance, which was upset by the onset of unrestricted submarine warfare in 1917. The Twenties were characterised by a desire to return to 'normal conditions' but the crisis of global depression affected agricultural exports and many farms were hard hit. Several thousand farms were forced to sell up, and in the Thirties many of the 200,000 farms existed under the constant threat of bankruptcy. The crisis had organisational and political consequences, attracting people to right wing politics, but despite the large demonstrations (including the "Peasant March" on Copenhagen in 1935), the majority of the farmers remained loyal to their trade and political organisations and leaders. The pressure of the crisis also induced the farmers' and smallholders' unions to cooperate under the umbrella of "The Agricultural Council".

Denmark was occupied by the German Nazi regime from 1940 to 1945. Links to the traditional British export market were severed and supplies redirected to Central Europe. The occupying powers paid well, with cash taken from The Danish National Bank.

The post war years in Europe were characterised by reconstruction. The export trade to Britain was resumed, but price levels were lower than before. The increase in agricultural production all over Europe created problems for Danish agriculture, and efforts to secure free trade via OEEC and GATT proved fruitless. The number of farms was still quite constant in the Fifties, and they were normally run as mixed farms, with both cereal and animal production. Mechanisation was gradually introduced; the tractor was soon followed by more and more mechanised tools. Consequentially, agricultural workers left the farms and moved into urban areas, which, particularly in the Sixties, were easily able to absorb the new labour force.

The formation of the EC and EFTA

Danish agricultural exports are greater than ever. The implementation of improved breeding techniques and strict quality controls help to ensure the satisfaction of consumer demands. Export pig with the stamp of quality. 1980s.

markets (Denmark belonged to EFTA), did not solve the problems of agriculture, and the agricultural organisations sought compensation for the increased standard of living which the rest of society was enjoying. A number of support measures were introduced, gradually increasing to comprise one third of the total agricultural income, which was untenable in the long run. Agricultural interests were

47

therefore in favour of Denmark's entry into the EC, which took place in 1973, together with Great Britain and Ireland. The terms for production and sales are now shared by Danish agriculture and farmers in the rest of Central and Western Europe alike. Approximately half the Danish agricultural exports are sold within the EC.

Agriculture Today

Since 1960 Danish agriculture has undergone a massive process of rationalisation. Two thirds of the total area is still arable land, but the number of farms has decreased from almost 200,000 in 1960 to 77,000 in 1990. It has largely been the smallholdings which have been given up or amalgamated into other farms. The average farm size has therefore grown from 15 to 35 hectares in the same period. "Mixed farming" no longer exists either. Only 20% of farms have both cattle and pig production. 25% have cattle only and 20% have pigs only. One third of all farms are run solely for cereal production, and often with speciality crops. In 1992 only 5% of the working population are directly employed in agriculture, and an additional 2% are employed in the processing industries (dairies, slaughterhouses etc). Nevertheless production is now greater than ever before, and has increased by 45% since 1970 alone. A contributory factor has been the increased use of chemical fertilisers, which, together with the uneven distribution of animal manure, has caused environmental problems in some areas.

What is the future for Danish agriculture? Only half of the current 77,000 farms are run as "full-time" farms, supplying the farmer's total income. However as these 39,000 farms cover two thirds of the acreage and supply 80% of the total production, it is not difficult to predict the future of the industry. The rest, the "part-time farmers", are those who either have rural roots or are city dwellers with romantic ideas about "life in the countryside" - an illusion which can only be maintained as long as it does not become necessary to live off one's production, but can be enjoyed as a recreational activity.

Environmental and Physical Planning

by Kai Lemberg

MIDDELFART, THE LITTLE BELT AND THE NEW LITTLE BELT BRIDGE. PHOTO: SVEND TOUGAARD / BIOFOTO.

The Cultural Landscape

The foreign visitor arriving in Denmark by air or by ferry, or touring the country by train or car, will see Denmark as a small country, broken up into the Jutland peninsula and many large and small islands by the watery fjords, sounds and belts - more or less just as the last ice-age left it.

The country has no mountains, yet neither is it completely flat. It is largely undulating, with the scenery alternating from fields and meadows to heathlands, small forests and lakes and finally, excellent beaches. It is a cultivated landscape, shaped by man's use for agriculture, forestry and habitation, with scattered villages and many small towns, close to each other. Only three provincial towns, Århus, Odense and Aalborg, have populations of around 200,000, and the only metropolitan city is Copenhagen.

Excellent road and railway networks link the small and medium-sized towns. The domestic air routes link up at Copenhagen.

Only a few of the domestic shipping routes are still in operation, ferries sailing between Zealand and Jutland as well as to the east of the country, to Bornholm. In addition, there are small routes connecting those islands which are not linked to the mainland by a bridge. There are still a considerable number of overseas routes, to Norway, Sweden, Poland, Germany and Great Britain, as well as to Iceland, The Faroes and Greenland in the North Atlantic.

Environmental Problems

Denmark has no minerals such as coal, iron or other metals - only salt as well as chalk, clay, sand and gravel, which can be used in the construction industry, and therefore the country has but a very modest mining industry. This fact, coupled with the limited size of the country, has meant that no heavy industry of any consequence has been developed. And this has also meant that Denmark has been spared the severe environmental problems caused by mining and heavy industry. Since the 1980s there has been a considerable expansion of the Danish offshore industry focusing on the extraction of oil and natural gas from the North Sea.

Until the Second World War Denmark was largely an agricultural country with a number of medium-sized and small industrial and craft-based enter-

The slums in 19th century housing developments have created environmental problems in Copenhagen. Demolition of houses and inner courtyards have alleviated the problem. Photography of a tenement block in the "bro" (bridge) district.

prises, whose environmental nuisance factor was minimal with regard to air, water or noise pollution.

Industrial urbanisation had also been modest, compared to Great Britain and continental Europe. This limited the extent of environmental problems caused by slum districts, traffic congestion and pollution, which are inherent in large cities. Refuse and human waste disposal improvements were initiated in the late 19th century with the installation of toilets and sewerage.

It can thus be maintained that, until recently, physical problems relating to the external environment were practically non-existent, or were extremely limited and of purely local significance in the open countryside and in small villages and towns. Environmental nuisance factors were caused by individual large industries such as shipyards, other iron and metal works as well as cement factories and local gas or electricity works. These largely took the form of problems related to the working environment.

During the second half of the 19th century tenement blocks for workers were constructed in Copenhagen and a few of the larger provincial towns. The flats were small, poorly equipped and built too densely to allow air and light circulation, or play facilities for children. This heritage of (limited) slum areas has presented Copenhagen and a few provincial towns with the problem of slum clearance and urban redevelopment.

After the Second World War the country was subject to a massive wave of industrialisation, particularly in the chemical industry, electronics and pharmaceutical industries as well as oil refineries and power stations. It was the power plants and chemical industries which were the chief cause of new and more serious pollution. This was even more true of road traffic which increased at a

dramatic rate from the 1950s onwards, and which particularly threatened the urban environment.

The Environmental Awareness of the Population

During the 1970s a new environmental awareness developed which led to increasing demands from the people to stop or reduce the pollution of water, air and soil, to reduce noise levels in traffic and industry and to incorporate measures of long-term significance for the ecological balance. It had been adequately demonstrated that the unrestricted growth of urbanisation, production and traffic in pursuit of a higher material standard of living had led to a poorer quality of life. Worst affected were the larger towns which suffered increasing environmental nuisances, and the destruction of historical areas in town and of valuable countryside areas in their immediate environs. This general awareness amongst the people reflected the new international understanding of the fundamental conflict between economic growth and ecological and environmental considerations, as expressed in publications such as "Blueprint for Survival" and "Limits to Growth" in 1973. In Denmark this awareness led to the formation of a cross-party green movement, stimulated by the publication "Oprør fra Midten" (Revolt from the Centre) in 1975, and to the establishment of a green party.

Planning of Growth

The conservative and liberal scepticism of planning, regarded as a kind of "socialism by the back door", was gradually superceded by an interest in using physical planning as a means to promote economic growth via public infra-structure investments. These took the form of extensive

51

Both the Conservative and the Social Democrat parties were enthusiastic about the major building projects which were designed to create better housing for ordinary people and promote economic growth. High-rise development at Bellahøj, 1952. Photo: Erik Gleie.

house-building and major construction projects. This actually matched the policies of the Social Democrats quite well, as they prioritised economic growth, full employment, better housing for the working classes and redevelopment of the old tenement blocks.

The planners were generally extremely enthusiastic about enormous new town projects, massive investment in the road network, the establishment of regional megacentres etc. These projects were to be incorporated in major overall plans for towns and regions, involving enormous architectural and engineering challenges. This planning process stimulated the already dramatically accelerated growth in private transport.

Clearly, the motives for this increased

interest in the environment and physical planning were by no means without conflict. On the contrary, two strongly opposing factions soon emerged: an economic growth faction, supported by the Conservatives and the Social Democrats, and an ecology and environment faction supported by sections of the left wing, centre and green parties.

New Signs in the 1970s

The favourable global economic climate deteriorated abruptly after 1972 into economic recession, which was deepened by the two energy crises of 1973 and 1979. The great expectations of economic benefit from the new membership of the EEC began to pale, industry started making cutbacks and unemployment figures began to rise. Industrial growth and increased production levels shifted from the capital city and the larger towns to peripheral areas in western parts of Denmark. Government policy consistently favoured development in the provinces at the expense of Copenhagen. And in addition the negative population development meant that there were fewer young people around to get married, set up house and have children.

Despite strong political demands for budget cuts and reductions in taxation, it proved impossible to restrict the massive expansion of the public sector, which took on additional pace after the local government reforms of the 1970s. This led to increasingly tight public finances and the necessity to give up plans for major roadworks and housing projects for new areas.

The experiences harvested from the numerous expansions of suburban areas carried out hastily in the 1960s had not always been favourable, despite all the detailed planning, involvement of architects and provision of diverse urban facilities. The industrially constructed blocks of flats were often faceless and lacked amenities, and thus soon became run down, with a high turnover of residents, vandalism and petty crime. Complex designs for new district centres never left the drawing board or were abandoned before completion.

After a glorious period from the 1950s to the beginning of the 1970s, where no plan could be big enough, planners now found themselves discredited; both by the left and the right wings of the political spectrum. The task was now to trim down the expansion plans, retain existing buildings, preserve areas of historical interest and tone down the harsh demolition slum clearance methods in favour of more moderate methods by improving existing premises.

These new ideas gradually became accepted. The construction industry statistics show a drop from 50,000 homes per year in the early 1970s to 15-20,000 per year. This drop was partially compensated by more urban renewal and home improvement work, but developments in this field were slow. Demolition and new construction work still dominated the order books in 1980, but the introduction of the Urban Renewal Act in 1983 brought about a swing to more moderate and user-friendly renewal projects with a greater variety of less drastic designs.

From Social Democrat to Conservative-Liberal Politics

The trend in the 1980s and early 1990s has been influenced by the shift in political power from the Social Democrats to the Conservative-Liberal coalition which took place in 1982. This also coincided with a new international economic boom and the fact that Denmark was entering the process of European integration. There was a long period which was dominated by the deficit on the international balance of payments, a high interest rate and high unemployment, matched by massive cut-backs in public sector spending.

Conservative and Liberal policies on winding down state responsibilities, deregulation, removal of bureaucratic systems and privatisation are receiving more support. In town planning, political interest has shifted from overall plans and environmentally friendly housing developments to individual projects, such as large office blocks and hotels. On the environmental front Denmark is in an awkward position vis-à-vis the EC, since we often stand alone in our demands for stricter measures against pollution, toxic substances, nitrate emissions into the sea, car exhaust emissions etc. The majority of EC countries tend to regard these demands as measures creating unfair competition and technical barriers to trade. The EC has no powers of jurisdiction over town or regional planning as yet, but these areas, together with major transport projects, are included in the proposed political areas of interest of a federal union, adopted by the Heads of State and Government at Maastricht in December 1991.

Reorganisation and Reduction of Energy Consumption

Denmark was always a country without natural sources of energy, and thus had to import all its energy requirements from Sweden or Germany in the form of coal, oil or electricity. Since the Second World War production of electricity supplies for both industrial and domestic use has been concentrated in the inter-municipal coal and gas-fired power stations. These are inter-connected via the distribution grid. The economic growth of the 1960s and the international oil crises of the 1970s provoked a thorough examination of the use of other sources of energy: this included natural gas from the North Sea piped from off-shore drilling platforms, nuclear energy and renewable energy sources such as sun, wind and wave power.

After a very open public debate, initiated by the new Ministry of Energy, private production coupled with semi-public distribution of natural gas from the North Sea was started up. However, proposals for the construction of Danish nuclear power stations (for which land had already been earmarked) were dropped by the Social Democrat government in the mid 1970s, following widespread public opposition to the plans and doubts regarding operational safety and disposal of radioactive waste.

The major development in the energy sector was thus concentrated on the exploitation of natural gas and the construction of combined power and heating stations (which harness the heat produced during the production of electricity). This enabled many households to convert to the district heating supply system, rendering their individual oil-fired boilers redundant and thereby reducing the extent of polluting and socially less efficient energy consumption.

In recent years a number of decentralised alternative energy systems have been developed, despite protests from the central power stations. These include modern windmills, which have proved to be successful products for Danish export, solar panels on private houses, straw-fired burners, and biological gas plants. These are all, apart from the windmills, still in the experimental stage.

Extensive campaigns for energy-saving in the home have been successful in promoting better insulation in private homes and the use of energy-efficient equipment. Campaigns directed at industrial enterprises have also been moderately successful. It has been significant that in Denmark the population at large is both environmentally aware and willing to accept the Brundtland report's requirements for a sustainable global development, which entail a 50% reduction in energy consumption by the wealthy industrial nations by the year 2010. A more traditional policy has however been followed in the transport sector, based on individual free choice of transportation (i.e. the private car) and increasingly expensive charges for public transport.

Major Bridge Projects in Denmark

There have traditionally been a large number of ferry routes in this country with its many islands. However, modern requirements for quick and convenient long distance transportation have, ever since the 1930s, resulted in the construction of numerous short bridges for road and rail traffic.

The most prominent of the transport projects of international and national significance are the plans for permanent land links between Denmark and overseas, and between East and West Denmark. These projects cover distances of some 20 kilometres over or under water.

First there were decades of reports and debates. Then political consensus for the Great Belt Bridge was reached in the 1970s, only to fall apart a couple of years later. Finally in 1989, after heavy pressure from the car lobby and important Danish and international commercial interests, Parliament finally agreed to the construction of a combined rail and road link across the Great Belt between Zealand and Funen. This was to be both a train tunnel, low road bridge, and combined high bridge. There was considerable opposition to the road bridge for environmental, traffic and energy consumption reasons. The construction of the railway tunnel commenced in 1990, but has been heavily delayed due to technical problems. The road section is due to be started shortly.

The IC3 high-speed train at a platform in Copenhagen Central Station. Photo: Peter Thornvig/DSB.

The next campaign was for the link across the Sound between Copenhagen and Malmö, the two largest conurbations in the area. It has been a high priority for the Swedish export industry, who regard it is a transit route to the continent of Europe, as well as amongst other car users and commercial interests. The project has provoked a very hefty debate between these interest groups and spokesmen for the ecology, marine environment, nature preservation and urban conservation. They accepted the railway tunnel, but attempted to prevent the road bridge. But also here the political decision reached in 1991, in consultation with the then Social Democrat government in Sweden, included the construction of both the rail and the road link.

Political guarantees for these mega-projects have come principally from the Conservative and Social Democrat parties.

Following the decisions to go ahead with the Great Belt and Sound projects, the campaigners are now, in cooperation with the German government, pressing for a similar link to be constructed above or below the Fehmarn Sound between Lolland and Fehmarn.

In addition to the railway works connected to the above projects, the major innovation in the railway sector has been the introduction of the new diesel-electric IC3 high-speed train (Inter-City train units of 3 coaches) on the long-distance domestic routes. This has reduced the travel time and is also more comfortable than the old trains. The ferry routes run by the Danish State Railways have however been running into major technical problems.

55

Copenhagen's international airport at Kastrup plays a crucial role in ensuring fast and convenient links to overseas destinations. The airport also has a large domestic terminal, and both terminals have been extensively developed during the course of the 1980s, providing new traffic, shopping and other facilities. The airport is one of the cheapest and best in Europe.

The City of Copenhagen

Metropolitan Copenhagen serves as a concrete example of environmental and physical planning problems and their political manipulation since the Second World War.

Copenhagen is the capital city of Denmark and its only metropolitan city. The population of the municipality reached its highest level in 1950, with 770,000 inhabitants, and has since dropped dramatically to 470,000 inhabitants in 1991. People have moved out to the suburbs and outlying districts. Since it is mostly young families who are moving way, the proportion of elderly people and students is increasing. And there are more deaths than births. Greater Copenhagen does however comprise a large number of municipalities, although this is not evident to the commuter on his way to and from work. The built-up areas tend to merge together, and there are few features to distinguish one suburban municipality from another or one Copenhagen district from another. The whole area of Greater Copenhagen had a population of 1.7 million inhabitants in 1991, slightly below the 1973 total.

The major municipal amalgamations in 1901-02 left the separate municipality of Frederiksberg as a 'municipal island' in the middle of Copenhagen. Beyond the municipality of Copenhagen there is the County of Copenhagen, then Frederiks-borg County to the north and Roskilde County to the south-west. These five local government units make up the Greater Copenhagen region.

The Greater Copenhagen Finger Plan

During and immediately after the Second World War ideas for an overall plan for the development of the rapidly expanding capital were crystallised. Hitherto, growth had largely been confined to the municipality of Copenhagen, but it was correctly estimated that this growth would soon overflow into the suburbs and outlying districts. In 1947 the country's first regional plan was therefore devised, designed to prevent uniformly concentric urban growth in all directions as well as the spread of built-up areas all over Northern Zealand. The plan was adopted by the Folketing in 1951 with its full support. The principal idea of the plan was to channel developments along the lines of existing and proposed local railway routes, the S-train network, emanating from the town centre in a star formation. Green wedges between the "fingers" were to be reserved for agricultural and recreational areas, including forests. Given the geographical outline of the region, the design resembled a hand with five fingers spread out, thus giving rise to the name The Finger Plan. The legislative power required to enforce this plan was the 1949 Urban Development Act, which designated the town centre and the fingers as urban zones and the wedges as rural areas, where urban developments were forbidden. It was this principle which, in 1969 under a non-socialist government, was extended nationwide in the National Development Act on Urban and Rural Zones.

Some of the wedges became narrower than was originally intended, and the northern sector was already so well covered with middle and upper-class residential areas, that here the fingers lost some of

their shape, but apart from that, the original design of the Finger Plan has been
fairly well maintained, as illustrated on the map, which indicates built-up and designated urban zones.

The Greater Copenhagen Region 1974-1989

The Finger Plan only covered an area approx. 15 km from the city centre, and it did not anticipate the extent of growth in private motor traffic which accelerated from the late 1950s onwards. The plan seemed viable until well into the 1960s, when it was recognised that the area to be covered by the regional plan had to be extended to the whole of North Zealand, and a new regional structure was therefore considered. This led to the establishment of an inter-municipal collaboration in 1967, which was legislatively formalised in 1974 with the establishment of the Greater Copenhagen Council. In 1973 a new, very growth-oriented regional plan was presented, and this was passed by the Ministry of the Environment in 1976, though not without major curtailments to the extent of planned growth. The plan included 4 new regional mega-centres to relieve pressure on the old city centre in Copenhagen. Only one of these, Høje Tåstrup Centret, has been constructed. And this centre is also considerably smaller than originally envisaged, partly because 1973 was the year when the population in the Greater Copenhagen conurbation peaked at 1.8 million inhabitants, since when it has fallen off slightly. The number of jobs peaked in 1987 at 987,000 and is also falling again. In 1989 there were 956,000 jobs in the region. It is thought-provoking that the figures for the municipality of Copenhagen reached their peak as early as 1960, with 765,000 jobs. In 1989 the figure had dropped to 332,000.

In 1989, despite protest from the Social Democrats and the left wing parties, the government dissolved the Greater Copenhagen Council and assigned the responsibilities of the regional plan individually to the two central municipalities and the three counties.

Town Planning in the Municipality of Copenhagen

The first overall town plan for the municipality of Copenhagen was presented in 1954, and then only as a "blueprint master plan". It was far-sighted and vi-

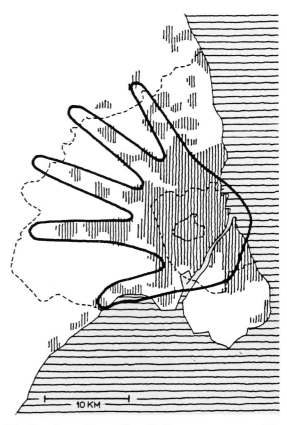

The Copenhagen Finger Plan, 1947.   **57**

sionary. It put the brakes on any further expansion in the city with more high-rise commercial buildings and breaking up of existing streets and went in for less dense developments, conservation, residential building and less car traffic in the city centre. For the old, densely built-up districts surrounding the city centre the plan proposed extensive urban renewal projects, whilst the outer districts remained 'status quo' areas. Recommendations were made for a main network of arterial roads for through traffic, and for the expansion of the S-train network with underground trains in the central municipalities.

Some of the recommendations of the blueprint master plan for the city centre were adopted by the town council after 1959, and more suburban S-train routes were established along the fingers, but no underground lines were built in Copenhagen. The 1960s were a period of frenetic growth in both economic activity and private car transport. People and jobs moved out to the suburbs, to towns further out in the region, and to the provinces. This provoked intensive activity in planning for the Copenhagen area. This included plans for housing, roads, the transfer of the airport to an island in the middle of the Sound, the construction of a road and rail bridge to Sweden (Malmö), a comprehensive underground railway network, a large new East Port and the clearance of the central district of Vesterbro, parts of which had deteriorated into a slum, to a vast new satellite city, City Vest, as well as

In recent years many Danish artists have been commissioned to decorate the Copenhagen buses. HT local bus, decorated by Lise Malinovsky in 1985. Photo: Torben Liebst/ HT Museum.

a major urbanisation project for the empty, reclaimed polders of Vestamager. This was the Swinging Sixties, the era of total faith in the blessings of unlimited economic growth.

The backlash came in the problematic decade of the 1970s, with international economic recessions, energy crises, protests from the general public against noise, pollution and lack of concern for the natural environment. The plans for Vestamager, City Vest and the major transport investments collapsed like houses of cards. Practically none of the big plans were implemented, despite their approval by a large political majority.

Car Transport Takes the Lead

The number of cars on the roads in Copenhagen rose dramatically from the 1960s onwards, and this was exacerbated by a distinct political dragging of the feet with regard to plans for public city and local rail transport.

Efforts to relieve traffic congestion in Copenhagen city centre began in the 1960s when the main shopping street, Strøget, was successfully converted into a pedestrian street in 1962, to be followed by a number of other central streets. In the 1970s a number of residential streets were converted from traditional mixed traffic, largely dominated by cars, to either play and recreation streets (max. speed 15 km ph) or quiet streets (max. speed 30 km ph) with mixed forms of traffic, but giving priority to children and pedestrians.

After decades of discussions and reports, a combined regional body for collective transport in the capital region was set up in 1974. It was called Hovedstadsrådets Trafikselskab (The Greater Copenhagen Traffic Agency), commonly known as HT. It assumed responsibility for all the bus and train routes in the entire region, the overall planning, expansion, control and finance. HT owned and ran most of the bus routes (the last tramlines were closed in 1972) and held the concessions for the rest. In the 1980s the Conservative-Liberal coalition government privatised many of the bus routes and transferred the S-trains from HT to DSB, the Danish State Railways, who were already responsible for the technical operations.

Urban Renewal in Copenhagen

After the slow-down in new housing and the dropping of the vast building projects in the late 1970s, municipal interest began to focus on the redevelopment of old, antiquated and unsuitable residential districts. This work had been on the agenda ever since the presentation of the blueprint master plan, but little action had been taken. Legislation on slum clearance passed in 1969 facilitated the establishment of semi-official non-profit clearance companies. The Nørrebro district in central Copenhagen was top of the schedule for extensive urban redevelopment, with demolitions and new housing developments. This project was implemented ruthlessly in the early 1980s, despite strong protests from local residents against the "bulldozing clearances". The district became airy and spacious, with modern apartment blocks, but it lost its character. And the industrially constructed flats were criticised for being monotonous and characterless as well as too expensive for the original residents.

Later on, redevelopment work carried out in the Vesterbro district incorporated a variety of renewal projects, with fewer mass demolitions and more improvement work on existing properties, whilst redevelopment in the oldest, historical parts of town consisted largely of conservation projects .

Municipal Planning in Copenhagen since the 1980s

Work on a municipal plan for Copenhagen and individual plans for local district building and renewal plans featured heavily throughout the 1980s. A draft municipal plan was published in 1985, with supplementary reports and proposals over the next few years, and the final plan was published in 1989. The plan consists largely of a registration of the current situation and of existing plans and proposals for new housing and service facilities. It is pragmatic and considerate of the current economic constraints with a limited public investment budget. The planning process has been criticised for the almost consistent rejection of all objections from residents, associations and other local interest groups.

The most urgent current town planning and environmental problems in the 1990s include the forthcoming conversion of the large inner harbour areas from industrial to another, as yet undetermined use, the rail service to Amager, the plan for a large satellite office development on Vestamager ("Ørestaden") and the establishment of a landlink to Sweden, which has been discussed in the section on the bridge plans. A draft revised municipal plan was published in January 1992. This has been criticised by environmental activists as an expression of the continued emphasis on economic growth.

The Mutually Supportive Welfare Society

A welfare society was gradually built up during the inter-war years and after the Second World War. Although chiefly the work of the Social Democrats, the principles gradually also gained the support of the other parties. This development was based on the principles of social solidarity with the least fortunate groups in society and was implemented via comprehensive social welfare legislation based on the principle of care, coupled with state regulation and control of market mechanisms, cooperative ideas incorporated into commercial enterprise - particularly in connection with agriculture, housing developments (massive state subsidies, low interest rates etc) and the retail trade, as well as strong interest groups. This social system necessitates the imposition of high and progressive taxation on personal income and company profits and high consumer taxes such as general VAT (1992: 25%) and additional excises on goods such as spirits, wine, beer, tobacco, cosmetics, cars and fuel.

The welfare state prioritised full employment, worker protection, improved occupational and living environments and municipal planning of urban development, new construction and urban renewal.

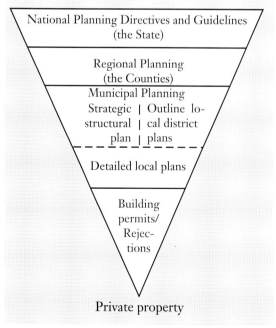

The Planning Pyramid in Denmark following the Planning Legislation Reforms, 1973-1975

National Planning Directives and Guidelines (the State)

Regional Planning (the Counties)

Municipal Planning
Strategic | Outline lo-
structural | cal district
plan | plans

Detailed local plans

Building permits/ Rejections

Private property

The Danish Administrative System

The Danish administrative system is a three tier system: the state, the counties and the municipalities, as illustrated here.

The political power of the state is divided on a tripartite basis between the legislative Folketing (parliament), confirmed by the signature of the monarch, an executive government, whose ministers are appointed by the monarch, and an independent judiciary.

The counties occupy an intermediate role with responsibility for main arterial roads, conservation, hospitals, pollution control etc. as well as regional planning and (partly) transport. Elected county councils are headed by a county mayor and raise their own property taxes. In addition, a county governor, who is a civil servant, is appointed to each county by the state. In the municipalities of Copenhagen and Frederiksberg the county responsibilities are handled by the municipal council.

In the Danish democracy there has been a longstanding tradition of extensive self-determination in local government. Local councils are directly elected by the local population, and councils raise their own taxes, largely via taxation on personal incomes. All local affairs are determined by the local councils, though with a degree of state control. Municipal responsibilities include town planning, building permits and control, urban renewal, energy supplies and local environmental control.

The Faroes and Greenland belong to the Kingdom of Denmark, but have their own special Home Rule agreement and are not covered by the Danish administrative system.

In 1970 a local government reform was implemented, whereby approx. 1300 municipalities were restructured geographically to form 275 new municipalities, and 27 counties were restructured into 14 units. Outwith the Greater Copenhagen area there was a comprehensive amalgamation of towns and their adjacent suburban districts into larger municipal units. This reform was followed by a revised distribution of responsibilities and a revision of the system of financial allocation between the state, the counties and the municipalities. The old state system of reimbursement of specific expenses was replaced by advance allocations of block grants from the state, calculated on the basis of certain objective criteria such as the total length of the road network, the number of old people, the number of antiquated dwellings etc.

The development of planning legislation - even the most far-reaching measures introduced in the Planning Legislation Reform in the 1970s was generally supported by a wide cross-party political majority.

This was partially due to the acceptance of a degree of official control and intervention in building, transport and other plans as necessary for the smooth operation of a modern, complex society. It was also recognised that planning could be instrumental in promoting economic growth. There was also an increasing awareness of the environmental and ecological dangers of uncontrolled growth, and the larger municipalities created by the local government reform in 1970 proved to be capable of administering the task of decentralised physical planning. Meticulous state control was replaced by the increased involvement of the local population. This was put into practice in a variety of ways in the individual municipalities, and in some places evoked strong local protests against plans for projects like new highways, extensive slum clearances and large commercial centres.

Environmental and Physical Planning in the Future

Despite considerable economic and political uncertainties, it is possible to indicate a number of probable developments in environmental and town planning in Denmark in the coming decade.

With the trend towards stagnation in population growth, there will no longer be as great a need for new housing as before the economic recession of the 1970s. Urban expansion will proceed at a slower pace, and urban renewal will become more important than new housing. This will feature renovations rather than demolitions and new developments, as well as locally implemented environmental improvements. A possible renewed economic dynamism may however stimulate increased industrial building activity, especially office blocks and service industry buildings.

Perhaps, and this is dependent on political developments, the process of decentralisation will be taken even further in the capital region and the largest provincial towns. Maybe decision-making authority in town planning, urban renewal, local transport and environmental issues will be devolved from the municipal councils to elected local community councils. The major financial problems experienced by the Greater Copenhagen region may lead to the increase of tax compensation by local authorities within the region to each other, but a reduction of their remittances to other areas of the country.

The new ideology of economic growth, coupled with the advent of the EC internal market and the free movement of capital, may lead to less regulation and supervision of commercial enterprises, and thus also less intervention from town planning authorities.

If Denmark had become a full member of the European Community Union, very sizeable losses in national revenue, without recourse to compensatory revenue increases, would have been incurred due to the requirements for budgetary discipline (no 'disproportionate' budget deficits), for the harmonisation of VAT and specific purchase taxes, the transfer of all monetary, foreign exchange and interest policies to the Union and the proposal for Union citizenship status for all citizens of the Community with certain rights. This will necessitate considerable public sector reductions and cuts in welfare expenditure affecting the social, health, housing and educational services.

The awareness of the general public of ecological threats and the deterioration of the environment will provoke political demands for more active environmental and energy policies. But these may conflict with the European Community's ban of trade barriers and unfair competition.

There will hardly be a need for further major reforms on the legislative front following the 1991 revised Planning and Environmental Acts, but this is subject to regulations and directives which may be passed by the Council of Ministers of the European Community Union.

The completion of the railway and motorway links across the Great Belt and the Sound and (at a later date) the Fehmarn Belt will, together with lower car taxes, imply even more cars on the roads, thus increasing air pollution, chiefly of carbon dioxide, which unlike sulphur and lead, cannot be reduced by catalysators.

Learning
in Denmark

by Harry Haue

The Danish Learning Process

Denmark's distinctive form of education has been influenced by theories from other countries. Comenius, Rousseau, Basedow, Dewey and Piaget are some of those educators who have been used and interpreted in Danish educational theory. The adaptation of foreign models to a Danish context has produced some original results. The most fundamental innovation has been the development of a non-authoritarian formative approach, and teaching methods which facilitate the respect of individual needs and interests. The non-authoritarian, individual approach in both the home and school has necessitated the delegation of considerable freedom of choice to the individual to determine the direction of his own education as well as its content and study methods.

This freedom of choice and co-determination has contributed to the reduction of social inequality in schools and has given girls genuine equality within the educational system.

The development of the three fundamental constituents of the Danish learning process - the non-authoritarian method, co-determination and equality - has at best resulted in the allocation of equal status to the general formative aspects of education in relation to the attainment of qualifications. The current trend emphasises that the process is just as important as the product, and that individual interests may not summarily be set aside in deference to the requirements of the system. Where this works well, participation in teaching becomes as important as received learning. Learning objectives at different times of life in Denmark must be evaluated with the above in mind and in terms of the pupil's own situation.

The tangible results in the classroom depend on the extent to which the teacher is able to incorporate the experiences of the pupils and to select relevant methods to achieve the overall objectives.

In principle the Danish school and educational systems are based on a decentralised and democratic structure. The prerequisites for successful implementation are the allocation of sufficient funds and a user-driven exigency. The decentralised and democratic trend is reinforced by the numerous alternatives to publicly administered education. Independent schools, leisure-time education and the many Folk High Schools are evidence of the multiplicity of choice available to the individual for learning in Denmark.

A non-authoritarian upbringing is fundamental to the Danish School. "Can you see children, what I have?" Illustration in "Nye Billed- og Læsebog for børn" (Children's Reading Book), 1808.

Educational Choice
A Non-authoritarian Tradition

There has never been compulsory school attendance in Denmark, but since 1814 there has been compulsory education. Parents who are dissatisfied with the public system have always had the option of either teaching their children themselves or finding other like-minded parents to establish an alternative school with state funds.

The alternative to the local authority school could be a private school where traditional educational norms are upheld, or a non- authoritarian independent school, which stresses the interests and needs of the individual child in a more systematic way than in the local authority school. Finally there are the independent schools with well-defined religious or political objectives.

The Folkeskole is the local authority-run 9 or 10 year basic school. In the Danish school system parental interests are allowed to play an important role in drafting the main educational guidelines, and this is possible firstly because the system is geared to allow parents to have a real influence, and secondly because its organisation is decentralised.

Continuity and concensus have thus characterised school developments and there have only been a few striking instances of confrontation between parents and the system. Legislation for schools has primarily served to codify alterations which have already been introduced, and thus legislative proposals have always enjoyed considerable backing, whilst the small opposing minority has been obliged to accept the fait accompli, already introduced by the pilot projects.

In 1967 corporal punishment was banned in schools. This ban had already been implemented in the municipality of Copenhagen in 1951. Attitudes to the use of discipline in schools had changed, and the most common form of discipline became the giving of detention.

There is obviously some connection between the degree of urbanisation and enforcement of discipline. A study just carried out by the Danish National Institute of Social Research has revealed that Copenhagen parents rated "good behaviour" lower than parents in the rest of the country on a list of six objectives for the education and formation of their children.

The nationwide abolition of corporal punishment in 1967 came as a consequence of the general reduction of corporal punishment in the home. The above-mentioned study also reveals that rather than "good behaviour", Copenhagen parents rate "responsibility" higher than parents in the rest of the country. The reason for this must be that the degree of occupational sophistication plays a significant role in methods of upbringing.

The statutes of the majority of the private schools, right from the 18th century pietist schools and later ministerial circulars on discipline in schools, all call for lenient disciplinary methods. But these guidelines were very rarely implemented, due to the fact that parents were practising corporal punishment themselves in the belief that the qualifications which most children had to attain all required the acceptance of an authoritarian system. Parents who opted to place their children in independent schools often based this choice on a desire to avoid traditional harsh discipline. It was not until the qualitative changes took place in industrial development in the 1950s that the expectations of children's future occupational roles also changed. This new departure stressed creativity, flexibility and ability to cooperate as its fundamental concepts. Children were no longer to be trained to enter a lifelong state of duty

65

In 1951 corporal punishment was abolished in Copenhagen. "He's got withdrawal symptoms". Drawing in "Socialdemokraten", 1951.

versus authority, but were to become acclimatised through open discussions to participate in problem solving and cooperation. In this context physical beatings did not serve a very useful purpose in the longer view. The non-authoritarian attitude manifested itself in many ways. It could be the tone of a school newspaper, a reluctance to stand up when the teacher came into class or to address him/her in the "De" (formal You) form. The wave of student unrest in 1968 was part of this process and stimulated the idea of an anti-authoritarian education. This anti-authoritarian educational ideal only found a foothold in a few marxist independent schools, but the critical attitude to traditional authority was adopted by the mainstream and came to influence both the Folkeskole and further education establishments.

Choice and Co-determination

The baby-boom of the war years resulted in overcrowded schools in the 1950s, and the nation's economic development was interpreted by many parents as a reason to allow their children to remain in school for the 8th and increasingly also the 9th grade. Progressive educational circles lobbied for the introduction of 9 years of compulsory education, but it was not until most parents had voluntarily opted to extend schooling for their children that broad political support could be mobilised. This happened in 1972. The nation's dynamic economic development sparked off radical reforms in 1958, which also had repercussions for the structure and content of the Gymnasium (Upper Secondary School). Since 1903 pupils wishing to take an academic education had transferred to a Middle School after the 5th grade, provided that they could pass a number of national tests. The new school legislation introduced a postponement of this division of pupils into practical and academic streams until the 7th grade. This gave late developers the chance to take the academic route . Pupils who wanted to take exams could however go to a 3-year Realskole (lower secondary school), and it was possible to transfer from here to the Gymnasium after the 2nd year.

The reform introduced greater subject orientation into the three-year Gymnasium course. Students could choose between a language and a mathematical line. After the first year it was possible to select specific subject branches and thus adapt the final matriculation exam (Studentereksamen) according to individual interests. The Studentereksamen gave access to universities, and provided a certain minimum average mark had been achieved, also to other establishments of higher education. This distinctly liberal admissions policy was amended in 1976 when it became obvious that the turnout of graduates in certain subjects would far exceed the demand. The prevailing economic climate also affected educational

The Danish School System, 1850-1990

approx. 1850, following the 1814 Act

In the country and small towns   In larger towns

Pupil's age			Free School	Municipal School	Grammar School
18					7th Grade
17					6th Grade
16					5th Grade
15					4th Grade
14					3th Grade
13				7th Grade	2th Grade
12				6th Grade	1th Grade
11	Top Class			5th Grade	5th Grade
10				4th Grade	4th Grade
9				3rd Grade	3rd Grade
8	Bottom Class			2nd Grade	2nd Grade
7				1st Grade	1st Grade

7-year school with two classes and teaching every other day

7-year school with 4 - 7 classes and half-day teaching every day

7-year school with 7 classes and full-day teaching every day

5 year preparatory school and 7 years grammar school with full-day teaching every day

1940, following the 1903 and 1937 Acts

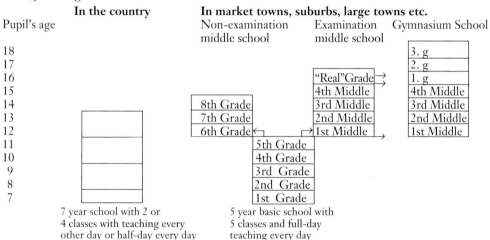

In the country   **In market towns, suburbs, large towns etc.**

Pupil's age		Non-examination middle school	Examination middle school	Gymnasium School
18				3. g
17				2. g
16			"Real"Grade →	1. g
15			4th Middle	4th Middle
14		8th Grade	3rd Middle	3rd Middle
13		7th Grade	2nd Middle	2nd Middle
12		6th Grade ← →	1st Middle →	1st Middle
11		5th Grade		
10		4th Grade		
9		3rd Grade		
8		2nd Grade		
7		1st Grade		

7 year school with 2 or 4 classes with teaching every other day or half-day every day

5 year basic school with 5 classes and full-day teaching every day

1990, following the 1958 Act with later amendments

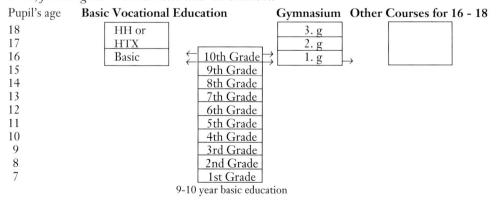

Pupil's age	**Basic Vocational Education**		**Gymnasium**	**Other Courses for 16 - 18**
18	HH or		3. g	
17	HTX		2. g	
16	Basic	← 10th Grade →	1. g →	
15		9th Grade		
14		8th Grade		
13		7th Grade		
12		6th Grade		
11		5th Grade		
10		4th Grade		
9		3rd Grade		
8		2nd Grade		
7		1st Grade		

9-10 year basic education

policy which moved away from a 'social demand' consideration to a more 'manpower' based attitude. The years of the baby boom coupled with the extended school attendance produced a demand for more qualified teachers, and a special two-year preparatory course for entry into teacher training college was established in 1966, called HF (Higher Preparatory Exam). This course was also open to the numerous adults who had not had the opportunity to go to a Gymnasium. This new course assumed a significant role in the overall educational spectrum and gained popularity as a qualifying exam for other forms of higher education, in competition with the Gymnasium.

The HF course was designed for mature students, and it was thus natural to allow more choice than in the Gymnasium, giving students the right of co-determination on choice of subjects and teaching materials. In 1968 legislation was passed to promote the establishment of student councils in the Gymnasium and the HF courses, which was partially due to the contention that the rights of organisation and formal influence on the day-to-day affairs of the course enjoyed by the mature students on the HF course, should be extended to the Gymnasium. In 1971 a minor reform of the Gymnasium to introduce the five-day week also contained measures which provided for the introduction of student co-determination on subject content and the organisation of teaching.

Student co-determination had a major impact on arts subjects such as Danish, history, religious education and modern languages. There was a change in educational models. In the 1960s students were still expected to learn the chronological development in history and literary history. But the disruptions in society - economic, social and cultural, removed all agreement on what it was considered essential to learn. In this breakdown of values the decision-makers, the experts, educationalists and politicians, decided to let the students make their own choices. So it was the fads of youth culture which came to dominate the subjects and methodology. The cultural revolution in China was a popular subject choice and group work a supplementary study method. The objective was no longer knowledge as a well-defined portion of proficiency but knowledge as part of a process.

Methodological insight as well as documentation and evaluation skills thus assumed highest priority, especially in the arts subjects.

This educational ideal also influenced the Folkeskole. During the 1970s, a 9 year comprehensive system evolved, which permitted the pupil to delay any decision regarding choice between 10th grade, vocational training, or Gymnasium-HF to be left until after the 9th grade. A final option open to pupils at this stage is to drop out of the educational system altogether and join the residual group which currently constitutes some 10 - 15% of an age group.

The major reform of the Folkeskole system in 1975 included the introduction of subject choice within the comprehensive school. After consultation with parents and teachers, 7th grade pupils can now choose between a number of electives to be taken in the 8th and 9th grades. This splits up a class which has had joint lessons in all subjects for 7 years. Only children with special learning difficulties are withdrawn from the class for remedial lessons for a number of hours a week. The final school leaving examination at the end of the 9th grade is offered at two levels, the basic course and the extended course. Classes are still unstreamed, but the exam requirements for each level are different. Thus, despite the comprehensive nature of the Folkeskole, there is an element of streaming.

The 1975 Schools Act outlined a new mission statement for the Folkeskole, which included the following: "The Folkeskole prepares the pupil for participation and codetermination in a democratic society and for the assumption of co-responsibility in the solution of joint tasks. The teaching and day-to-day affairs of the school must therefore be based on intellectual liberty and democracy". Parental influence on the Folkeskole and on the children's subject choices is extensive. In the introduction to the 1975 mission statement it is specifically stated that all the activities of the school must be organised in cooperation with the parents. Parental influence manifests itself in the active collaboration between teachers, children and parents in the individual classes. A weekly class meeting is held right from the 1st grade stage through to 10th grade. This provides the forum for teachers, especially form teachers, to discuss teaching content, form and methods, as well as social events, with the pupils. Parents, especially in the younger classes, are invited several times a year to participate in meetings, discussions and consultations on educational standards, behaviour etc. Since 1990 parents' paramount influence has been channelled via the school boards, which have decision-making powers in a number of vital areas affecting school life. But as already mentioned, parents may still opt to teach their children themselves or send them to a private school. They have also now been given the option to select a municipal school outwith their local catchment area. Finally they have a certain influence on the starting age for their children, as they may either postpone school entry or bring it forward a year.

It is also the parents who decide whether a child should repeat a year and, together with the children, which subjects

are to be taken in the 8th and 9th grades and at what level the exam is to be attempted.

In 1985 an OECD report on the Danish Folkeskole concluded: " The system does work: the teachers and parents do cooperate: the system is effective because of the high degree of *trust* which exists between the parties. In Denmark there is a very delicate balance between parents, the teachers and the authorities. The Danes are very aware that the system works and its works because of the relations of trust. In consequence all the parties are reluctant to disturb the balance of forces, for to do so might disrupt the effectiveness of the system in which all parties currently achieve a high level of satisfaction."

Liberty and Equality

In 1991 the Danish National Institute of Social Research published a major study which included a survey of parental ideals on upbringing. The results of this survey provide the basis for a reliable assessment of the ideals held by contemporary Danish parents. 1858 parents of schoolchildren were given a list of six attributes which should be promoted in children in their domestic upbringing. Each family had to select 3 of these attributes. Of the six options, 86% selected independence, 79% a sense of responsibility, 44% tolerance, 44% good manners, 35% active imagination and 5% thrift. It may be assumed that most parents approve of thrift, but when forced to prioritise, this attribute receives least emphasis. When the weighting is analysed according to social groups it emerges that unskilled workers gave a far higher priority to good manners and thrift than parents with a background of higher education. The liberation of a child from its social heritage through education can therefore

69

be inhibited by strong parental influences.

But it cannot be a realistic objective to insist on everyone being equal, with the same interests and values. A democratic school must respect differences, and insist on liberty over and above equality. It is however important that parents and teachers interpret the individual choices as equally valuable from a human point of view. In my opinion the Danes have made considerable progress in this area in recent years, but this progress is difficult to demonstrate in figures and percentages. It is unsatisfactory that between 10 and 15% of a class do not continue any form of education after the 9th or 10th grade.

The equal status of girls within the educational system is a concrete example of how liberty can break a traditional social pattern.

In 1960, 10% of all adult Danish women were registered as available for the labour market. In 1990 this percentage had risen to almost 90%. This development has had a fundamental influence on the educational choices and learning orientations of girls.

Girls now make up the majority of students taking the academically oriented courses offered by the Gymnasia/HF, as well as a number of higher education courses. There are several reasons for this real equality. Firstly, girls are now being brought up by mothers who themselves are working, and who in many cases have also completed some form of further education. Secondly, the Feminist movement has strongly emphasised the need for education. Thirdly, the divorce statistics have demonstrated that marriage cannot be regarded as a form of social insurance, and finally the introduction of equal opportunities in society and the labour market has helped to remove sex discrimination in

Girls now make up the majority of students taking the academically oriented courses. Group work in the Gymnasium school. Photo: Peter Olsen

the educational system.

In the 1980s much attention in schools was focused on the concept of "quiet girls", but this concern seems to be waning, and new research shows that girls perform better in exams than boys. In the equal opportunities debate it has been pointed out that a feminisation of upbringing methods has evolved as a result of the dismantling of the authoritarian role of the father. Whilst this may benefit girls' interests, there are now insufficient challenges for boys. 75% of Folkeskole teachers are women, and there has also been a shift in favour of women on the teaching staff of Gymnasia. Despite these developments however, equality has not been achieved in all areas of society, neither in politics, nor in business management, nor in the distribution of work in the home.

Teaching Objectives - Pupils - Results The Folkeskole

The teaching objectives in the Folkeskole remained unaltered from 1814 to 1937. As the nation became industrialised and urbanised, the requirement arose to provide the same basic educational opportunities for rural children as were enjoyed by those in towns.

The objectives formalised in 1937 state that the Folkeskole's aim ".... is to foster and develop children's aptitudes and abilities, to reinforce character development and provide them with useful knowledge". It was further laid down that religious education should be in accordance with the doctrine of the Danish Lutheran-evangelical church. However, the acceleration of industrial development since the 1960s has produced the need for a different kind of qualifying and socialising environment for children. Public awareness heightened, creating the need for a revision of the objectives of basic

education, which took place after years of intensive debate. The revised Schools Act of 1975 states that it is "the task of the Folkeskole, in collaboration with parents, to provide pupils with the opportunities to acquire knowledge, skills, working methods and modes of expression, which will contribute to the all-round development of the individual. In all its activities, the Folkeskole must seek to establish opportunities for experience and self-direction, which will encourage pupils to increase their eagerness to learn, to use their imagination and to develop independent judgement and views."

In addition the Folkeskole is also required to prepare the pupil for living and participating in a democratic society.

The educational and philosophical considerations underlying the concepts of experience, self-motivation, eagerness to learn, development of the imagination and independence are innovations in the mission statement, but not actually in practical teaching. Individual teachers have long regarded many of these concepts as important objectives for their own work, as teachers and pupils alike may recall from their own experience. The concepts of knowledge and character development contained in the 1937 mission statement were probably indicative of the priority given to the product, knowledge, over and above the process, character development.

The major 1958 school reform did not include a revision of the 1937 mission statement, but the White paper, published in connection with the reform and including the requirements for the revision of the objectives of individual subjects, had the objective of enabling children to learn to learn as its underlying idea, in other words it underlined the concept of process. In the 1975 reform the process was singled out for central emphasis. The objective is now the all-

Children should have the opportunity to use their creativity and imagination. Physics lesson at Enghøjskolen in Copenhagen. Photo: Lars Bahl/2.maj.

round development of the individual pupil. And the means to further this end are knowledge, skills, method and powers of expression.

The 1975 mission statement was influenced by examples from other countries. Progressivist educational theory has had a few, articulate spokesmen over the last century. Its origins go back to psychoanalytical psychology, and its objectives were the liberation and independence of children. Between the wars a few experimental schools were established which operated on progressivist principles.

A number of other educational models have also played an obvious role. But the Danish "folkelig" tradition of a liberating education as practised in the independent schools run on the principles of Grundtvig and Kold has provided the prerequisite framework within which theories from abroad could be interpreted for Danish use. The synthesis of progressivist educational theory from abroad and the Danish independent school tradition facilitated a broad political backing for the new mission statement. Support for progressivist ideas was strongest on the left wing, whilst the Danish traditions were supported by the right. Mission statements are normative, and in Denmark they are characterised by a high degree of compromise. They can often be contextually correct whilst also being devoid of content, but in an age when the Danes needed new values and guidelines, the statement proved to contain more than empty headings.

The 1975 Schools Act required instruction to be offered in 15 compulsory subjects and several electives. Each school is responsible for pursuing the objectives of the individual subjects, as laid down by the Minister of Education. The subject

72

contents are detailed in the curriculum which is drafted for each school by the municipal committees. The curriculum is drafted along the guidelines provided by the recommended curricula issued by the Ministry. Local authorities have some freedom to determine the number of weekly lessons for each subject.

Children's Domestic Environment

For the 1975 objectives to have any chance of fulfilment, the pupil's own situation and interests must be taken into consideration. Many pupils are accustomed to institutions prior to school entry; they are used to functioning in a group, to cooperating and to having other adult role models in addition to their parents. About 15% of the under-twos are looked after in creches, and nearly half the 3 - 6 year olds attend kindergarten. When they are six, most children start in the voluntary nursery class at school, which is designed to acclimatise them to school life, rather than providing any formal education.

The findings of a study published in 1991 by the Danish National Institute of Social Research reveal that 80% of Danish children live in a traditional nuclear family, i.e. together with both their biological parents. 10% of children live with one parent alone and only 5% live in families where one of the biological parents has been replaced by a step-parent. Schoolchildren (7 - 15 year olds), spend a lot of time with their families. Studies reveal that adults spend on average 4 1/2 hours a day with 7 -11 year olds and 4 hours with the 12 - 15 year olds. Mothers spend more time with children than fathers. Nearly all children eat dinner with their parents, but only two-thirds eat breakfast with them. When the school day finishes between 2 and 3 pm children often return home to an empty

house, since both parents are at work. Most urban districts provide fee-paying after-school clubs for the under-tens. Here the children are looked after by trained staff, who keep them occupied with games and hobbies. For the over-tens, and especially in larger towns, there are adventure playgrounds with adult supervision.

The survey also showed that most adults had watched TV in the preceding week and chatted with their children. 68% had played with them, 54% had gone for a walk, 47% had read aloud to them , 24% had taken them to a sporting event, 14% had been to the library with children and 5% had taken them to an exhibition.

TV and Video

TV and videos occupy a central position in family life. A 1987 survey on children's video viewing habits by the Social Research Institute revealed that 30% of schoolchildren had video recorders at home, and that these children watched video programmes almost every day. As they grew older, their interests diverged and it was revealed that boys watch more than girls. However it is considered that the amount of time spent watching videos was mostly within reason. This also applied to TV viewing. A 1980 survey reveals that 7 - 14 year olds spend an average of 1 1/2 hours a day watching TV, whilst parents watch approx. 1 1/4 hours per day. Danish children thus watch an average of 10 hours a weeks, which is far less than children in the United States, where the average is 25 hours. Boys are more interested in TV than girls. The study also revealed that those children with the highest TV consumption were also those who read most books, comics and magazines. It therefore concludes that children use TV primarily as an

73

exciting and relaxing pastime, rather than an educational aid. Nevertheless TV is the most educational of all the mass media. It expands children's knowledge of the adult world and familiarises them with foreign languages. It would therefore be reasonable to assume that teachers can draw on children's TV experiences to develop associations and new perspectives. All schools possess video-equipment, including recorders, thus enabling them to work critically and creatively with this medium.

Libraries and Play

A 1987 survey of children's library use reveals that 75% of the 7 - 11 year olds and over 80% of 12 - 15 year olds are regular users of public libraries. Urban children borrow more books than rural children and there are other social differences. However 55% of library users come from homes where the parents are non-users. These new clients have obviously been inspired by familiarisation with the school library and by encouragement from teachers of Danish. The survey also analysed schoolchildren's reading habits and found that boys start reading 'real books' later than girls. Boys read more comics than girls, and even though reading rates level out somewhat in the early teens, the boys never quite catch up with the girls. There appears to be a male preference for pictures, which applies to TV and videos as well as comics.

In addition to playing in school breaks, in the after-school clubs and with their parents, children meet their need to play by inviting friends home after school. The 1987 report includes the results of interviews with children about their playing habits and these reveal that nearly one third of children invite friends home almost every day. Three out of four have friends home at least once a week. Gen-

der-specific toys are still predominant in the younger age group, with boys playing with cars and girls with dolls. Only 5% of children never play with friends at home. Of course this pattern changes as the children grow up, and by the age of 14 to 15 children show an interest in socialising, also with members of the opposite sex, outwith the watchful eye of their parents.

The study also reveals that four out of five schoolchildren participate in a leisure-time activity, on which they spend an average of four hours a week. 65% of both girls and boys play some form of sport. The remainder spend time on music, singing, dancing, riding or scout work. Boys typically do not display as much variety in their leisure-time activities as the girls. More girls continue these interests after they reach puberty than boys. One boy in every four in the 13-15 age bracket does not participate in any leisure-time activity.

Young People at the Gymnasium

The 1987 Gymnasium reform confirmed its dual purpose; both to provide an all-round education and a preparatory base for higher education. The Ministry of Education has the overall responsibility for the Gymnasia, which are operated under county administration.

As with the Folkeskole, each Gymnasium has a board which wields considerable authority. Many of the Gymnasia also run HF (Higher Preparatory) courses. Pupils normally progress to the Gymnasium after the 9th grade of the Folkeskole, but may also be accepted after the 10th grade. Acceptance is normally conditional on a recommendation of suitability provided by the pupil's first school, but if this is not available, aspirants may also sit an entrance examination. The reform of the Gymnasium which was implemented in 1988, removed the system of subject

Most of the Gymnasia run annual Theme days, with the whole school participating in the project. Carnival at Tornbjerg Gymnasium in Odense. Photo: Lars Poulsen.

departments which had been introduced in the 1960s. The pupils now have a greater choice of subject combinations than was previously possible; for instance they can now take both English and Mathematics at an advanced level. New subjects have also been introduced, including Philosophy, Technical studies, Computer studies and Business Economics. The two basic streams of Mathematics and Languages Lines have been retained, but the natural sciences have been given greater emphasis in the Languages Line and more priority has been given to English in the Mathematics Line. The syllabus contents of the individual subjects have been revised with a higher priority given to coherence and general knowledge at the expense of the predominantly methodological requirements contained in the 1971 reform. The 1987 reform increased the requirements to produce independent written work. One paper has to be submitted in the 1st Year in Danish studies, one in the 2nd Year in History, and a major assignment in the 3rd Year in either Danish, History or one of the two advanced level subjects.

The reform has reinforced the strong position enjoyed by the academically-oriented courses, attracting some 40% of lower secondary school leavers.

The EFG (Basic Vocational Education) courses were formalised in 1977 after an initial trial period. They were established as a result of the decrease in numbers seeking traditional apprenticeships as well as the demands being made by industry

75

and commerce for a more flexible workforce. The aim of these foundation courses was to augment the theoretical dimension and to introduce pupils to more general subjects. Several abortive attempts have been made to integrate the EFG courses with the Gymnasium and HF. The Labour movements and associated political parties were in favour of integration, along the lines implemented in Norway and Sweden in the 1970s. But the more conservative parties and the employers were unwilling to integrate the theoretical and vocational upper secondary courses. Pupils may progress to the EFG courses after either the 9th or 10th grade of the Folkeskole. A 40 week foundation course covers the nature and function of the subjects under several main areas. The pupils then start a 3 to 4 year period comprising practical vocational training alternating with modules of formal theoretical education at school. This ensures a comprehensive vocational grounding and thus enables the pupil to select the vocation which best suits his or her interests. Whilst it has not been possible to integrate the theoretical and the vocational basic education courses for young people, advanced vocational courses have been established, including elements from both the EFG and the theoretical gymnasium studies. The HTX (Higher Technical Exam) is designed for pupils wishing to take up engineering studies, and the HHX (Higher Commercial Exam) for those who wish to progress to the Higher Colleges of Business Studies.

Youth Awareness

When young people in the final years of the Folkeskole and the higher secondary courses start breaking free from parental influences, they do so in a climate of rapid social change. The gap between their parents' horizons and the opportunities they envisage for themselves can appear so great that they make a complete break with the traditions of their parents and feel culturally liberated.

The Danish Institute for Future Research and the Ministry of Education have published a joint survey on young people's attitudes to the future. Pupils attending Gymnasium and various EFG and HF courses were asked to write an essay on their expectations of the future. An analysis of the 1487 answers produced four distinct categories of young person; the ordinary pragmatic group, the horror-stricken group, the anxious group and the enterprising group. The ordinary pragmatists constituted the largest group, comprising 48% of the answers. These young people hoped for a future focusing around a happy family in a secure environment. It is clear that they were copying an idealised version of their parents' life. In a way they have rejected a 'liberation' by repressing any break with tradition. 28% expressed a genuine fear of the future in their answers. They feel that "the future is devoid of any hope or opportunities, dominated by dismal concrete jungles, voluntary childlessness and human isolation". Some even believed that the world would be destroyed before they reached the age of 35. The 10% who fell into the anxious group believed that the negative aspects of modern life would probably dominate their future. The threats included unemployment, nuclear warfare, pollution and AIDS.

15% of the respondents could be categorised as entrepreneurs. They regarded the future as a challenge, and believed that they could exert a considerable influence on their own future. They expect to enjoy exciting experiences and demanding challenges at work. Young Danes thus display very diverging reactions to the challenges of a disintegrated culture.

Whilst the ordinary pragmatist attempts to solve his problems by hoping for security and a firm framework, the horror-stricken look to intimacy, warmth and contact. Both groups are introverted, and if their descriptions of their expectations of the future correspond to their real attitudes, then they are hardly suited to tackle the social challenges which lie ahead. On the other hand, the entrepreneurs were prepared to use their liberation in the solution of future problems. The overriding concepts which apply to this group are dynamism, fascination and intensity. There is much evidence to indicate that the upbringing of their parents' generation in a culture of logically structured opinions and beliefs clashes with the more aesthetic experience-oriented culture of the youth of today. They are marked by a lack of adult sparring partners and opponents and influenced by a media-oriented peer group of friends perceiving the world around them like a remote scanning device. The teachers of upper secondary education are confronted with these different groups of pupils and have to unite their interests working with theoretical problems of a very traditional nature.

There is an increasing emphasis on subject proficiency in the Gymnasium. Swotting for exams. Photo: Peter Olsen.

Teachers' Qualifications and Additional Resources

The teachers are equipped with a good hand of cards for the task of uniting the educational goals with the interests of the pupils. Folkeskole teachers all complete a 4 year teacher training course, covering theoretical educational studies and practical teaching skills as well as advanced studies in two school subjects of their choice. Supplementary in-service training is also available. Gymnasium and HF teachers are university graduates (which normally takes five to six years, and requires two subject specialities) who have also completed a theoretical and practical educational course. Both categories are thus entirely professional and they enjoy reasonable conditions of pay and social status. Applications for Colleges of Education consistently exceed the number of places available. Both categories of teachers enjoy considerable methodological freedom. Choice of themes and methods is only restricted by the syllabus requirements for external examinations and teachers thus have a pretty free hand. The school principals are responsible for the administration but not the supervision of the teaching, but they do have the right to intervene if objectives are not met. There are no school inspectors, but there are a number of advisors, whose function is to provide guidance rather than to carry out inspections. Unannounced visits by advisors are rare. All counties run a teaching resource centre, from which teachers may

77

borrow sets of books and audio-visual material. Subject and teaching advice is also available.

All schools are well-stocked with technical aids, including good photocopying equipment, so that teachers can produce their own material or supplement the literature available.

The Downside of Restricted Admission

The essential prerequisites for success in the learning process should thus be present. Most teachers agree that this is so. But the system also harbours some adverse elements, which at worst can turn the learning process into a negative experience. This may have a number of origins; personal. educational, structural or subject-based. Only a couple of possible negative factors will be discussed here. One of them is the policy of restricted admission to higher education, introduced in the late 1970s for economic reasons. There were no longer sufficient national resources to allow unrestricted rights of admission and it was therefore decided to channel admissions into subjects where the greatest demand for graduates was anticipated. Nowadays one third of applicants from Gymnasium and the HF courses are rejected. They are usually advised to improve their qualifications by getting some relevant work experience or taking supplementary courses. The competition is tough. This naturally affects the atmosphere in the upper secondary schools. The overriding interest of teachers who had started up experimental teaching projects in the 1970s had been to create cohesive relationships between the various subjects, either by interdisciplinary collaboration or by initiating more ambitious pilot projects. The idea was to employ the subject contents as vehicles via which the pupils could attain a higher degree of functional development. They would thereby acquire an understanding of the world which would enable them to solve complicated problems with a global perspective. Insight into the various subjects would be achieved by a process of committed and responsible cooperation.

The aim was thus to accord a higher priority to participatory learning than to received learning. But the introduction of restricted admissions produced the demand for more structured teaching, where there was no room for experimental educational approaches and issues. This happened quietly and gradually but the trend towards individuality had penetrated completely by the mid 1980s. Maybe this would have happened even if admission restrictions had not been introduced, but it is difficult to dismiss a link. In any case it is recognised by many Gymnasium teachers that pupils' involvement in individual subjects has increased at the expense of the desire to experiment with various modes of cooperation. Subject-oriented work is preferred to broader perspectives and the importance of marks has taken on a governing and dominating role. The latest reform of the Gymnasium system with its plurality of options has reinforced subject orientation at the expense of broad interdisciplinary work, but on the other hand the emphasis placed on arts subjects in the final year helps to provide an awareness of cohesion.

It has maybe also been this increasing subject-orientation in the Gymnasium which has influenced pupils at Folkeskole level to opt for the advanced school leaving exam and concentrate on the compulsory subjects at the expense of optional electives. A 1985 OECD report indicates that this trend will impede the achievement of the prime objective: the all-round development of the individual pupil.

The considerable weight of parental influence will hardly bear favourably upon the optional subjects, and there is no tradition for central intervention against parental interests. There are not enough work-based training posts for the EFG trainees, and every year thousands of young people completing the foundation course fail to find an employer who will offer a traineeship. This results in frustration and resignation and these youngsters easily drop into the youth unemployment category, from which they can only be rescued by new educational initiatives.

Alternative Learning Paths
Lifelong Education

The early 19th century "folkelig" consciousness-raising movement of the people prepared the foundations for the establishment of the first folk high schools. The first one was started in the Duchy of Schleswig in 1844 as part of the nationalist endeavours. The target group was the young rural population, who were encouraged to supplement their basic Folkeskole education with liberal studies, thereby creating a counterculture whose members would be in a position to exploit the instruments of democracy which were introduced with the new Constitution in 1849. The idea was to develop the peasantry from a group of subjects to a group of participating citizens. The folk high schools normally offered a five months' course during the winter for young men and a three months' course in the summer for young women. Up until the 1960s most students came from a rural background, and folk high school people regarded this liberal education, unrestricted by national curriculum requirements, as an alternative to the vocational and aca-

The 'folkelig' revivalist movements in the first half of the 19th century not only paved the way for the folk high schools and the free schools, but also exerted a profound influence on teaching methods in the Folkeskole. The two central figures were the priest N.F.S.Grundtvig (1783-1872), who developed the theories, and the educator Christen Kold (1816-1870), who realised the theories. On the left N.F.S. Grundtvig, drawn by C.W.Eckersberg in 1829. On the right: Christen Kold. 1860's Xylograph.

demic courses offered in towns. In contrast to the bookish learning of the Gymnasia and the universities, the folk high school teachers used the spoken word in the presentation of the main subjects, which were history and literature.

The industrialisation and urbanisation process of the 1960s led to the need to recruit students from urban districts. These new target groups wanted study groups as well as the traditional lectures. They wanted to have a say in the choice of subjects to be dealt with, and nowadays most folk high schools have a specifically defined orientation. The Environment, The Third World, Sport and Art are some of the special interest areas available for study. The courses have also been adapted to suit the occupational structure of the new user groups, and many short courses have been designed. The folk high school's system of liberal education served as an inspiration for the development of the independent schools for children as an alternative to the local authority schools. The educational philosophy guiding these schools aimed at developing the child's talents and aptitudes by appealing to its imagination instead of employing the rote-learning and disciplinary methods of the local authority schools. Parents who had encountered the free teaching methods of the folk high schools made certain demands of the Folkeskole. Where these could not be met, many parents decided to set up their own schools. The schools legislation enables these schools to be grant-aided and to be subjected to the minimum of control.

The Continuation Schools

In addition to the folk high school and the independent school there is also the Continuation School, which offered youngsters who had just been confirmed some form of further education. When

compulsory education was extended to 9 years, it was made possible to do the 8th and 9th grades at a continuation school and to take the standard school leaving exams there. The state refunds 85% of the teaching budget and provides favourable loans for building projects. The continuation school which is a boarding school, is a good idea for children who need to get away from home and the local authorities usually provide grants.

For those children who stay in the Folkeskole there is a local authority-run youth school, which offers evening courses in subjects not available at the Folkeskole. All those people who had been won over to the idea of a continuing learning process through their experience of a continuation or folk high school then found it quite natural to establish evening institutes. These would provide a local forum for lectures, debates, choir practices or handicraft sessions for people of all ages and occupations. In rural areas this was usually organised by the Folkeskole teacher, and in urban areas the trade union movement started arranging evening classes for members around the turn of the century. Increasing interest led to the introduction of legislation which ensured reasonable conditions for this voluntary educational work and secured payment for teachers and subsidies for the acquisition of books and materials.

Leisure-time and Adult Education

In the years between the two world wars, leisure-time education developed into the preferred form of continuing education in Denmark. In 1968 the Folketing passed "the best Leisure-time Act in the world", as it was called by one of its proposers. Broad political support had been mustered to ensure the provision of generous grants to the ongoing educational work of the politically affiliated educational associations and to new initiatives such as interest groups.

This provided for the public subsidy of any activity, including hobbies, supported by at least 12 participants, who were also required to pay a fee, which though initially very modest, has become proportionately greater in recent years. The 1984 revision of the Act was accompanied by a major pilot project instigated to investigate the demand for leisure-time education. Interest groups with members of all ages, sexes and education were formed and, in particular, numerous initiatives were taken to gather groups in a single local school or community hall. People were obviously interested in turning the schools into local cultural centres and thus the forum for leisure-time education as well as teaching for children.

A new Act on leisure-time education was passed in 1990. Whilst local authorities previously had been obliged to subsidise anyone who wished to organise a course, the new legislation provided for allocations within a fixed budget. Each municipality has established a special "folkeoplysningsudvalg" (committee on Folkeoplysning - informal education and cultural activities) to advise the municipal council and be responsible for the allocation of grants within the limits set by the council. The committee is made up largely of representatives of various societies, including sports clubs, with a minority representation of municipal councillors.

The new legislation also included measures for the day folk high schools which have evolved in recent years for the benefit of adults who, as a result of unemployment or personal problems, need a new start. These are day schools running courses of a minimum of four weeks duration.

The Folk High School still plays an important role in Danish education. Ryslinge Højskole on Funen.

Production Schools

A special kind of start-up activity is organised in the production schools, where instruction is provided in specific areas of production. The target market for these schools is the group of young unemployed who are not sufficiently motivated to embark on a formal education. These schools evolved from a number of pilot projects initiated by the independent schools in the 1970s, working systematically to combine theory and practice. The need for these schools was created by the drop in demand for unskilled workers and a disturbingly large residual group who received no further education after leaving the Folkeskole. This type of school is the latest branch to sprout from the folk high school tradition. The production

81

schools do not provide any formal qualifications, but aim at giving participants the necessary confidence to embark on a formal education or to get a job.

Adult Education Centres

During the 1970s the Adult Education Associations started to offer courses based on the 8th and 9th grades of Folkeskole. This was supplemented by the development of Single Subject Courses at HF level, which enabled adults, many of them in full-time employment, to gradually build up a HF qualification. This proved to be a dynamic innovation and today there a numerous adult education centres (VUC) where thousands of adults manage to obtain qualifications and the confidence to continue with their education.

Adults who pass the HF exams can progress to courses of higher education on the same terms as younger students. But many do not wish to give up their jobs and a new option is now available to this group, through the Open University, which was developed in the late 1980s along British lines. This is primarily based on distance-learning and has been most popular for the arts subjects. Employed people who wish to improve their professional qualifications may apply for study grants, but not for paid leave. The trade unions have been unsuccessful in their campaign for paid study leave. Perhaps the coordination of adult education within the European Single Market will improve the chances of the introduction of paid study leave. After a certain period of unemployment, beneficiaries are obliged to take up a course of study in order to maintain their right to unemployment benefit.

Conclusion

The learning process in Denmark is non-authoritarian, decentralised and democratic by nature. This allows for the natural evolution of alternatives to the publicly run institutions. The right of free choice and co-determination are fundamental values which bridge existing social and cultural differences in Denmark.

Work and Leisure Time

by Torben Fridberg

The Danes do not consider themselves to be a particulary industrious or hard-working nation. The Germans are hard-working. They practically flog themselves. And the Swedes are efficient. The Danes are more relaxed, and place more value on their quality of life, comfort and well-being. Or so we think. Of course work provides the basis for our material well-being, and over the last 30 years the Danes have been able to enjoy a tremendous rise in wealth and consumption, the achievement of which has been a high priority for the population at large. But in addition to income, work is also important to the individual in other respects. It influences his image of himself and of society. Work provides status and the security of self-reliance. In Denmark every able-bodied adult is expected to work to provide for him/herself and possibly other members of the family. The target of work for everyone is not only based on arguments for equality/democracy but also on individual/social demand factors. In practice therefore, the Danes do attach considerable importance to work in many ways, and what is more, they are quite industrious. This is demonstrated by the size of the labour force, the long working hours put in by the average family, the general attitude etc. The average day is pretty hectic for the modern family with children, and even their leisure-time is being exploited more intensively.

The Labour Force

The most striking manifestation of the industriousness of the Danes is the high proportion who belong to the labour force, either working as wage-earners or self-employed, or possibly unemployed but available for work. In 1987, 86% of all men and 76% of all women in the 18-66 age group belonged to the labour force. This is a very high labour market partici-

pation by international standards, because so many women are economically active. In fact the male labour market participation has fallen slightly over the last 30 years. In 1960 95% of men of normal working age were part of the labour force.

Table 1. Labour Market Participation for Selected Age Groups. 1960-87

	1960	1970	1980	1987
Men				
20-24	91.3	82.2	89.7	88.5
35-39	98.7	97.9	95.3	94.2
50-54	97.0	94.8	91.4	90.8
60-66	83.3	77.6	55.0	46.7
18-66	94.9	90.8	86.8	85.9
Women				
20-24	58.9	67.5	85.5	85.2
35-39	35.8	56.6	83.3	89.9
50-54	37.4	50.5	76.2	76.3
60-66	20.5	23.0	27.6	24.3
18-66	39.2	52.5	70.9	76.3

Source: Danmarks Statistik

There was a drop in labour market participation amongst the younger age groups until the mid 70s, which was due to the increase in numbers taking up further and higher education, as well as the replacement of the traditional apprenticeships by the Basic Vocational Education courses (EFG), which include long periods of training at schools rather than at places of work. EFG students are therefore not included in the work-force statistics, whereas apprentices had been. However since the late 1970s the labour market participation amongst young people has risen again. This is due to the fact that it has become more common for students to also have some form of paid employment.

The decrease in the labour market participation in the oldest age group is due to the fact that the effective retirement age for large sectors of the population is falling, despite the fact that the official retirement age in Denmark is still 67. The acceleration of this trend was sparked

More and more women work full-time, and some are even penetratring the male strongholds! Female welders.
Photo: Henrik Saxgren/2.maj.

off by the introduction of early retirement pay in 1979, and today less than half of the men aged between 60 and 66 are still in employment. Early retirement pay is available to members of Unemployment Insurance Schemes aged between 60 and 66, if they have been members for at least 10 years within the preceding 15 years. In the first years of early retirement the pay corresponds to the standard unemployment benefit, and thereafter it falls to 80%. The early retirement scheme was introduced as a measure to counter the rise in unemployment after 1974. The objective was to redistribute the available jobs, to facilitate access for more young people, and to allow older workers, perhaps worn-out, to withdraw from the labour market without having to apply for a government early retirement pension on health grounds. The scheme proved to be

a great success and today 29% of all those in the 60-66 age group receive early retirement pay. A further 35% are in receipt of some form of early retirement pension, and 2% have opted for semi-retirement schemes. Thus only a third of the 60-66 year olds are still active in the labour market. The early retirement pay solution is most common amongst men, whilst the pension is the most common option for women.

There has also been a slight drop in labour market participation for men in the principal age groups apart from those young people in education and the elderly on their way out of the labour market. Increased demands at work have probably contributed to the increase in numbers of people of all age groups who are unable to hold down a job, and thus transfer to early retirement pensions. This problem has been exacerbated by the reduction of sheltered workshops.

The earlier retirement of the oldest age-group and the overall lower participation rate for men has however been more than outweighed by the development of female labour market participation. Their participation rate has doubled over the last 30 years, and is almost level with the male rate in the younger age groups.

Part of the increase has been due to the uptake of part-time work, but this trend has also waned in recent years. There has been a progression towards an extension of the working week for part-timers. Also more women have full-time jobs. The increase in numbers of women working full-time is particularly marked in the younger age groups. Approximately one third of the current female work force is employed on less than full-time terms.

The increase in women working full-time also applies to households with small children. The trend in Denmark today, in contrast to both Sweden and Norway, is that the younger the children are, the more likely the mother is to have full-time work. This must be due to a generational effect. Young women today enter the labour market with different expectations than their predecessors. And they are also better educated than their mothers. The economic situation in Denmark in the 1980s has also meant that the younger generation have had to put in more hours than their predecessors in order to make ends meet. And this affiliation with the labour market will probably mean that this generation will continue to work full-time on a par with men.

Historically only a small proportion of men have been employed on a part-time basis, but the incidence of part-time male employees is now on the increase, whilst that of women is falling. In 1990 approx. 10% of men were working part-time. On the other hand there is a significant group of men who work more than the standard full-time working week. In 1987 one in every four men with children under the age of three worked more than the standard week, which was 39-40 hours at that time. In families where the youngest child is three or more, approx. 30% of the fathers work more than full-time. Altogether this means that in half the families with young children, both parents are working at least full-time.

The largest group in the labour force is the group of 25-59 year olds, comprising over 2.1 million people. This means that 87% of all men and women in this age group belong to the labour force. The high incidence of women in employment also means that there is no longer any difference between the incidence of married and unmarried women in the labour market. This has also meant that the category of „housewife" is almost extinct in Denmark. And this development has been extremely rapid. In 1965, 66% of mothers of young children were housewives. By 1987 this percentage had plunged to only 7%. The increased female labour market participation is one of the most significant developments of recent years, and has had repercussions in numerous areas. One of the most obvious consequences has been the increased transfer of childcare and care of the elderly to the public sector.

Moonlighting

There is also a lot of work which is not included in the official Danish employment statistics. A lot of time is spent on housework and on home maintenance tasks. And then there are the 'moonlighting' jobs, which obviously cannot be included in the statistics. Moonlighting is defined as the production and sale or exchange of goods and services, on which the payment of income tax and excises is avoided. As the level of taxation and excise duties is very high in Denmark, moonlighting has become an attractive proposition for an increasing number of people, as far as it has been possible to calculate.

Research surveys carried out in the 1980s have demonstrated that the number of people who admitted to having done moonlight work in the previous year rose from 8% in 1980 to 13% in 1988, and this percentage must be regarded as a minimum figure. In some sectors the proportions are much higher: skilled workers (36%), unemployed (20%), and students and schoolchildren (18%). The percentages are considerably higher for the younger age groups than for the older, and also higher in the provinces than in the metropolitan area of Copenhagen.

About one fifth of the population admit to having purchased moonlight work. The main categories of work commissioned are housing construction and maintenance jobs as well as childminding, cleaning, gardening, hairdressing and car repairs.

In 1984 it was estimated that the sum of all moonlighting work corresponded to 110,000 full-time jobs, but it is of course not possible to convert moonlighting to regular jobs.

Unemployment is one of the main socio-political problems in Denmark. "The dream of work". Photomontage by the photo-group 2.maj.

Unemployment

Unemployment is one of the greatest social and political problems in Denmark. Unemployment is measured as the registered unemployment, i.e. the number of people between the ages of 16 and 60 who are registered with the official employment service as seeking work.

In 1990, 737,000 people were affected by unemployment. Most of these only experienced short periods of unemployment, but 224,000 were unemployed for more than half the year. On average there were 272,000 people unemployed, which means an unemployment rate of 9.7% of the labour force. Following a period of full employment, the unemployment rate has risen considerably since 1974. It peaked in 1983, fell slightly for a few years, but has been increasing again since 1987. In 1991 the average unemployment was over 10%. Until 1976 the unemployment rate amongst men was higher than amongst women but since 1977 women have been most affected by unemployment, but this trend must viewed in the light of the enormous in-

87

crease in women seeking work.

The vast majority of unemployed people are members of an Unemployment Insurance Scheme. Membership of such a scheme is voluntary in Denmark, but most employed and also many self-employed people are members. In 1990 the Insurance Schemes had almost 2 million members, which corresponds to approx. 70% of the total labour force. About one sixth of the unemployed are not covered by insurance, but these usually receive social security benefits instead of unemployment benefit.

Unemployment benefit is paid by the Unemployment Insurance Schemes. The benefit is partially financed by members' subscriptions, but mainly by central government funds. The high rate of unemployment thus also creates a considerable extra financial burden for the state, which is already struggling with a large budgetary deficit. The debate has therefore been launched to consider the reorganisation of the funding and transfer of the financial burden to the Employers and Employees, as is common in other countries. However the all-important problem to be solved is that of unemployment itself, which the Danish government has sought to alleviate primarily through its overall economic policy.

In addition there are a number of measures which have been introduced in order to help the long-term unemployed, as well as young people and other special groups. All unemployed people are entitled to a job offer to avoid being cut off by the 26 week regulation (i.e. have had less than 26 weeks work within the preceding 3 years). Members under the age of 25 are entitled to a job offer after 1 year, and ideally other unemployed members of insurance schemes should also have received job offers by that time. The legislation stipulates that job placements should principally be in the private sector, but in 1988 only 14% of the job placements were secured in the private sector. The employer pays the normal contractual salary for the job, but receives a subsidy of 39 D.kr. (1990) per hour from the state. The state is supposed to find job placements for 10% of the unemployed but usually takes on a slightly higher proportion. The majority of unemployed are allocated placements in sectors run by the regional or local councils, who may also claim the subsidy from the state.

The long-term unemployed are also entitled to pursue various courses, with an education grant. Young people up to the age of 25 may follow a course of study for up to 2 years and claim a grant which corresponds to 50% of unemployment benefit. Between the ages of 25 and 50, unemployed people not in possession of vocational qualifications may retain the right to full unemployment benefit if they take a course of study lasting between 3 months and 1 $^1/_2$ years, with a possible extension to 2 $^1/_2$ years.

The chronically unemployed may also apply for an enterprise grant if they start their own business before they reach the age of 60. The grant corresponds to 50% of unemployment benefit for a period up to 3 years.

Job offers are taken up by almost all the unemployed, whereas educational grants have not been exploited very much. This is largely due to the fact that the long-term unemployed, many of whom have a poor educational background, are more motivated to getting a job than an education. However the long-term unemployed need a better education in order to survive in the labour market, and so the educational opportunities have been improved several times.

The local municipalities have been granted special powers to initiate job creation projects for young people on condition that the projects do not distort local industrial competition. It is quite a challenge to comply with this demand whilst also attempting to make these jobs resemble normal salaried work. Young people may also be posted via the municipalities into private companies, who receive the 39 D.kr. per hour subsidy, for a maximum of 12 months. In addition there are a number of production schools, non-residential folk high schools, counselling courses, single subject courses leading to examinations, etc, which the young unemployed can attend whilst retaining the right to unemployment benefit or social security benefit. The social services can also award rehabilitation grants for education and vocational training or retraining, the level of which corresponds to unemployment benefit.

With this relatively generous benefit system an increasing number of chronically unemployed people been able to receive unemployment benefit for 6 to 8 years, interspersed with a number of job offers. It has however gradually become evident that long-term unemployment was in itself a barrier which increasingly prevented the individual from getting a permanent job. Vocational qualifications were lost together with self-respect. It has often been necessary to instigate the rehabilitation process, or even anticipatory rehabilitation to make the chronically unemployed capable of commanding a job again. In recent years the endeavours have concentrated on more active efforts for the unemployed, which are aimed at reducing the length of the unemployment periods. In 1990, a special youth allowance was introduced for all youngsters under 20 in receipt of social security cash payments. The municipality has to find a job for them within two weeks, and the young recipients have to take up an offer. This could be on a job creation project or in a private company, which receives a salary subsidy for up to 5 months. Prior to

this, the municipality can organise a six week vocational introductory course on the same conditions. This scheme also applies to 20 year olds from 1991 and an extension to include all under 25 year olds is being considered.

There are thus many efforts underway to provide young people in particular, but also others, with an occupation instead of a more passive existence collecting social security benefits, unemployment benefits or other transfer payments.

Use of Time

Both the adults work. They live a long way from their place of work and often have to spend a lot of time travelling to and from work. The children have to be looked after, taken to day-care and school and collected again, there is the shopping to be done, the cooking, washing and cleaning. There is the car to be repaired and the house to be fixed. And there has to be time for further education. This is the general picture of the harrassed family in the 90s, and there is not much leisure time during the week for the working family, and especially for those with children. This is also clearly demonstrated by the major surveys on people's use of time in Denmark, carried out by the Danish National Institute of Social Research in 1964, 1975 and 1987.

On an average working day in a household with small children, there will normally be 3 1/2 to 4 hours left over out of the 24 hour cycle, after deducting the time used for the essential functions of life. These include the primary personal needs (sleep, personal hygiene and meals), work-related time (inclusive of commuting time and education) as well as time spent on domestic chores, including shopping, cooking, cleaning, childminding, gardening etc (Andersen, 1988). Just over one hour of this leisure time will be spent

89

outside the home, where the most frequent occupation is activities (meetings) in clubs and associations, and transportation in this connection. Within the home most leisure time is spent on watching TV (nearly 1 hour daily on average) and on socialising with the family.

The busy life of families with children means that they have to spend part of their days off doing housework. Fathers spend over 3 1/4 hours and mothers 4 3/4 hours on housework. Fathers with small children thus have 9 hours and mothers of small children 8 hours leisure time at their disposal on days off. Both spend approx. 4 hours outside the home, mainly on visiting others and physical exercise. Fathers tend to spend the rest of their leisure time at home watching rather more TV (2 1/2 hours) than mothers (1 1/2 hours).

Families with children are obviously particularly tied by jobs and housework, and the single parent even more so. Other social groups have far more leisure time available, and some have more than they care for. The groups which have the most leisure time on average are young people before they start a family and the older generations, as gradually the children leave home and they start withdrawing from the labour market. In addition there are those groups who, whilst of normal working age, are either temporarily or permanently out of work.

Young people spend much of their leisure time visiting friends, visiting relatives, engaging in sport or physical exercise, going out to enjoy themselves etc. Older people spend more time at home watching TV, reading newspapers, books etc, practising a hobby or just relaxing. The unemployed spend more time on housework, especially the women, and more leisure time on watching TV, various hobbies, and visiting others who are not relatives. The long-term unemployed

spent proportionately more time on do-it-yourself jobs and gardening.

However on the basis of a seven day week, the adult Dane has an average of between 6 1/2 and 7 hours of leisure time per day. This applies both to men and women. It is quite thought-provoking that this pattern has not changed much since the first time studies were introduced in 1964. Even though the contractual working week had been reduced from 45 to 39 hours by 1987 (in 1991 it was reduced again to 37 hours), we now appear to have somewhat less leisure time than before. The average time spent on paid work has only been slightly reduced. On the other hand we spend more time on education and especially on commuting to and from work. The total work-related time is therefore longer than before. Even if we spend slightly less time on sleeping, eating and personal hygiene, as well as marginally less on unpaid housework, the end result is that we have less leisure time on average.

Table 2. The average daily use of time for men and women
Trends from 1964 to 1987

	Men	Women	All
1964			
Sleep, hygiene, meals	9.45	10.19	10.03
Work/Education	6.17	1.53	3.51
Transport	0.29	0.19	0.24
Housework	0.29	4.29	2.42
Leisure	6.58	7.01	7.00
1987			
Sleep, hygiene, meals	9.37	10.01	9.48
Work/Education	5.07	3.21	4.15
Transport	1.02	0.59	1.00
Housework	1.36	3.09	2.22
Leisure	6.36	6.28	6.33

Source: Danish National Institute of Social Research. Survey on Use of Time

It is not surprising that the time spent on essential primary needs such as sleep and meals has not altered much over time. It is however more surprising that the time spent on essential unpaid housework is still nearly 2 hours per day, even though a large number of labour and time-saving devices are widely used. The reason is that we use more time for shopping and do-it-yourself jobs in the home. In addition we have experienced an overall improvement in living standards: we have more clothes, which are washed more often, we have large and better furnished homes, equipment etc, all of which require maintenance and repairs.

The car is also a good example of an amenity which in principle is designed to make transport easier and quicker for us all, but it also opens opportunities for taking up activities which require transportation, which in the end leads us to spending more time on transport. Nowadays we not only spend more time travelling to and from work, we also spend more of our leisure time travelling. In leisure hours the improved travel facilities are used for pursuing more activities outside the home both on a working day and on days off.

However, the apparent stability in the total average use of time since the mid 1960s conceals quite large shifts between the use of time by male groups and by female groups. The reduction in total working hours which men have experienced through the general reduction in the working week is nearly balanced by the increased economic activity of women. On the other hand, men have had to take over some of the housework, and spend over an hour more on this than in 1964. This more or less corresponds to the reduction in time spent on housework by women in 1987. Even though the total amount of time spent on paid and unpaid work is still more or less the same for both sexes, there has been a considerable reallocation between the two categories of essential work. This reallocation will probably continue its current trend as the

During the last few decades men have had to take on more housework, but there is still some way to go before complete equality on this front is achieved. Photo: Sonja Iskov/2.maj.

differences between male and female labour market participation continue to diminish.

The trend towards a slight reduction in total leisure time is also common to both sexes. An examination of the total average leisure time of the adult population negates any expectations of a trend towards a leisure society. And there are few indications to point to a shift in this trend in the future.

The Attitudes and Wishes of the People

If the economically active groups in society have experienced an overall increase in total time spent on paid work and unpaid work over the last thirty years, despite a considerable increase in productivity in this period, it must mean that the Danes

91

have preferred to convert this productivity gain into a higher standard of living rather than into more time for family life or leisure activities. In the 1970s and 1980s the Danes have spent more time on achieving a higher housing standard than previously, and on equipping these homes with all the new consumer durables which have appeared on the market, some of which were designed to save time, but which also create new time-consuming needs. This has also resulted in many people feeling that there simply are not enough hours in the day.

A shorter working week has also featured strongly in the political and public debate throughout the 1980s, and large segments of the population have expressed the desire for some action to be taken in this respect. The length of the working week in Denmark is negotiated by the employers' and trades union associations as part of the collective bargaining agreements. During the 1980s a 35 hour working week equally distributed over 5 working days was established as a high priority demand by the employee unions. This resulted in a reduction of the working week from 40 hours, which had been the norm since 1974, to 39 hours as from the beginning of 1987, and in the following years up to 1991 a further reduction to 37 hours was introduced. Discussions on an additional reduction have currently been removed from the agenda.

The arguments for a reduction in working hours have been based both on socio-political concerns for family welfare and equality, and the desire for a fairer distribution of work amongst the employed and the unemployed. However various calculations have demonstrated that it is doubtful whether small reductions in working hours could create an increase in jobs. Also the social welfare concerns which claim that a reduction of working hours would provide more leisure time for recreation, social life, more cultural and other leisure time activities, have been countered by the argument that a shorter working week would only lead to greater pressure at work, as the same amount of work would have to be accomplished in a shorter time.

The political arguments for a reduction of working hours based on family welfare interests have been particularly aimed at alleviating problems experienced by families with children. An overall reduction in working hours for everyone, instead of individual solutions where the mother works part-time and the father has an even longer working week, would appear to give parents more time together. The family welfare and equal opportunities lobbies are closely linked here, since this overall solution would counteract any uneven labour market participation by male and female groups. We are still waiting for evidence of the effect of the last reduction in working hours on the use of time in families with children.

In recent years a special inter-ministerial children's commission has been examining the situation of families with children. The commission has also looked at what is called the parental time jigsaw puzzle, that is, their attempts to coordinate their working hours both with each other and with the opening hours of childcare institutions and shops. A survey has shown that it is chiefly young people, families with small children and women, who do not have the option of flexible working hours, so that they can vary their daily working hours. A large proportion of this group, and in particular single mothers, would therefore welcome the introduction of flexible working arrangements at their place of work.

Another section of the survey on use of time by the economically active segment of the population dealt with the question of whether people preferred more leisure time rather than a larger pay packet as a means to better welfare. Since 1964 the proportion preferring extra pay has remained fairly constant, namely approx. one in four women and one in three men. However the proportion who would prefer extra leisure time has increased steadily at the expense of the don't knows. Nevertheless, as previously demonstrated, the total amount of leisure time available has not increased since 1964, and one may well ask why more people have not fulfilled their desire for fewer hours of work. Part of the answer may lie in the fact that the Danes, and especially families with children, feel more pressed by their financial situation than by lack of time. Another reason could also be that for most Danes affiliation to the labour market by way of a full-time job is a high priority.

A survey carried out in 1989 revealed that, when asked how much they value various activities, the people of Denmark value paid work higher than anything else. Only women with children under the age of 15 rate being together with their children higher than paid work.

This prioritisation of gainful employment for everyone is also diversely underpinned by our family, social and taxation legislation. We have very few regulations on the obligation to support members of the family, and we have very few regulations which encourage or give preferential treatment to those members of the economically active age groups who do not want to take paid work. For many years the individual principle has had a higher priority in Danish legislation than the concept of the family or the household. In reality this individualisation means that every single adult is normally expected to be capable of supporting him/herself through gainful employment. Where this is not possible due to age or other reasons the individuals will nevertheless usually be guaranteed their own means of support.

Even though not all adults in the economically active age groups actually are working, almost all adults now have their own income, their own means of support. However, neither the unemployed themselves nor the social welfare system regard the replacement of the lost income by a cash benefit as a solution to the problem. Affiliation to the labour market is not only necessary for economic reasons, but also for social and human reasons. There must be a use for everyone, and as mentioned earlier, there is currently much effort being devoted to finding ways of channelling the passive transfer incomes into more active resources.

All in all therefore, there is not much that points to the Danes having much more leisure time in the future than we have today, which is still more or less the same as in the mid 1960s. It would even appear that other interests have been allocated a higher priority.

Leisure Time

On the other hand we know that nowadays we use the leisure time which we have in a slightly different way than before. For instance more leisure time is spent outside the home. It has been demonstrated that increasing proportions of the population are taking up the numerous opportunities on offer for cultural activities such as theatre visits, playing music, going to concerts, visiting art exhibitions, reading books, newspapers and magazines, using the libraries etc. Also active participation in the work of clubs and associations as well as participating in sport and other forms of exercise have seen a considerable upturn since the middle of the 1960s.

This marked growth in the leisure-time activities of the population is partially the result of the expansion of opportunities offered to the public, and partially that people now have a greater surplus to exploit these opportunities. This surplus is in form of better education, better communications and transport facilities, better health amongst the older generation, and improved economic circumstances for most people.

It is notable that there has been a marked reduction in the differences between town and country and between different parts of the country. There has been an 'urbanisation' of leisure-time activities in the small towns and rural areas. This is due to the 1970 local government reform, which resulted in the amalgamation of all the small municipalities into larger units, now totalling 275 in all. The individual municipalities thus attained a reasonable size, which allowed them to develop their library service, sporting facilities, including the construction of centres, which could also be used for theatrical performances, concerts etc. The migration of jobs away from agriculture also played a role. Most of the people who live in rural areas actually have urban professions, and probably go into town on a daily basis to work. In any case the roads have all been improved, and the car can quickly transport everyone to see a performance by touring company in the nearest market town.

It is also notable that the older generations are much more active than they used to be. This is particularly true of the 67-74 year-old group, both with regard to spectator activities as well as active participation such as playing music, singing, or exercising. The reason for this is that every new generation reaching this age group is generally more educated and healthier than the previous one.

Thirdly, it is also notable that the links between the level of education and leisure time activities which were demonstrated above still apply, but the overall increase in educational level for all population groups can explain some of the growth in the leisure-time activities of the younger age groups.

Fourthly, it is also notable that some of the differences in the level of activities practised by men and women are gradually being evened out. But there are still considerable differences in the content of these activities. Men and women do not read the same sections of the newspaper, and do not practise quite the same forms of sport or exercise. Women are greater consumers of fiction and less likely to watch films than men.

Part of the reason for this increase in activity, despite the fact that we have not witnessed an overall increase in leisure time, is probably due to the fact that we have more whole days off than before. Most people now have longer holidays, and in particular the extension of the weekend to comprise two whole days means that people have more aggregate periods of time to spend on activities outside the home and for transport to and from these activities.

A Few Facts about Leisure-time Activities

In 1987 one in every four adult Danes either participated in singing or played an instrument. This is a far higher proportion than in 1964, when it was only 15%. This increased interest in music is also evident in concert-going or other musical activities. 39% of the population had been to a concert in the previous six months, including 12% who had been to a concert of classical music.

One in every four Danes had been to an art exhibition or to an art gallery in the previous six months. Interest in this field also appears to be on the increase.

On the other hand, cinema-going has been falling drastically in line with the spread of television. Apparently it is not a smaller proportion of the population who count themselves as cinema-goers, but rather the frequency of attendances, especially amongst young people, which accounts for the decrease.

83% of the adult population are daily newspaper readers. The number has been falling over the last few years, because more people read a newspaper just once or twice a week. On the other hand there has been an increase in the number of people reading more than one newspaper every day.

One in four Danes reads books on a daily basis. Another 19% read books once a week, and 22% once a month. Thus 2/3 of the population are regular book readers. There has been a stagnation in the consumption of fiction, since men, and in particular younger men, are reading less fiction than previously. On the other hand women are reading more fiction, and both men and women are reading more non-fiction than previously.

This great interest in reading is demonstrated by the fact that 64% of the adult population use the public libraries at least one a year. In 1964, when the first survey of leisure-time use was undertaken, only about a quarter of the population used the libraries. There has thus been a considerable increase in the use of libraries. Library loans are not confined to books and magazines. 11% of the population borrow music tapes and records, even though far from all local authorities offer this service. A large number of people are also attracted into the libraries by the art exhibitions, lectures, concerts and other events which take place there.

Sport and exercising is rapidly becoming more popular amongst people in all age groups. In 1964, 15% practised a sport. In 1987, 42% of the adult population regularly participated in some form of sport or exercise. The greatest increase in participation levels has occurred in the

One in four Danes participates in singing or plays an instrument. Amateur choir giving a concert in Århus. Photo: Marianne Grøndahl.

activities related to physical exercise such as swimming, walking, jogging, bicycling etc. The most popular activities organised by sports clubs are badminton, gymnastics and football. Other popular sports include handball, tennis, sailing, rowing and skating and skiing.

The Danes have a long tradition of club and society work. And even the level of participation here has been increasing. Sports clubs and other clubs related to youth work have attracted the most volunteers. But clubs and societies with other missions have also witnessed increases in voluntary contributions. Almost one in three Danes has been to a club meeting within the last month and nearly one in five hold some sort of committee post in a club or society. The 40-49 year olds are those who are most heavily engaged in this work. One in every three men and

95

17% of women in this age group are committee members of a club or society.

Even though there are differences in growth rates in the various areas, it is evident that there has been an increase in activity in most fields, and this increase has been consistent for all groups regardless of age, sex, income level or education. Increasing proportions of the population in all parts of the country are taking up the multitude of opportunities available. And last but not least there are more people in all groups of society who are actively participating in various cultural activities such as music and drama, actively participating in sport and exercise, and are active volunteer workers in clubs and societies, all in their leisure time. The Danes have become quite industrious in their leisure time too!

Living and Working Environment

by Birgit Jeppesen

Kaare Klint's Measurements

The groundwork for the world-famous Danish furniture production of the Scandinavian Design period in the 1950s and 1960s was started as early as 1917, when Kaare Klint began his systematic measurement programme, carrying out studies of the human body and using these to work out the proportions for furniture, for instance seating and table heights for various different purposes. Then in 1927 the Copenhagen Cabinetmakers' Guild staged the first of a series of annual exhibitions, which exerted a tremendous influence on Danish furniture production.

Kaare Klint's furniture, with their simple designs and beautiful upholstery, demonstrated perfect craftsmanship, and the designs were based on human measurements and movements. In 1924 he was appointed director of the Furniture Department at the Royal Academy of Fine Art in Copenhagen and a whole generation of furniture design students were influenced by Klint's efforts to create harmony between form, materials, construction and use. They measured cutlery, glass, dinner services, clothes, books and other articles which are normally stored in drawers and cupboards, and they designed furniture to suit these measurements.

This is the way in which Functionalism was gradually introduced in Denmark.

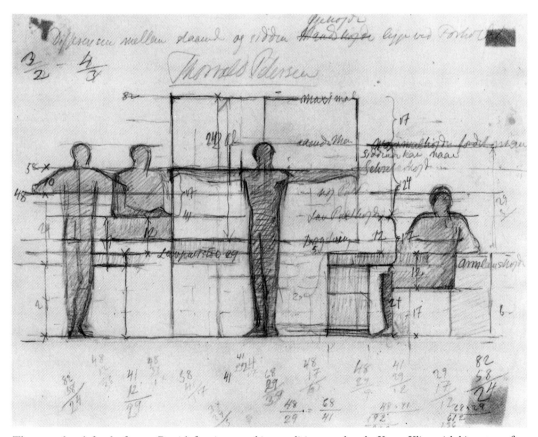

The groundwork for the famous Danish furniture-making tradition was done by Kaare Klint with his system of measurements. Studies of human proportions underly industrial production of office furniture. 1916-17.

The Functional Tradition

Functionalism introduced new forms for houses, furniture and household articles based on the requirement that the function of a thing should dictate its form and appearance. Functionalism was an international movement which was adopted with a distinctive Danish flavour.

Many Danes dubbed this style Funkis. The ideas stemming from overseas were adapted to the Danish building tradition and lifestyle. One of those to introduce the new ideals in housing with flat roofs, white walls and steel window frames was Arne Jacobsen. He applied the idiom of Functionalism to the design of the apartment complex "Bellavista" on the Øresund coast north of Copenhagen, but he did not use Functionalism's construction methods - the plasterwork and paint cover a traditional brick house. In his later works the style was meticulously applied down to the smallest detail. Mogens Lassen was another of the leading functionalists in the house construction field, but his Funkis houses were not very cheap, and it was thus only the avant-garde who acquired them.

The ideals of Functionalism - harmony of form, construction and content - were however not very dissimilar to the sober Danish building tradition, and although there were a number of Danish architects who sympathised with these ideals in the Thirties, they were not prepared to reject their own traditions. The traditional building material - brick - had proved its superlative qualities for Danish climatic conditions for hundreds of years; bricks were weather-resistant and good insulators. Kay Fisker and Ivar Bentsen were two of the architects who managed to successfully transfer Functionalism's ideals of form to brick buildings. Kay Fisker believed that the Nordic tradition was healthy and functional and he said "It is

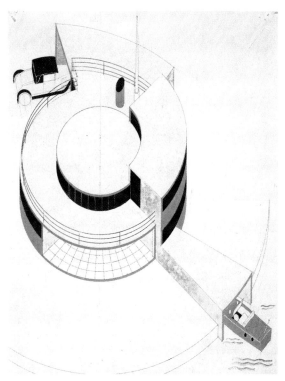

Arne Jacobsen was one of the architects who introduced Functionalism to Denmark. "The House of the Future". Water colour by Arne Jacobsen and Flemming Lassen. The house was constructed at the Building and Homes Exhibition organised by the Society of Architects in Copenhagen in 1929. From a catalogue for an exhibition on Arne Jacobsen at the Aarhus College of Architecture.

not pretentious and ostentatious as in the mediterranean countries. Monumentalism is not a goal in itself. We are seeking a building style which will serve life and people, which will fit into nature, which does not try to stand out, but on the contrary, seeks to remain anonymous." Kay Fisker and his fellow architects C.F. Møller and Povl Stegeman were the winners of the 1931 competition for the design of Århus University. This building complex combines the solid Danish building tradition with the best aspects of Functionalism.

99

PH

Poul Henningsen, also known simply as PH, was a true functionalist. He wanted to improve everyday life by changing physical surroundings, and his PH-lamp is based on the functional principle. It emits the right amount of light without dazzling the eye. The PH-lamp was first shown at the Paris World Exhibition in 1925. From then on and for the rest of his life Poul Henningsen sought to improve and develop the lamp, which is available in a number of different versions, and which has been on sale ever since 1925. PH also designed furniture, including some items which were closer to international Functionalism than anything else produced in Denmark.

Social Housing

From the turn of the century the action programme of the small local housing associations called for new, healthy and attractive living areas for ordinary people - without noisy, smoke emitting factories as neighbours. They gradually amalgamated and organised themselves as cooperatives or self-governing non-profit housing associations, most of which developed into nationwide organisations. The social housing units which they built

The PH-Lamp. From a series of stamps on Danish applied arts, issued in 1991.

for lower income groups were usually quite small units of 2-2$^{1}/2$ rooms, but well furbished, well designed and well built.

Functionalism prioritised good physical living conditions, and in Denmark the pioneers in this area were the social housing organisations, which commissioned large complexes of socially oriented modern dwellings interspersed with large open and green recreational areas. This heralded a break with the traditional closed courtyard system and the introduction of freestanding parallel apartment blocks, the line of which allowed each apartment to capture the sunshine, as in Ivar Bentsen's 1932 Blidah project in Copenhagen.

The Detached House becomes the Ideal

The first decades of the 20th century saw the development of smaller single family houses with gardens for the middle and upper working classes. In the Twenties terraced housing appeared, to be followed by other forms of high-density, low-rise building projects. During the post-war years the government encouraged the construction of private houses by issuing state loans, thus enabling many families to acquire a detached house.

During the Fifties and Sixties Denmark transformed from an agricultural society to a largely industrially based society. The towns expanded, new residential areas evolved to absorb the influx of population from the rural areas, and the so-called "dormitory" towns with their endless rows of single family houses appeared on the landscape. The Dane wanted to live in a house with a garden, and this form was considered the ideal family dwelling. The houses were constructed of bricks and wood, and people experimented with open-plan and split-level designs. There was always close cooperation between the

The functionalist architects cooperated with the social housing associations to create healthy and attractive dwellings for ordinary people. View of Ivar Bentsen's 1932 'Blidah Park' in Copenhagen.

architect and the owner on these one-off, architect-designed houses, which resulted in a string of well-built, attractive and practical houses. Personal preferences could be incorporated in the individual design, which was seldom the case in the manufactured standardised houses which took over the single family house market in the Sixties and Seventies.

Monotonous Concrete Buildings

The construction of apartment buildings was also industrialised, which meant the rational exploitation of series repetition - in contrast to the earlier practice of smaller, brick-built constructions with individ-

ual variations. There were not enough qualified bricklayers to meet the demand for brick constructions and this resulted in the appearance of miles and miles of monotonous grey concrete constructions with an endless repetition of standardised dwellings. The residents had no influence on the design of their homes, and the problems soon became evident - nobody wanted to live in a concrete jungle, even though the actual apartments were of a fairly high standard.

Both the concrete constructions and the standardised house industry were criticised for being monotonous and unimaginative - there was a need for new thinking in the housing sector.

101

New Housing Ideals

"Houses and municipal districts should be administered by the people who live there. As far as possible, decisions on the programming, planning and day-to-day operations should be taken by the residents themselves." This was the mission statement for a competition launched by the National Building Research Institute (SBI) in 1971. Its aim was to produce new ideas for alternative housing schemes for high-density, low-rise housing projects.

This was the time when women were beginning to enter the labour market in earnest, which brought about enormous changes in the interactive roles of work, home and family. The family was voided of its social functions, and the tasks which previously had been carried out within the framework of the family were now transferred to the nursery schools and creches. The life-long duration of the nuclear family could no longer be taken for grant-ed, and thus there was a need for greater flexibility in the housing sector. More and more people rejected the isolated nuclear family and looked for an alternative form of housing and social life. It should be possible to live alone - or together - and with or without children, and all this without having to change one's home environment. In other words it should be possible to change one's lifestyle without changing one's housing style.

The competition's winning proposal described a user-run housing project, which provided flexibility according to the changing needs and requirements of the residents. The project had been worked out by the Vandkunsten architectural studio, and it saw the light of day in the Tinggården project in Herfølge by Køge. 79 dwellings and 900 m^2 of communal facilities were built on a 26,000 m^2 site. The homes were constructed in small units around communal recreational areas and community buildings with lounges

The Tinggård project in Herfølge near Køge. Group of houses with family housing and communal buildings. Photo: Tegnestuen Vandkunsten.

and dining rooms. The project was classified as an experimental project, and it was developed in close cooperation with a tenants' group in Køge. However, as the project progressed it proved difficult to realise all of the ideas; some people objected to established legislative and financing practices. The end result was therefore a compromise.

New Cooperative Housing

By 1980 the idea of high-density, low-rise communal living had caught on in earnest and there were numerous housing communities all over Denmark. Until then they had almost all been started by private initiative and with privately owned houses. In 1981 a law was passed facilitating public subsidies for new cooperative building projects, which offered a halfway house between owner-occupation and tenancy.

From then on most of the housing communities were constructed as cooperative projects. One qualifying condition for public subsidy was a restriction on the maximum size of a dwelling, which was not to exceed 110 m^2. However there were no lower limits, the only requirement was that the dwellings should be independent of one another, each with their own kitchen and bathroom. There was therefore nothing to prevent the construction of one room flats, although another requirement was that the cumulative average size of the dwellings must not exceed 95 m^2. Support could not be given for a project of less than 8 units, except in very small rural communities, where 6 units would suffice. No upper limit was set, and there are instances of cooperative housing communities with over 100 dwellings.

The main principle in the housing community is the idea of a community building, which facilitates many communal activities and thus reinforces the whole basis of a communal project. The community building is usually used for meals, parties, lectures etc. A typical community building comprises a kitchen, dining room, lounge, TV room, music room, playroom, laundry, workshop and hobby room as well as bedrooms for guests or young people living in the housing development.

Alternative Ways of Living

The majority of the Danish population still live in single family houses or in flats designed to accommodate the traditional nuclear family of 2 adults and 2 children.

But housing communities constitute an attractive alternative. They have been proclaimed the housing form of the Eighties, representing new ideas in housing and innovation in the Danish house-building industry. Denmark has become world-famous for its housing communities, which are characterised by the fact that they are not based on either religious or political ideologies. When the first housing communities appeared in the early Seventies the residents tended to constitute a relatively homogenous group. But gradually the diversification of residents increased.

Many people opt to move into a housing community in order to simplify and rationalise their day-to-day life - for instance by doing less childcare or cooking. The age spread has increased, and there are now housing communities with a preponderance of older and middle-aged residents, whose children have grown up and moved away. In Denmark it is normal for the elderly either to live in their own homes or in specially constructed houses for the elderly. This new housing form has become so popular that the social housing associations have adopted the idea and integrated housing communities into their housing developments.

Most of the housing communities are established in new building developments, but there are some examples of alternative living styles introduced into existing buildings. The "Free Town of Christiania" in the heart of Copenhagen, is located in a former military barracks complex which was taken over by squatters 20 years ago, and despite numerous problems Christiania is still in existence. The Svanholm Estate on Zealand has been converted into a commune, based on ecological farming.

The New Apartment Block

During the Eighties there was a renewed interest in city life, and the high-density, low-rise housing community is not a practical solution for everyone. Especially not for those who need to live in town, close to shops, cultural facilities, public amenities and workplaces. The changes in the structure of the family has led to smaller households; there are many single people with one child or with no children, and the demand for smaller, more flexible dwellings has therefore grown.

The necessity to improve housing in the suburbs and in the city centres was recognised. New types of apartment buildings have been developed and old ones refurbished and the residents have been granted greater say, enabling them to influence the design of their own homes.

In 1988 the need for new ideas in the apartment building sector inspired the Ministry of Housing to launch a competition for the development of the apartment block of the future. The requirements included the following: "Flexible internal design, suited to industrial production and construction, adaptable to various applications, from new developments to urban renewal projects and the export of Danish architectural expertise".

Odinsgården

The most recent of the projects to be constructed as a result of this competition is the Odinsgården in the Århus suburb of Brabrand. The development was designed by the architectural firm Arkitektgruppen in Århus, and it comprises 83 dwellings financed by non-profit organisations and 20 dwellings for young adults, as well as a communal building. The construction is based on concrete decks supported by pillars. Since neither the facades nor the partitioning walls are load-bearing, each floor and each individual apartment can be divided up according to the resident's own particular needs.

To a certain extent the residents can even determine the location of the kitchen and bathroom, since all the technical installations are grouped together in a central area.

The construction of the building also facilitates alterations according to future needs. Two small apartments could easily be converted into one large one, and conversely a large one can be divided into two small flats. In contrast to the grey concrete facades of the Sixties, the concrete used in the Odinsgården development is an ochre yellow colour and the structure of the surfaces has been livened by the insertion of squares. Another attractive feature of each flat is the addition of a loggia with large glass surfaces. The Odinsgården project enables a more interesting distribution of rooms according to the individual needs of the residents and represents the very latest in Danish apartment building.

The Danish Interpretation of "Isms"

Housing communities and the new types of apartment buildings are prime examples of one of the main trends characterising Danish architecture in the Eighties.

The concepts of community, grass-roots democracy and user-influence have been part and parcel of the design remit of housing developments. The high-density, low-rise housing communities are reminiscent of the old Danish village system. The organisational structure of these estates is conducive to community living and democratic co-existence. In addition, a steadily increasing awareness of environmental, ecological and energy problems has resulted in the use of solar energy systems etc.

However, international architectural trends have not completely by-passed Denmark. There have been major debates between the Danish supporters of Neo-rationalism and Post-modernism. The Post-modernists were accused of frivolousness and superficial decoration, and the work of Neo-rationalists has been called petty-fascist!

The Odinsgård project in Brabrand near Århus. The column construction allows each dwelling to be adapted to the individual requirements of the residents. Photo: Arkitektgruppen i Århus.

Post-Modernism and Industry

Post-modernism was introduced with the 1981 architectural exhibition at Louisiana, entitled "The House as a Picture", and it successfully disrupted deeply rooted architectural norms. Many people felt that the unity and integrity of Danish architecture was now to be replaced by "external scenery buffoonery" and regarded Post-modernism as a threat to the foundations on which generations of Danish architects had been working. Post-modernism was an American reaction to the industrial society's rationalised mass-production of buildings. In the United States there is no close link between architecture and society, as is the case in Denmark, where there is a strong architectural tradition.

But as one of the Danish advocates said, "Denmark is not the United States and so - according to a Post-modernist philosophy - our houses must differ from those in America . They must be Danish".

The industrial building industry willingly adopted Post-modernism. Expanding companies were interested in using architectural features to create new corporate images and thus attract attention to their products. The administration building built for the H.S. Hansen Group in Lem in 1983 was one of the first Post-modernist buildings in Denmark, presenting an almost scenographic facade. The project was designed by the architectural firm of C.F. Møller.

105

The Family House of the Eighties

The uniformity of the suburban areas of single family houses was broken when Tage Lyneborg introduced columns, bay windows, enormous glass facades and curved walls to the design of Danish family houses. The idea was to give the houses a visual identity. There are also elements of Post-modernism in the striking house designed by 3 x Nielsen in 1989 in the Århus suburb of Risskov.

The architects' first Post-modern house "Villa Atzen" by Horsens Fjord is distinguished by the enormous window which is the focal point of attention. In general the Eighties have witnessed an increased inter-

Høje Tåstrup was designed as a modern version of the old Danish market town. The town square in Høje Tåstrup with Bjørn Nørgaard's tower.
Photo: Lars Skaaning/Polfoto.

est in architecture in this sector. For decades the single family house market had been dominated by the standard-type manufacturers, but during the Eighties the architects regained a foothold and started to influence the design of individual homes again.

New Town on an Empty Field

Neo-rationalism continues the classical tradition and attempts to rationalise architecture to enable it to express its fundamental basic types. Danish followers of this movement regard Neo-rationalism as a means to carry on the development of the architectural heritage of the country.

Høje Tåstrup on the outskirts of Copenhagen is one urban housing estate, whose strict, classical and pure lines are heavily inspired by Neo-rationalism; it is also an ambitious attempt to create a new town out of nothing on the basis of a single comprehensive plan. The town plan covers an area of some 280,000 m^2 and has been worked out by Jacob Blegvad. The aim has been to construct a modern town, with a physical mixture of housing complexes, shops and public institutions, and with lots of open squares and parks - a modern version of the old Danish market town. A number of Danish and foreign architects have been invited to design the individual neighbourhood blocks. The new town is being built in yellow brickwork and is centred around a new central railway station, a modern version of the traditional railway stations built in the infancy of the railway era.

Neo-rationalist Housing

Henning Larsen is a prominent exponent of Neo-rationalism.

The College of Commerce at Frederiksberg in Copenhagen built in 1988 is an example of strict stylistic consistency. The nearby housing estate "Dalgas Have" was also designed by Henning Larsen, and together these complexes form a unified whole. Dalgas Have was completed in 1990 and consists of two curved buildings as well as a small U-shaped building and some square tower blocks. The shape of the curved buildings is accentuated by the open semi-circular greens which face the College buildings.

A good example of a Neo-rational single family house is the 2 storey square house in Risskov on the outskirts of Århus designed by Jan W. Hansen and Elisabeth Schmidt-Nielsen. The key word is simplicity, which is evident in every aspect of the house, from its proportions to the choice of materials and colour.

Foreign Inspiration and Danish Building Tradition

Some of the architectural projects of the Eighties could be classified as Regionalism, where the emphasis has been on the adaptation of the proportions, materials, shapes and colours of a building to the surroundings in which it is to function, and foreign impulses have been assimilated into the Danish building tradition. The firm of C.F. Møller created simple and yet beautiful structures in the design of the housing development "Sandbakken" in Skåde on the outskirts of Århus. The yellow-brick houses with their yellow tiled roofs merge gracefully into the surrounding countryside.

Jørn Utzon

In contrast to these main trends there are projects like Jørn Utzon's 1987 design for the Paustian furniture store in Copenhagen's old North Harbour area. It was built on 3 split-level floors right on the waterfront, and Utzon's design for the building was inspired by something typi-

The simple Neo-rationalist house in Risskov in the suburbs of Århus, designed by Jan W. Hansen and Elisabeth Nielsen.

cally Danish, the fringes of a Danish beechwood forest!

Blangstedgård

1988 was designated Danish Home-Building Year. The most prominent event to mark this was the housing exhibition at Blangstedgård. A master plan for the project, to be located on the outskirts of Odense, was worked out by the architects Boje Lundgaard and Lene Tranbjerg. 600 dwellings were built, comprising public housing units, cooperative dwellings, apartment blocks for private ownership, single family houses as well as special units for young adults and for the elderly. Together they constituted a catalogue of

107

3 x Nielsen's housing development at Blangstedgård with innovative attic areas. Photo: Lone Mengel.

Danish house-building in the Eighties. One of the most exciting projects was the block of flats designed by the 3 x Nielsen company, which included many exciting features. A number of dwellings were two-storey buildings with unusual attic areas which allow daylight to enter the house from two sides.

Working Environment and Architecture

The Dane insists on good physical conditions at work. The work-place environment has received a higher priority in recent years and an understanding of the importance of the physical surroundings has developed. This has resulted in the construction of a number of industrial

buildings of architectural interest, including C.F. Møller's design for a knitwear factory in Skjern in 1986, the Crimp Electronics company building in Allerød designed by Vandkunsten, and the Purup Electronics building in Lystrup near Århus by Arkitektgruppen, both in 1985.

New Uses for Old Buildings

The reconstruction of derelict industrial areas and buildings has presented architects with something of a challenge in recent years. Under the guidance of Christian Isager, "Brandts Klædefabrik" in Odense's city centre, has been converted into a cultural centre with museums, a cinema and restaurant. Christian Isager was also responsible for the conversion of

Odense's old cattle market buildings into the TV2 station headquarters. The 19th century warehouse "Gammel Dok" in the Copenhagen harbour area now houses the Danish Centre for Architecture and Building Exports, and the housing community Vejgaard Bymidte in Aalborg is located in an erstwhile factory complex.

Urban Renewal

Finally there is the ongoing task of urban renewal, which will last well into the next century. After the era of mass demolitions, where a whole street or housing block was simply cleared, an awareness of the positive qualities of old houses in the townscape developed, and during the

Eighties efforts have been made to conserve the old town centres. The old residential areas of town are now being preserved, as demonstrated by the projects in Dragør and Christianshavn in Copenhagen and by the Jutland towns of Haderslev and Tønder.

The 1982 legislation on urban renewal earmarked billions of Danish kroner for this work. The objectives were to retain the character of an area and its residential mix, and highest priority was given to the renovation of individual buildings.

Danish people have become more energy conscious and ecologically aware, and the provision of green areas is considered very important. Many old dwellings have benefited from kitchen modernisa-

Christian Isager was responsible for this exciting conversion of the old cattle market in Odense into the headquarters for the TV2 television station. Drawing by Jes Fomsgaard.

109

tions and the installation of bathrooms incorporated into glasshouse extensions, which also supply passive solar energy. Other features included in many urban renewal projects have been the treatment of waste water, domestic water supplies heated by solar energy, sorting of household waste and new courtyard garden areas.

"Healthy Town"

New housing developments also reflect the growing interest in healthy and green issues. Both Copenhagen and Horsens are participating in "healthy town", WHO's project for health in European cities for the year 2000. So far most progress has been made in Horsens, where a whole new district, Thorsted Vest, is being designed along ecological principles. The Vision Villa, prioritising energy efficiency, the environment, health and flexibility, is one of the latest designs for the house of the future. The house is scheduled to be constructed at Høje Tåstrup in 1993.

Architectural Exports

In the Danish architectural tradition a number of elements combine, which are unknown overseas. The quest for order and the ability to achieve simplicity and harmony constitute important elements of the Danish architectural heritage.

In many countries it is not the architect who designs all the details of a project. These may be left to engineers or contractors, and their solutions are sometimes technically incorrect or architecturally inappropriate, when compared with the Danish building industry. The system of order-sharing, often practised overseas, where one architect will look after the external aspects of a building, whilst another will concentrate on the interior, is like-

wise unheard of in Denmark. The international fame of Danish architects must be seen in the light of the training of architects in Denmark, where craftsmanship and creativity receive equal attention. This background enables them to arrive at solutions which are both beautiful and durable as well as technically viable.

Danish Competition Winners

In recent years the stagnation in the Danish building sector has meant that Danish architects will increasingly seek orders overseas. They have already created a number of imposing monuments, some as a result of international architectural competitions. In 1957 Jørn Utzon won first prize in the competition for the design of the Sydney Opera House; Utzon owes his international fame to the design of this expressive building with its enormous white concrete scales, the like of which has not been seen either before or since. In the Fifties Arne Jacobsen was one of the most internationally minded Danish architects. In 1964 he designed St Catherine's College in Oxford, including much of the furnishings and fittings. Dissing + Weitling have attracted attention with their design for the Düsseldorf Art Museum, which opened in 1986. The enormous open cube, "The Triumphal Arch of Mankind" in Tête Défense in Paris, was also the product of a competition, won by Johan Otto von Spreckelsen in 1983.

The panel of judges selected this project "because of its clear concept, its symbolic strength, its simplicity of expression, its geometric precision as well as the lyricism of the proposed design".

The list of Danish competition winners is long. It is noteworthy that Danish architects seek to adapt their projects to local conditions as far as possible. A clear example of this is the project for a museum in the Rovaniemi arctic wilderness in Finland, which was won by Claus Bonderup, Ellen Waade and Søren Birch in 1984. It is a strikingly simple project, where the exhibition rooms have been sunk into the ground due to the fact that the ancient ethnic artefacts cannot tolerate sunlight. A domed glass roof stretches down over the hillside like a light strip and makes the building visible from far away during the dark arctic winter.

Danish architecture is represented far and wide. In London's dockland development the firm of Kjær & Richter have made a major impact with the Greenland Passage housing estate. The Scanticon conference centre in Princeton in the United States was built in 1981. The architects Friis and Moltke chose to give this project a very Danish appearance. This cannot be said of the Denver Scanticon, built in 1989, which bears a closer resemblance to an American building. The Scanticon centres are not competition projects, but are based on a Danish concept for conference centres.

Henning Larsen

Henning Larsen's international career started with a competition project for the Freie Universität in Berlin. The University in Trondheim in Norway is based on the idea of a street. Henning Larsen designed glassed-roofed streets between three-storey blocks, with stairwell towers, bridges and plants, to form external areas which could also be used in the dark Nordic winter. The Danish attention to detail and thoroughness is demonstrated in the Foreign Ministry building in Riyadh, which was constructed in 1982-85 as a result of a competition win. Henning Larsen has succeeded in incorporating Islamic architectural traditions into a very modern building, and with deference to local climatic conditions. In keeping with

Johan Otto von Spreckelsen's "Triumphal Arch of Mankind", at the Tête Défense in Paris, is an excellent example of Danish architectural exports.

Islamic tradition the external facades of the building are closed, but internally it opens up with cool halls and light courtyards. Amongst the most recent of Henning Larsen's projects is Churchill College in Cambridge, built to commemorate Winston Churchill's contribution in the Second World War. Here too Henning Larsen has sought local references and was inspired by aspects of King's College, another of the many Cambridge colleges.

Large Projects

New large projects involving Danish architects include designs for the British

111

The Danish pavilion at the World Fair in Seville can be regarded as a symbol af modern architecture. Photo: KHRAS.

Crown colony of Gibraltar, where the firm of Kieler is designing a hotel, offices and financial centre as well as shopping and housing complexes. Another giant project is for San Francisco's harbour front and includes shopping malls and an exhibition centre as well as a hotel and park. It is scheduled for completion in 1995, and is being designed by Hvidt and Mølgaard.

Finally, the Danish pavilion at the World Exhibition in Seville in 1992 stands as a strong symbol of Danish architecture. The firm of Krohn and Hartvig Rasmussen have used four elements in the design of the pavilion; the disc, the sails, the islands and the water, which together create a beautiful and striking entity.

The Era of Scandinavian Design

Scandinavian Design is the international term for a style which became world famous in the Fifties and Sixties. The ideology of the Nordic welfare states promoting a better life for their citizens had a great impact on design for the home - its physical design, interior decoration and furnishing. The home plays an absolutely central role in Scandinavian countries; the climate encourages indoor activities and thus there is a greater interest in interior design.

Beauty, utility and construction - the old trilogy which was also pointed out by Vitruvius in the first century B.C. - appropriately cover Scandinavian Design.

112

A sense of beauty, and the utility requirement were combined in a construction which was adapted to a simple and rational production method, resulting in carefully designed objects which were made by expert craftsmen with a thorough knowledge of their materials .

This principle found universal application, and made a considerable international impact. Modern Scandinavia design avoided exaggeration and provided the answer to basic human needs for things and surroundings which were both functional and attractive.

The spirit of Functionalism permeated Scandinavian society in the post-war years.

Scandinavian Design, with its emphasis on man in the centre, became a model for many people who believed in the advent of a new age. An American author raised the question of why Scandinavian interior design was "so well designed and so full of meaning for us?". He then stressed our traditions and our Nordic sense of beauty and utility requirement and continued, "their design is human and warm, therefore it is personal, national and universal.

Domestic Goods

There were several factors which contributed to the success of design in Denmark. There was an explosive economic development underway with a tremendous demand for labour. Hundreds of thousands of women joined the labour market and men who had formerly been agricultural workers now went into industry. The urban districts expanded and large new residential areas appeared to absorb the influx of people from the rural areas. All these new homes had to be furnished, and since a family now usually enjoyed two incomes, there was a notable increase in the standard of living, which was applied to the furnishing and equipment of the home - the haven of recreation after a long working day.

The harmony and order in Danish homes reflected the Danes' new position as members of a welfare society. There was an increased interest in household goods and a heightened quality consciousness.

Furniture is one of the most important groups of household articles in terms of our social life, and as an ever increasing sector of the population had more income at their disposal to spend on the home, it became a matter of prestige to create a tastefully furnished home with modern, architect-designed furniture. A Børge Mogensen sofa or Hans Wegner chair was a stamp of good taste and status.

Everyday household items also bore the mark of quality, being both durable and practical as well and beautiful to look at. The mass-produced, simple and practical "Blåkant" dinner service, designed by Grethe Meyer, is a good example of these criteria. Each piece can be used for several purposes, and the service stacks and washes easily. The "Margrethe" melamin mixing bowl, designed by Sigvard Bernadotte and Acton Bjørn, has been in production since 1950. The bowl is strikingly simple, it "is curved, just like the spoon which will stir in it" and a rubber ring in its base prevents the bowl from slipping. Nearly all Danish homes possess one, and it is sold all over the world.

Arne Jacobsen was responsible for the design of the "Cylinda-Line" series, a collection of stainless steel utility items including jugs, an ice bucket and tongs, ash trays etc, all in strict and simple geometric shapes. Amongst his many other designs is the "Vola" collection of fittings, where extreme simplicity has been applied to a series of water taps and fittings. The design is based on a valve unit which allows the adjustment of water flow and temperature with one single handle. Arne

113

Jacobsen was one of the greatest advocates of the concepts of quality for which Danish design is renowned. "Boligens byggeskabe" solved storage problems, whether this was for suitcases, shirts or porcelain. The architects Børge Mogensen and Grethe Meyer designed this flexible storage system after intensive studies of a family's storage needs. They were both pupils of Kaare Klint.

Denmark becomes the Leading Furniture Nation

A number of outstanding furniture designers contributed to Denmark's reputation as the world's leading furniture nation over a twenty year period from about 1950. The cabinetmaking craft had been well preserved, and furniture design-

John F. Kennedy sitting in a Wegner chair during the TV debate with Richard M.Nixon in the 1960 U.S. election campaign. Polfoto.

ers, who trained alongside craftsmen, now began to design furniture for mass production, which in reality were simplified versions of the hand-made products. The architect Kaare Klint was a central figure in Danish furniture design; nearly all the famous furniture designers of the Scandinavian Design era had been pupils of Kaare Klint.

These furniture designers had been taught a working method which covered both practical and aesthetic aspects, and Danish furniture design assumed very special characteristics, associated with quality, beauty and durability. These designs were founded on a democratic tradition - and they were not aimed at a limited wealthy elite. The designs were adapted to the ideology of the welfare society and implemented for the nice middle class home; elegant, beautiful and fairly modern without being provocative.

Furthermore, the annual exhibition of the Cabinetmakers' Guild, for which cabinetmakers continued to collaborate with young architects to create exciting new pieces of furniture, also played an important role in Danish furniture production.

Hans J. Wegner was the supreme chairmaker, and the chair which the Americans simply dubbed "The Chair" became world famous when it was used on television in the famous debate between John F. Kennedy and Richard M. Nixon in 1960. Poul Kjærholm combined hard steel with natural materials such as round pith, wood and leather to create perfectly finished pieces which displayed simplicity and integrity. In 1950 Finn Juhl was commissioned to design the interior of the UN Trust Territory council chamber in New York. In 1951 Arne Jacobsen designed the extremely simple three-legged dining chair "the Ant" for industrialised production, and since then several million copies have been sold the world over. The Ant chair marked a significant break with the contemporary Danish furniture-making tradition. Whilst its technical qualities match the very best in hand-crafted pieces, it was designed specifically for industrial production.

From Combine Harvester to Dental Equipment

Design evolves - as does society, and the concept of design has diversified. During the Scandinavian Design era, the main focus of attention was on the home, but in the course of the 1970s and 1980s the design concept has been adopted by the industrial sector. Designers have found a new market in product groups such as office equipment, building components, electronic equipment, sports equipment and machine tools.

In industry the main emphasis is on the solution of functional problems, and designers have found they have a contribution to make. The complexity of these problems is such, that the designer's role is usually that of a generalist within a team of specialists.

In a country like Denmark with so few natural resources, the appearance of a product can be a decisive competitive factor, and the range of the products which bear the obvious stamp of professional design is impressive - everything from electronic medical apparatus, high-pressure cleaners and combine harvesters to famous brands such as B&O and Lego, where the design factor has played a considerable role in their long-term market prominence. The Lego brick is a children's toy, produced in numerous versions to permit endless combinations and variations. Lego has managed to be consistently innovative, and has thus become a world-wide household name. B&O was one of the first Danish companies to apply modern design to technological innovations. Its designs are strictly timeless

and functional. The pick-up arm designed in the early Sixties is an example of the combination of good design and technical innovation.

This is also true of a number of other products. Danish industry is becoming increasingly aware of the importance of design, and there has been a gradual change in attitude extending far and beyond those sectors closely linked to the applied arts industry, for whom it is natural to think in terms of design. Dronningborg Maskinfabrik has managed to introduce both practical innovation to the construction process of a complicated piece of machinery such as a combine harvester as well as an overall visual harmony. And an almost exemplary incidence of good industrial design is demonstrated by the Flex 102cc Dental Unit, where designers, dentists and technicians have collaborated to produce total unity of form and function.

The Danish Design Center

The Danish Design Center is one of the prime movers in stimulating interest in good industrial design, and it organises a wide programme of activities aimed at increasing the understanding of and the priority given to design. DDC acts as a bridge between industry and the design profession and has become a model for design centres all over the world. The programme covers areas ranging from consultative work and information to courses, publication of books and journals as well as the organisation of exhibitions and competitions. Finally the Danish Design Council, under the DDC, is responsible for the annual nominations for the ID prize, which is awarded in recognition of good industrial design. This award was launched in 1965, and every year it is bestowed on one or more companies, who have launched new product developments which demonstrate excellent structural, 115

B&O`s advanced design has secured them a market niche. TV and stereo unit produced by the factory in Struer.

aesthetic and utility features.

The aim of the ID prize is to stimulate interest in product development and to encourage the efforts of Danish industrial enterprises to improve their image via detailed and functional product design.

Public Services Design

Design for public sector facilities is often aimed at promoting an overall identity. DSB (The Danish State Railways) is a company working for society as a whole, and this fact has influenced its design concept, which aims to convey a genuine Danish product which one can rely on. The architect Jens Nielsen was hired by DSB in the early 1970s and from then on DSB began to work systematically with design. A design manual was produced first, laying down guidelines for DSB's

visual presentation, and one of the first tangible results was a clearer and technically more efficient sign-posting system.

In the course of the Eighties DSB began to collaborate with a number of Danish artists, designers and architects. The new Inter-city train, the IC3, which was awarded the Danish Design Council's ID prize, is the result of a team effort. The attractive exterior of the train is matched by advanced technology beneath the surface. This train, which has already found markets in several other countries, is quite an innovation. A train unit consists of 3 coaches, which can be coupled to one more unit; the front of the train can also serve as its rear, since the front contains a driver's seat which can be swung to one side when not in use.

"The Question Mark" is a telephone booth which has been designed by Klavs

A superb series of posters was produced as a result of DSB's cooperation with a number of Danish artists. DSB posters 1975-91.

Helweg-Larsen. The elegant design of "the Question Mark" was responsible for its selection for exhibition at the Centre Pompidou in Paris, for purchase by The National Endowment Fund for the Arts, for an award bestowed by the Cultural Fund of the Municipality of Copenhagen, and for its first prize award in a competition for a new telephone booth. Unfortunately it has suffered a rather sorry fate, in that it was declared "not user-friendly for the disabled".

Fortune has smiled more kindly on another public service design product, the F78 telephone, "danMark". Technological developments have allowed the good old telephone to change its shape completely, and the "danMark" is an example of innovative, beautiful and detailed design. This product is even on display in the Museum of Modern Art in New York.

Interior Design

New designs for domestic interiors and goods continue to appear. The architect Nanna Ditzel was already working during the Scandinavian Design era; she has been influencing Danish design for over 40 years. Her latest product is the "Intimacy" furniture set - which consists of two striped, lightweight chairs which slot together easily to form a pair. She has been awarded a Japanese prize for this chair. The younger furniture designers who have made an impact include Anders Hermansen, who has created unusual metal wire furniture.

The Danes' growing interest in gastronomy has been exploited in the design of a range of high quality kitchenware, for instance the EVA Trio Gourmet Series, which comprises a range of pots, casserole

117

dishes and frying pans, which are constructed along similar lines, but are made of different materials. Ole Palsby, the designer, has shaped the lids so that the pots can be stacked whilst on the hob, thus keeping the contents hot. Mads Odgaard's two white triangular pepper and salt cellars stand out amongst thousands of other sets. He is one of the younger generation, and has also designed cutlery, casserole dishes, pots and bowls as well as beds, tables and chairs.

The new designers are all-rounders. Torsten Thorup and Claus Bonderup not only design buildings, but also lamps, pens, porcelain, bags and time-pieces, as for example the watch designed for Georg Jensen in matt steel and matt gold with a knitted metal strap.

Tradition and Innovation

Interest has now turned to individuality. The lifestyle of the Eighties has accentuated interest in the home and its interior. It has become fashionable to surround oneself with beautiful things, and the Danish artist-craftsmen produce very beautiful things. They have inherited a tradition of skilled craftsmanship, which they combine with a confident feeling for form and colour.

A hundred years ago there was little difference between artistic crafts and trade crafts, but industrialisation, though relatively late to arrive in Denmark in comparison with other European countries, meant that a number of craft trades were made redundant by industrial mass production. The artistic crafts developed as an independent sector, where the artist-craftsmen continued the traditional methods of the old craft trades. Denmark has a strong tradition in ceramics, backed up by artists and architects, and Georg Jensen's silver has blazed a trail for the concept of Danish design. Contemporary potters still sit at the

wheel, the goldsmith's work-table and tools have not changed much, and the weaver's loom is constructed in the same way as in bygone times.

Danish artist-craftsmen have kept up with the times and have taken up new challenges, have created new forms and used new materials together with the traditional ones. The old norms for combinations of materials and techniques have been broken, and the result is innovation and daring experiments. Today Danish artistic crafts are characterised by vitality, rich inventiveness and imagination. Some artist-craftsmen have made a radical break with the pure simplistic designs of the Scandinavian Design era; the dissolution of social values and norms has provoked in them the need to express themselves with greater force in their use of colour as well as form.

Decorative Art

The traditional sphere of crafts has been the production of domestic articles for everyday use. Nowadays the range has increased, the boundaries between everyday articles and decorative art have become blurred, and more artist-craftsmen are involved in the decorative arts. 1988 was the Home-Building Year, and this provided many opportunites for the decoration of buildings. Furthermore, many public housing associations make a budget allocation for decorative assignments in connection with new housing schemes.

Acrylic and Rubber Jewellery

The goldsmiths' traditional sphere of operation has expanded too. "Razor" is the name of an untraditional tear-shaped shaver, designed by the young goldsmith Flemming Bo Hansen. Some years ago it was exhibited at the Louvre, and President Mitterand commented on it as an expression of typical Scandinavian design. Simplicity and beauty are also hallmarks of his stainless steel digital watch, simply called "Watch".

Birgitte Støvring uses anything but gold in her sculptural pieces. In recent years she has won several prizes from the German Ivory Museum, Erbach, the latest for her sculpture "Seven Sisters", in concrete and whale baleen.

Jewellery is artware, and modern jewellery in aluminium, acrylic, rubber and plexiglass is designed primarily for use. These items are not investment objects, which is often the case with jewellery made of precious metals. With her imaginative and unorthodox attitude to materials, Lisbeth Nordskov combines Bingo tokens, painted bamboo sticks, cable netting and scuba-diving suit material and transforms them into fun jewellery. Jan Lohmann's jewellery belongs to the space age, and Kim Buck's work is also a complete contrast to purist and traditional goldsmith's work.

Gold and diamonds have not been completely forgotten, but when used the results are untraditional, as in Annette Kræns' bangle where they are combined with white horse-hair and oxidised silver; and Ole Bent Petersen's bracelet with houses in a Danish street is also more reminiscent of traditional goldsmith's jewellery.

Ceramics with Angular Shapes and Strong Colours

Nowadays an old craft such as ceramics is no longer covered by one single definition; some ceramicists do traditional work, some work sculpturally, some create classical forms and others work with decorated surfaces, some have started working on decorative commissions for the building industry and finally there are those who do not fit into any catego-

Numerous new public art projects have been commissioned in recent years. Frederikssund Station decorated by Susanne Ussing and Carsten Hoff. The sculpture, which is part of a decorative project encompassing the whole Frederikssund Line, was designed with the aid of a CAD programme which can create fractal pictures. Photo: DSB.

ry. The boundaries between ceramics as a form of handicraft and as free sculpture are inceasingly vague, and this is a trend which has also found a foothold in College of Arts and Crafts in Kolding, where combinations of techniques, angular shapes and strong colours are being used.

One of Denmark's best known ceramicists, also abroad, is Alev Siesbye, whose bowls display a classical purity. In 1990, the Arts and Crafts Council's annual prize went to Bente Hansen, who works with complicated geometric decorations. Gun- **119**

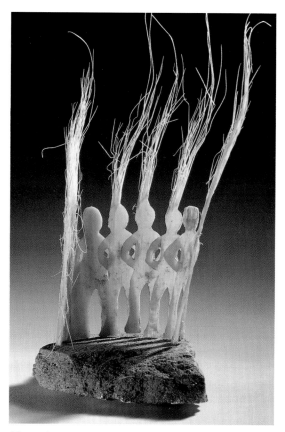

"Seven Sisters". Sculpture in concrete and whale baleen by Birgitte Støvring. 20 x 13 cm. Photo: Ivar Hjell.

hild Aaberg and Jane Reumert create decorative artware in bold simple shapes. Sculptural tendencies are evident in the work of Richard Manz.

Lin Utzon works with costume design, scenography, porcelain and last but not least, with large decorative commissions. One of her largest projects is a wall for the San Jose Convention Center in California. It measures 45 x 20 metres and consists of 9000 handmade porcelain tiles.

Textiles and Glass

The textile branch has been subject to a variety of developments in techniques as well as materials. New man-made fibres such as plastic have appeared, and weavers have abandoned the loom. They have gone from traditional flat woven hangings with decorative geometric designs to tapestries and on to free sculptures using willow branches entwined with feathers, horse-hair, wool, silk and paper.

The use of paper has fascinated a number of textile artists, some of whom have chosen it as their preferred material for the construction of textile sculptures. Paper has the same plastic qualities as material or clay, as demonstrated by Jane Balsgaard's three-dimensional light-weight mobiles made of hand-crafted paper and willow twigs. Paper production is a very ancient craft, which has only been used artistically in the last ten years. It is easy to make hand-crafted paper, and it has numerous artistic possibilities. The technique was introduced to Denmark by Anne Vilsbøll.

Britt Smelvær, Ann-Mari Kornerup, Jette Gemzøe, Bodil Bødtker-Næss, Annette Holdensen, Vibeke Klint, Kim Naver and Randi Studsgarth are only a few of the many talented and versatile weavers and textile artists who have made a name for themselves.

Anja Kjær and Darryle Hinz have consciously sought innovation within the Danish glass-making tradition, and their cobolt blue bowls with orange-coloured ornamentation are quite untypical of Danish glass. They exploit the traditional techniques of glass-making in a contemporary adaptation. They have collaborated on the creation of a number of beautiful dishes and bowls using a combination technique, whereby different colours of glass are carefully melted together. Before 1977, when Finn Lynggaard started to blow glass in his own workshop, the only other glass-blowing facilities in Denmark were located within the large industrial glassworks of Holmegaard. Since then, Danish glassmaking has undergone tremendous diversification; there are a number of small glassworks working with different techniques and in different idioms. Bente Bonne works with glass as a decorative art and produces sculptural reliefs in white glass. Torben Jørgensen also produces glass sculptures, using effects and techniques which exploit the special properties of glass, such as optical effects.

In short - the range in Danish arts and crafts is very wide.

The Future of Danish Design

Voices have been heard claiming that we "flogged our success to death" after the Scandinavian Design period with its simplicity, stringency and respect for the user. Danish design has always been characterised by its timeless qualities, and

it is therefore not remarkable that PH-lamps and Arne Jacobsen furniture are still popular, even though the designs may be 30 to 40 years old.

There is an increasing interest in design, and Denmark boasts many talented architects, designers and artist-craftsmen. The fact that Danish architecture and crafts enjoy a world reputation for beautiful design and perfect craftsmanship is due to the fact that the design-based educations emphasise a combination of the artistic and craftsmanship skills.

There is not much to indicate that eccentric novelties will dominate Danish design in the future. Innovation will more likely stem from those areas where there are still many outstanding problems, for instance within the field of ergonomics, environmental improvements and ecological or low resource products.

Glass by Anja Kjær and Darryle Hinz.

The Citizen and the Social System

by Jørgen Kock

There is a long tradition for social assistance in Denmark. When the local municipalities were beginning to take shape in the 18th century one of their most important tasks was to look after the weakest groups in the local area, i.e. the poor.

Two hundred years later, the task is the same, and now comprehensive legislation exists which sets out detailed guidelines for the obligations of society towards its individual citizens.

The development of the social system has been characterised by the assumption by central and local government of ever more areas of responsibility, to the point where the population of Denmark now enjoys a fairly close-knit, although not totally impervious safety-net, and this security also extends to certain groups of people who are not Danish citizens but who have taken up residence in Denmark.

Social Services: An important Feature of a Welfare Society

One of the most important features of a welfare state like Denmark is that, without adopting a socialist system of society, the state has taken on the responsibility of assisting citizens who land in situations where they are unable to cope. It could be said that a welfare society acts as a kind of

The Poor House in Fåborg, painted by Jens Birkholm in 1904. Fåborg Museum.

'social insurance company', which releases its benefits as and when the insurance incidence arises. The 'insurance premiums' are made up of of the tax contributions of its citizens, which are adjusted accordingly. The system depends on the principle of social solidarity, since the costs of 'social accidents', which hit at random and indiscriminately, are borne by the whole population. And this 'insurance system' is not only to be interpreted metaphorically, since many of the welfare schemes which comprise payments to clients are now structured on the same principles as insurance schemes. One of the advantages of this system is that recipients, just as in private insurance schemes (life insurance etc), know in advance what benefits they are entitled to in the event of an accident.

The social services can roughly be divided into 3 tiers; the preventive, the rehabilitative and the social security programmes.

The Preventive Programme

In recognition of the fact that "prevention is better than a cure" a number of schemes have gradually been introduced by legislation, which are designed to prevent the development of situations where the need for assistance arises, or which enable social clients to cope with less interventionist assistance than would otherwise be necessary.

A few examples will illustrate this principle:

When elderly or severely handicapped people are able to stay in their own homes, because a comprehensive round-the-clock home help service exists to make this feasible, and this is what the client wants - then this can be called a preventive measure, as it postpones the necessity for a possibly unwelcome transfer to a residential home.

The network of children's and young people's institutions (crèches, kindergartens, after-school clubs etc) is principally designed to give children and young people sufficient support during their development, to enable them to resist the dangerous temptations which await them in our modern society, including the risk of drug addiction and crime.

Then there is the outreach social work, which is characterised by the fact that the system and the client are linked via a third party mediator, such as the home help, the health visitor or the home nurse.

The industrial environmental legislation, with its regulations for the organisation of the work place, and the scheme covering free health examinations of women who are or have recently been pregnant, are also included in the preventive measures organised by the state.

Finally there is the preventive rehabilitation, which is an occupational scheme, which is initiated prior to any permanent damage being done, but at a point, when its onset may be anticipated, probably as a result of a health examination.

The 'Repairing' Social Programme

In the event of the failure of preventive measures, or in the event of social misfortune which occurs in areas where no preventive schemes exist, then the first concern of society's social system will be to examine whether rehabilitation is possible, and if so, what form it will take.

Rehabilitation work in Denmark, which got off to a "flying start" as a result of highly untraditional and effective legislation passed in 1960, covers many areas; from work assessment to retraining in special institutions and placements in the private sector, as well as educational opportunities at various levels and enterprise initiative schemes and grants.

Each individual rehabilitation pro-

125

Day-care centres provide support during childhood and adolescence. Adventure playground in Ballerup, Copenhagen. Photo: Henrik Saxgren /2.maj.

gramme will be worked out in close liaison with the disabled person, with due regard to his/her own interests, abilities, experience, educational background and health.

Special education of various groups of handicapped people and the distribution of physical aids such as specially adapted cars, also come under the category of rehabilitation.

Rehabilitation work is now a high priority area in Danish social work.

The Social Security Programme

Another main cornerstone of the social system is the network of insurance schemes, which by and large cover the majority of social risk areas; sickness, accidents, unemployment etc.

Industrial Injuries (Employers' Liability) Insurance covers injuries caused by accidents, occupational diseases and short term ill-effects resulting from the working situation.

The benefits which are payable under this scheme are retraining and physical aids, compensation in case of reduced working ability, compensation in case of permanent disability, compensation to dependants in cases where the injuries of the victim have been fatal, and a one-off payment to mitigate the reduction in living standards which the death of the main breadwinner will usually entail.

All employers are required to take out

Employers' Liability Insurance with a private insurance company. These companies are subject to the decisions of central government authorities regarding the amount of compensation to be paid, which prevents coincidences and variations in the assessment of compensation, which may arise due to different evaluation systems from company to company.

This cooperation between a state authority on the one hand and private enterprise on the other in the resolution of social tasks is quite untypical for Denmark.

Another kind of insurance scheme is the sickness, accident and maternity benefit scheme, which has been expanded during the last decade and now constitutes one of the main schemes within the social system.

Sickness and accident benefit is paid as soon as the inability to work arises as a result of ill health or accident, and provided that there is an ensuing loss of income. The right to this benefit is based on a degree of permanent affiliation to the labour market prior to the incident which provokes the demand for benefit. This restriction does not however apply to work-place accidents.

The benefit paid is geared to the current minimum wage, but it is less in those cases where the claimant's average income in the period immediately preceding the claim was less than the minimum wage.

The self-employed are also entitled to benefits, which may not exceed the level of benefits received by employees. And unlike employees, the self-employed have to wait three weeks before they may qualify for sickness benefit.

Maternity benefit is payable to the mother for a period of time before the birth as well as after the birth of her child, and may also be paid to the father after the birth. The regulations governing the payment of this benefit are very similar to those governing the payment of sickness and accident benefit.

Unemployment benefit is another related benefit scheme. It is administered by a network of unemployment funds run by trade and professional unions, whose operations are accountable to a state authority. The highest unemployment benefit rates are on a level with the maximum rates for sickness and accident benefit.

In special cases it is possible to top up the unemployment benefit by the award of social security supplementary benefits.

It is not compulsory to take out unemployment insurance, but it can be difficult to get work if one is not a member of a trade union, and union membership also covers membership of the affiliated unemployment fund, so in fact there is a certain pressure on the work force to join unemployment insurance schemes.

Anyone living in Denmark, regardless of nationality, is covered by a comprehensive health care programme, although in the case of immigrants there is a quarantine period of some weeks before they are entitled to benefits from the health service.

There is a choice of two kinds of health insurance, but by far the most popular is the kind which provides full cover of expenses for medical help. The majority of the population will thus be entitled to medical assistance, including specialist treatment, without payment. This also applies to treatment in the public sector hospitals.

The health service also provides fixed rate subsidies towards the purchase of medicine as well as dental treatment, physiotherapy and chiropractic treatment.

The existence of social pensions are vital for the provision of economic security for the population at large. There are all six different types of pension, ranging from early pensions for people with physical, psychological or social disabilities,

127

Rehabilitation is an important area of social work in Denmark. Sheltered workshop in Copenhagen. Photo: Nana Reimers/2. maj

semi-retirement pensions for the older generation wishing to cut down on their work input, to old-age pensions for those over the age of 67.

Pensions not related to old age are awarded after close consideration of each individual case, and are all adjusted to follow the country's overall wage level.

In the case of early pensions for people with various kinds of disabilities, these will not be awarded if it is estimated that the claimant has retained more than 50% of normal working capacity or if rehabilitation is considered feasible.

Social Security income support provides the most basic safety net for the population at large. Recourse is made to

benefits under this scheme in cases where the claimant is not entitled to benefits under one of the social insurance schemes, but where the need for economic assistance exists.

The level of benefits paid under this scheme used to be awarded on a discretionary basis, but they have gradually been standardised into fixed rates. The rates payable are now slightly above the West European minimum subsistence level.

In principle, individuals may continue to receive this form of assistance indefinitely, or until they qualify for a social pension, e.g. an old-age pension. But considerable efforts are now being made to reduce the period of assistance to minimum, by attempting to find means whereby the claimant would be able to support him/ herself by paid employment. In recent years major schemes have been initiated designed to assist young welfare recipients, in an attempt to nudge them out of their passive existence, with its obviously pointless and demoralising effects, into a state where they themselves can see the 'light at the end of the tunnel'.

Advice and counselling constitute an important complementary function in the economic assistance package. Expert counselling will often be the key to the successful resolution of individual assistance programmes.

This is particularly relevant for the problems affecting families with children and disabled people, when the counsellor must be aware of the full range of assistance provisions available, such as places at institutions, physical aids, foster families etc.

In addition to these main elements of the Danish social system, there are a number of other schemes, such as housing supplements, designed to reduce housing rents, and child benefits, which are designed to contribute towards the maintenance of the social balance in society.

The Administrative Structure of the Social Services

The Danish public administration system is, as in many other countries, a three tier system. The tiers consist of the national level (central government authorities), the regional level (counties) and the local level (municipalities). The administrative structure of the social services follows this pattern.

On a national level there is the Ministry of Social Affairs and two boards, the Industrial Injuries Board and the Social Appeals Board.

Each of the 14 counties is run by an elected council, which is assisted by a Department of Health and Social Welfare, and this pattern is mirrored in each of the 275 municipalities.

In recent years central government has gradually devolved responsibility for practical social work in the field and now concentrates its efforts on the paramount social tasks, including the formulation of guidelines for the social policy.

The areas of responsibility which have been devolved to the counties include an advisory service to the municipalities, the establishment and operation of residential homes for children and young people and of nursing homes for severely handicapped groups, as well as of rehabilitation centres. Aspects of the health service which are not geared towards the general public also constitute an important part of the work of the county departments of health and social welfare.

For the general public, the municipal departments of health and social welfare are the levers in the system. When social problems arise it is usually necessary to take these up with the local health and social welfare department. They deal with cases involving problems with children, loss of income due to ill-health or accident, the incidence of disablties which diminish working capacity, requests for the award of any of the 6 categories of social pension etc.

The municipalities are also responsible for the establishment and operation of various kinds of day care centres, including those for children and young people as well as for the elderly and the disabled. Applications for places in these centres are also dealt with by the local department of health and social welfare.

There are a few crucial areas of social misfortune where cases are not channelled via the local municipal administration. In the case of unemployment, the claimant is **129** referred to his/her unemployment fund, and in the case of an industrial injury, the claimant is referred to his employer's insurance company .

Private Social Welfare Initiatives

From the above outline it would be easy to get the impression that all social work in Denmark is carried out by public or semi-public organisations. This is however not the case, but it must be admitted that the incidence of private organisations operating in the social welfare field is less pronounced than in many other countries.

Examples of areas in which private organisations work, and do so with considerable idealism, insight and human compassion, are those related to the very weakest groups in society, such as alcoholics, and welfare work, such as the provision of visitor services for lonely disabled or elderly people.

Church organisations are active in this kind of work, as are other humanitarian associations, lodges etc.

There is a positive and trusting spirit of cooperation between the private organisations and the official social services in those areas where they both operate. Both parties tend to view the resources of the private organisations as an extension of the public authorities.

The Right of Appeal

One of the most significant features of the Danish social welfare service is that the award of its social benefits is regarded as the right of any citizen who meets the legal requirements for entitlement. They are therefore protected by legal guarantees ensured within the appeals system which is incorporated in the social administrative system.

The appeals system caters for the lodg-

ing of one and sometimes two appeals in cases concerning the award of social benefits.

On a regional level the appeals tribunals are held by a board, chaired by the state-appointed regional prefect, who usually has formal legal training, and on a national level claims are heard by the aforementioned Social Appeals Board. This Board arrives at its decisions via a consultative process between its appointed delegates, including representatives of organisations involved, and officials of the Board, who roughly speaking have the status of judges.

The legal rights of citizens in cases concerning the social services would thus appear to be well secured, but there is still the additional option of taking the decision of the appeals tribunal to be heard by a normal court of law.

Recourse to this court occurs extremely rarely, and mostly in cases relating to decisions concerning the forced removal of children and young people from the home in order to protect the interests of these minors, and decisions concerning compensation for industrial injuries.

Future Perspectives

The Danish social system is in continuous development, especially in areas of notable deficiency, but the rate of development has slowed down in recent years, due to the prevailing economic climate. And in certain areas, for instance in the care of the elderly, there is even evidence of a reduction in the level of service.

The coming years will probably see the intensification of the following trends:

Attempts to replace passive maintenance provisions, particularly for young people, by efforts to activate and resocialise the social clients;

Attempts to remove client groups without a clear-cut need for social benefits

Private organisations play a small but important role in social work. The Salvation Army's kitchen in Copenhagen. Photo: Tine Harden/Polfoto.

from the benefit system;

The emergence of new, less costly social work methods, resulting from the instigation of experimental projects;

Increased attention to the fulfilment of social clients' non-material needs and well-being;

Private organisations will assume a far more prominent role in the national social task force.

But whether these prophecies are fulfilled or not, developments in the social sector in the coming years will probably follow the pattern described by the English social historian E.M. Leonard:

"Administration and not legislation has always been the difficulty in laws concerning the poor".

And this has indeed been the Danish experience over the last 200 years!

Danish
Cultural Policy

by Ingerlise Koefoed

What is Culture?

In Denmark the word 'culture' has several meanings. This often adds confusion to the discussion of cultural policy.

As in so many other languages, the word 'culture' in Danish means the collective manifestation of the way of life, behaviour and patterns of social interaction of the Danes. Culture is expressed through the organisation of political life; through the way in which employment is structured; through the way in which the weakest groups in society are or are not supported etc. If, in accordance with this broad definition of the word, one interprets 'culture' as the total view of the traditions, forms of social and working life and social attitudes of a people, then cultural policy must be regarded as the most important single policy, which lays the foundation for the development of society.

There is however another, narrower definition of 'culture'. This definition relates to expression and content. Here 'culture' is interpreted as the manifestations which emerge in the creative arts, in the theatre, in literature, films, music and the dissemination of art and culture; as well as in less formal cultural activities and leisure-time educational initiatives, in sport and in the media. In this narrower sense, cultural policy constitutes the framework which the Folketing and the local authorities provide for the manifestation of culture via its legislation, regulations and grants. It means the way in which the visual arts, literature, film production, music and the theatre are supported; the way in which the media are organised; the degree of support given by the Folketing and the local authorities to the cultural professions as opposed to the local i.e. amateur initiatives in art, sport and the media. It also means the way in which the dissemination of culture is organised through the library system and the museums, and the extent to which access to cultural activities is facilitated.

Cultural Policy and the Development of Society

The emphasis which a society places on cultural policy is a reflection of the role it assigns to cultural activities and dissemination in the development of that society. Those people who live in a dictatorship, which has strong political views on which books may be published, which films may be produced, what the media are allowed to convey to the public etc, know only too well that the political system and its decision-makers can exert considerable pressure on the form and content of cultural manifestations. In a democratic society there is not the same concern about how the ideology of this society is reflected in its attitudes to cultural policy. It is regarded as 'natural' to allow any kind of cultural manifestation, provided an interest exists and people are willing to promote it. But of course cultural policy, just as any other policy, does reflect the ideology of the society, and cultural policy is an important and indispensable instrument in the process of democratisation.

The public library system and the folk high school movement have played significant roles as facilitators in people's efforts to improve themselves and their daily lives. In the previous century farm workers and servant girls attended the folk high schools. Here they listened to the myths about the Old Nordic gods, Odin, Thor and Freja, and they were better farmers on their return home.

The theatre, the visual arts, music, films and literature open up important avenues to new experiences and new ideas. For many people, participation in amateur activities and voluntary adult education has promoted individual personal

Danish culture according to the artist Claus Deleuran. Section of a poster for the exhibition "Danish, Danes" at the Nicolai Church in Copenhagen, Spring 1992.

development, provided new social experiences and injected them with renewed strength to cope with the daily problems of life. Children exposed to theatre performances, films and books specifically geared to their age groups, have likewise enjoyed enriching experiences, gained knowledge and been stimulated to engross themselves in the events of the world around them.

This was an attempt to put the 'narrow' definition of culture and the narrow definition of cultural policy in a wider context. An attempt to explain that cultural experiences are not simply the dessert to be relished after a hard day's work, but a

135

prerequisite for an active life. In the following I shall attempt to be more down-to-earth and shall describe the form and content of Danish cultural policy, the structure of its supporting legislation and the finances which enable its implementation.

Cultural Support

Cultural policy in Denmark has long been based on the principle that any form of cultural expression will need public support. But is it possible to maintain a democratic cultural policy with the freedom to create any kind of manifestation when culture is subsidised by the state and the local authorities? From my long experience in cultural politics and many years in the publicly financed library system, I can safely say that it is possible to work independently within a system subsidised by the state or other public finances. Of course it has happened that politicians have expressed their misgivings about the libraries' purchase and loan of a couple of children's books with overtly sexual or violent contents. There have also been strong protests against plans for the production of a film, which was considered to be blasphemous. There have been a number of protests against provocative programmes broadcast on radio or the television, which for many years included members of parliament on its governing bodies. But in most cases the protests subsided, and in Denmark there is only a tiny sector where censorship is imposed, the sector covering children's films. Film censorship may advise against viewing for children under the age of 7, and actually forbid admittance for the 12 to 16 year age group.

This law, which is highly unpopular amongst older children, but which is designed as a protective measure, is actually on its last legs, soon to be replaced by a general recommendation policy for this sector.

By and large freedom of expression is flourishing. The organisation of cultural life is based on a legislative structure whereby the politicians bear the financial responsibility - create the economic framework - whilst the decisions on the content of the activities rest with professionals. In the library system it is the Chief Librarian who is responsible for selecting the stock, and he or she is also authorised to delegate this responsibility to the individual departments within the library. The selection of material is partly based on an assessment of the composition of the local community and partly on the Library Act's requirement for "comprehensive balance, topicality and quality" in the selection of materials. In accordance with the appropriate legislation, the theatrical, music and film interests are supervised by professional committees appointed at national level. The grant allocations for creative artists such as painters, writers and composers are awarded by committees of experts in the various artistic fields, appointed for a three-year period. By and large this system works well - there is currently no shortage of ideas or management, only of funds.

A Forward-looking Legislation

There has always been some form of support for cultural activities in Denmark, though until this century this was chiefly provided by patrons, monarchs etc, who were quite generous. But in a democratic society it is not enough to subsidise a few great or at least promising artists and writers, or just a couple of museums. With the evolution of the Danish social-democratic welfare state and its philosophy of equal opportunities and mutual support, interest matured in the interpretation of cultural policy as another social sector and another social obligation. In this sector, the taxpayers' money was to be used to promote art and cultural manifestations and to provide equal opportunities for participation in cultural activities.

Denmark's first dedicated Ministry of Culture was established in 1961. It was headed by a social democratic Minister of Culture, who had formerly demonstrated considerable interest in working class culture and who used his period of office to concentrate on creating links between the cultural establishment and the community at large. This government created a forward-looking body of legislation covering grants for creative artists, the theatre, museums, and films. An excellent Libraries Act was passed, and an impressive Act on "Folkeoplysning" (adult leisure-time education and cultural activities), which guaranteed all adults the opportunity to pursue leisure-time educational and "oplysning" (awareness-raising) activities, and also partially covered leisure-time activities for children and young people.

Not all of this legislation was equally well received. The State Endowment Fund for the Arts was established to administer the award of annuities and grants to artists, writers and composers. When the first grants were awarded there was a public outcry, incited by people who could not understand, or refused to accept, that artists, unlike everyone else, could not exist on the income from their work.

These objections were not taken very seriously by the authorities, who also-declined to enter into a serious debate with the 'rebels'. This was probably a mistake, for it provided a fertile breeding ground for the widespread rejection of the so-called "fine arts". This rejection has since become one of the main hallmarks of the extreme right-wing party, The Progress Party, which in the 1970s and the early 1980s gained considerable influence on

Danish politics and still exerts a strong right-wing influence on the political parties.

Inspired by the recent debate in the country, the national and local authorities are attempting to give 'ordinary' people more influence on cultural policy, but there have been few changes, much to the dissatisfaction of the protestors.

It may also be asked, how much should be changed? Surely public funds should only be used to support the best in art, literature, music, films, "folkeoplysning", folk high schools and sport? On the other hand it is essential to provide this support, if only to counteract the wholly commercially run cultural activities and cultural products.

Cooperation between the State and the Local Authorities

Danish legislation in the cultural sector has long been based on the principle of close cooperation between the Folketing - the national instrument which creates the legislation and allocates some of the financial resources - and the local authorities where the legislation is implemented. For many years an excellent system of rebates operated, whereby the state refunded a certain percentage of municipal expenditure in the cultural sector. For instance, children's theatre performances organised by the municipalities qualified for a 50% rebate, there was a 20% rebate on library expenditure, and 40% rebate on a maximum municipal museum expenditure of D.kr. 500,000. This economic 'cultural' policy provided a good incentive for municipalities to increase their cultural activities. In the 1960s and the early 1970s there was also a considerable increase in the uptake of the cultural and educational opportunities. Attendance figures for museums, theatres and libraries soared, and despite a certain drop

137

since then, attendances are still high. This rise was due both to the rebate systems and to the overall increase in the level of education. For there is a clear link between education and an interest in cultural activities. It is primarily the more well-to-do, and thus more secure, as well as the better-educated groups in society which flock to art and culture, and to sport, amateur activities and to leisure-time education. This fact is of course exploited by those circles who do not wish to see the taxpayers' money spent on culture and cultural activities, to protest against the support of culture.

1.2% of the National Budget

In this country of some 5 million inhabitants, the state allocates between 4 and 5 billion kroner to the sector for which the Ministry of Culture is responsible; i.e. over 1.2% of the national budget. This amount covers the central grants to the folk high schools and other "folkeoplysning" (leisure-time education and informal cultural activities), various forms of youth education, as well as the whole of the traditional cultural sector, apart from the media, which receive no direct state support. The municipalities allocate between 1 and 2 % of their budgets to the public libraries, to sport and "folkeoplysning". An examination of the distribution of funds between the more elitist and the more "folkelig", community-based forms, disregarding expenditure on the folk high schools and "folkeoplysning" (which also includes sport), reveals that 98-99% of the funds are allocated to the more established and professional art forms, to the training of artists and art administrators, to the major cultural institutions, to some of the main research libraries, to support elite sports etc. Only between 1 and 2% of the funds reach the "folkelig", community-based, participatory activities. This

may seem like an uneven distribution, but then there is a difference between the cost of a professional theatre company and that of an amateur group, to name but one form of cultural activity. And many of the "folkelig", community-based groups prefer to be economically self-sufficient rather than seek public funds. They are afraid of official censorship.

A break-down of the cultural budget reveals that D.kr. 400 mill. of central funds are allocated to the theatre, including D.kr. 200 mill. to the Royal Theatre, and that another D.kr. 200 mill. are injected by the municipalities. D.kr. 160 mill. is injected into the film sector, covering both adult and children's productions; museum support accounts for D.kr. 285 mill. and the public library system is financed by approx. D.kr. 2 billion of municipal funds. Central and local authority funding for leisure-time education, including sport, amounts to approx. D.kr. 2 billion altogether.

Budgetary Constraints

These figures may seem impressive, but it is currently proving difficult to maintain the same level of cultural activities as in the better years. The system of grant-aid has been amended, and whilst the state still awards the odd subsidy here and there, it is no longer paid as a rebate. Many areas of responsibility have been devolved to the local authorities, without sufficient corresponding funds. The municipalities no longer have the same guarantees of central aid, and as they have received increased burdens in the health and social welfare sectors, they have been forced to implement cut-backs in the cultural sector.

Cultural administrators and those working in the cultural institutions and in central and local government are therefore looking more eagerly at the prospects

138

Danish children spend 12 - 14 hours a week watching television. The TV on board the ferry Peder Pårs. Photo: Søren Svendsen/Billedhuset.

of raising revenue from other sources, for instance from Foundations and business sponsorship.

Modest amounts are forthcoming from sponsors, but these funds are often targeted discriminatively. Commercial enterprises wish to see a return in the form of prestige or advertising exposure and therefore mostly sponsor the more spectacular art forms, the large museums and theatres, and occasionally experimental art forms which are likely to attract a lot of attention. Many new and imposing cultural centres are currently being constructed in Denmark, often in connection with commercial and conference centres and with massive sponsorship, which of course is not a bad thing. But it is regrettable that the more modest, more permanent experiences offered by museums,

libraries and small theatres, are being neglected. And that the important folk high schools, which also create considerable interest overseas, may soon be subject to cut-backs which will mean that some of the 105 folk high schools in the country, with their variety of philosophies and activities, will not be able to survive.

Radio and Television

Much of the population's time and thoughts are taken up by the electronic media, and this is true of children and adults alike. Until six years ago a single radio and television company was responsible for all broadcasting, and this was financed only by viewers' licence fees. This monopoly was been broken when, firstly, the go-ahead was given for the

139

establishment of independent local radio and TV stations producing all kinds of programmes, and secondly a second national TV channel, called TV2 , was set up, financed partly by the TV licences and partly by advertising. Finally, cable TV reaches all corners of Denmark.

The programmes are more or less the same on all channels, apart from a few places, where the local radio produces truly local material. None of it is particularly good, but the consumption of these media is steadily increasing. Children spend between 12 and 14 hours a week watching television. Because there is so much television and radio it is even more important to offer cultural activities which will entice people out of their living rooms to participate in activities with others. And this is at a time when Danish cultural policy is on a slight decline and more and more is left to private initiatives and private funds.

Danish Cultural Policy after 1992

Denmark possesses a structure and legislation for cultural policy which, even though these are faltering slightly at the moment, are worth telling others about. We have superb folk high schools, a sophisticated amateur and professional sports network, we have art, theatre, music and films produced in Denmark; and we have a population who use the libraries a lot, are avid readers, like to participate in leisure-time education and occasionally take the initiative to set up their own exciting cultural activities. We would like to show all of this

to our friends in the new Europe, who may want to learn something from us, just as we can learn a lot from them.

From this perspective it is a matter of some concern that central and local government interest in supporting Danish art and culture should be waning at this particular juncture. We are facing major changes in Europe, and from the 1st January 1993 cultural policy issues will be included in the provisions of the Treaty of the European Community. This implies a potential increase in the exchange of culture, art and artists between the member states and hopefully also between these countries and the other European countries. According to the Treaty of Union this also means that the national systems of cultural subsidy and promotion must be respected provided that these - and *this* is alarming - cannot be conceived as creating unfair competition or economic competition with the subsidy arrangements of other countries.

It is difficult to foresee what this will imply when it is implemented. But one thing is certain: it is vital to strengthen the economic basis of the national and regional cultural manifestations, if these are to participate in a worthy and independent cooperation with other countries. It will also be important to ensure that the European Community does not isolate itself on the cultural front, but that the cultural dissemination and cooperation which takes place goes beyond the boundaries of the Community, to the rest of Europe and the rest of the world.

Art and "folkelig" Culture

by Lise H. Skjøth

On the Danes, Art and Museums – and the Relationship between the Establishment and the "folkelig" (informal and community-based) Initiatives

Why start a chapter about art and culture with a discussion about mealtimes? Because it has been a Danish tradition for families to eat lunch at 12 o'clock sharp and dinner at 6 o'clock sharp. Lunch may consist of simple Danish open sandwiches taken to the office and eaten at work to avoid wasting time travelling to and from work at lunchtime. That is why the working day finishes at around 5 o'clock. The family is thus ready to eat dinner early and have the whole evening free for other activities. Denmark's flourishing club life, evening classes and the whole range of "folkelig" (informal, amateur and community-based) cultural activities would be unthinkable without this intensive exploitation of the day.

The evening classes and societies where people make new acquaintants, meet like-minded people who believe in the same things, are one of the cornerstones of "folkelig" cultural life. In clubs and assocations the route to direct influence is short. We learn democratic habits and "it does help" to put in an effort.

Denmark is called the land of clubs and associations. Yes, without the museum associations, the art associations, the music and theatre associations there would not be such widespread access to culture . Politicians have always recognised the significance of "folkelig" influence when planning new legislation.

The Typical Dane

From a cultural point of view, Denmark has always been a province in Europe. Stroll through one of our art galleries and you will see Danish versions of the great European masters. Danish art has however clearly been at its best when the artists have dared to be themselves and have translated what they have learned abroad into a separate artistic idiom. In some indefinable way it stands apart from the art of other countries. And we will substantiate this claim later in this article; but let us first take a step back to have a look at the Dane.

The Danes likes to think of themselves as informal beings with a relaxed attitude to norms. This is sometimes expressed through their informal attire, where they are most comfortable when 'underdressing' for an occasion. One of the many paradoxes one learns about the Danes is the tremendous difference in our self-perception. As soon as we are outside Denmark we are quite happy to be Danes - and to be ourselves - but at home it would be difficult to find people who are more self-critical and self-disparaging.

The Danes are a threat to no-one beyond their own borders. This allows us a certain leeway, for instance in international cultural cooperation, where the collaborative efforts of the Nordic countries have often succeeded in securing a sensible compromise, due to the trust which we enjoy in the Third World.

We have not won a war for centuries, and we take odd pleasure in celebrating the anniversaries of our defeats. This is reflected in our sense of humour, and in our sometimes somewhat sloppy language and in-talk, which we call irony. This latter is a weapon which sometimes makes non-Danes wonder, where we actually stand. On the world stage this is a weakness, but at home it is a strength, as the irony allows us freedom of movement.

The Danish philosopher and writer Søren Kierkegaard (1813-55), who wrote about the concept of irony, has contributed towards the formation of our idiosyncracies by saying that to be great was not to be one thing or the other, but to be oneself!

As we stand on the threshold of the European Single Market the question has been raised: If we become Europeans, will we remain Danish? Many peoples have tried to adopt a foreign identity for a while, until they one day realised, that the important thing is to be oneself.

Some Highlights in Danish Art

In this short review of certain periods which are generally held to be typically Danish, the focus is on those eras in Danish art in which strong artistic expressions, reflecting the Danish identity, have been achieved.

The Danish Golden Age

The period which we call the Danish Golden Age began, strangely enough, or maybe not - just after a period of economic decline which lead to the bankruptcy of the state in 1813. The Danes had "backed the wrong horse" during the Napoleonic wars; we had taken a beating by the English, who in 1807 had bombarded Copenhagen and sailed off with our fleet. The bottom had fallen out of the international grain market. It was a sorry plight. Denmark was a backward nation, especially out in the rural areas. The general state of health and hygiene amongst the population was appalling. At that time Copenhagen was no larger than a small provincial town today, and all the learned people knew each other. This was the climate in which Danish intellectual life flourished.

This development can be traced back to around 1770 when the influence of the European Age of Enlightenment reached Denmark, leading to social reforms and a change in the political structure as well as significant improvements for the arts and artists. The Royal Academy of Fine Arts, founded in 1755, was no longer primarily to serve the absolutist monarch, but was

Nicolai Abildgaard was inspired by early European Romanticism. Ossian. Copperplate engraving after a painting by Abildgaard, 1787. 32 x 23 cm. Kobberstik-samlingen.

to be an educational establishment for aspiring artists. The expenses were no longer to be borne by the royal purse, but by state funds.

Craftsmen, who needed to learn drawing for their trade, could attend the Academy, where lessons were free, and there was an open admissions policy for all men. Graduates were entitled to "practise their art" freely. In the summer months King Frederik V's art gallery at Christiansborg Palace was opened up to students for study purposes.

Whereas hitherto foreign artists had dominated artistic circles - important posts were gradually being filled by Danes, who continued to travel to Rome and Paris to further their education.

In 1772 the Academy's major overseas travel grant was awarded to the Danish

143

painter Nicolai Abildgaard, who travelled to Rome with instructions to continue working on historical paintings. Here he was greatly inspired by Michelangelo and the Romantic movement, whose sphere of interests went beyond classical antiquity.

It was of crucial significance to the Danish Golden Age that the sculptor Bertel Thorvaldsen, who travelled to Rome in 1796 to finish his studies, decided to stay there. He became one of the leading artists of Europe. He also became the pivotal figure for the colony of Danes, each of whom came to Rome after receiving the major travel grant. The intense life in Roman artistic circles and the fruitful fellowship of fellow artists induced a kind of forced maturation in each of them. But their work did not culminate until they returned to Denmark, had time to digest the impressions they had received overseas and translated them into their own idiom.

The painter C.F. Eckersberg was an exception to this pattern, since he went to Paris first and started studying under the artist David in 1811. This period proved to be crucial for his artistic development, which was then reinforced when he continued to Rome in 1813 for a 3 year stay, and where he found his artistic clarification. Back in Denmark he started teaching at the Academy, and a school of painters formed around him which developed a distinctive Danish style.

However, the prime exponent of the Danish Golden Age was the painter Christen Købke. His work with light and colour, his modest subjects, portrayed in great detail, catch the attention of the viewer. We believe that this is Danish art at its best. The paintings of the Danish Golden Age went on an international exhibition tour in the 1980s, and it was then that art lovers of the world first really discovered their qualities, with Købke's paintings creating the most interest. He

has at last been accorded the position in European art history which he deserves.

Denmark's first professional art historian, N.L. Høyen, was a teacher at the Royal Academy from 1826, and also at the university after 1856. He lectured on national art and stated that artists should portray the history, countryside and everday life of the country.

He interpreted the demands of the Sturm und Drang and placed themes from Nordic heritage on a par with the great traditions of classicism and religion. Art should not only be national and Nordic, but preferably be "folkelig", based on the traditional life and values of ordinary people.

The Northern Light

In 1982 another opportunity arose to present Danish art to a wider public. This was in connection with a joint Scandinavian cultural promotion, which included the United States. The title of the exhibition, "Northern Light" was not a random choice, for it was precisely the clear, stringent light of the north, particularly on the Skagen tip of Jutland, which had attracted artists a century ago. The exhibition was a resounding success in the United States. The Americans are keen on delving into the past, and probably many of those with Scandinavian roots found it easy to identify with the period which is portrayed here.

Skagen lies at the northernmost tip of Denmark, surrounded by sea on three sides, and endowed with such sparkling light, that it was irresistable to the Danish painters of light, the Danish version of Impressionism, who started settling there in around 1870.

A strange collaboration and conflict existed between the local inhabitants and what they must have regarded as somewhat eccentric artists. The fisherman,

Christen Købke's work is the epitomy of the Danish Golden Age. "View outside the Northern Gate of the Citadel", 1834. 71 x 93 cm. Ny Carlsberg Glyptotek, Copenhagen.

artisans and old folk acted as "exotic" models for the artists; but a more profound integration took place. Anna, daughter of the local merchant, who later married the painter Michael Ancher, became so interested in art that she travelled to Copenhagen in 1874 to study art at a private school - ladies were not accepted at the Royal Academy, which did not establish a department for women until 1888.

The painter P.S. Krøyer and the Ancher family became the central figures in the artistic circle at Skagen, along with the poet Holger Drachmann. P.S. Krøyer was a master of the impressionist tech-

nique, and Michael Ancher struggled to convey his acute understanding of his fellowmen through his psychologically revealing portraits. Anna Ancher's gentler, more detailed works, displaying a profound sense of colour and composition, did not earn her a leading position until much later.

The Journal "Kritisk Revy" and on to COBRA

A major exhibition in Stockholm in 1930 was the venue for the first appearance in Scandinavia of the German functionalist movement which had exploded in the

145

P.S. Krøyer painted "The Artists on the South Beach at Skagen" during his first summer there. The painting is dated 15th September 1882.

wake of the Bauhaus school. Danish architects and artists flocked to the exhibition and absorbed these new impressions. At the Royal Academy of Fine Arts they had been taught to draw from plaster-cast models, Ionic capitals and the entire classical idiom.

The architect Poul Henningsen did much to introduce the new ideas. He used biting satire, both in songs and the magazine "Kritisk Revy", which he published together with friends from 1928-1932, and in which they raged against the "stupidity of the age" and ridiculed the staid town planners and decision-makers.

On the visual arts side the director of the Museum of Art, Carl V. Petersen, drew the attention of his son, the painter Bjerke Petersen, to developments in the Bauhaus. He went to study in Germany and returned full of both the socialist ideas which prevailed in the school, and the theories of Klee and Kandinsky,

which he and his artist friends Richard Mortensen and Ejler Bille translated into a Danish idiom. In the years preceding and during the Second World War these ideas combined with the influences of Nordic mythology and Scandinavian mentality and evolved into a form of abstract expressionist art which had a major impact on the world of art, since it formed the background for the international COBRA collaboration in the post-war years, with an explicitly "folkelig" objective.

In modern times Danish thinking has been superimposed on the influences of incoming international art movements and in the COBRA collaboration it was responsible for launching a new art movement outside Denmark.

The outstanding name of this period was the spirited and innovative Asger Jorn. For a number of years he exhibited boundless energy, throwing himself into the organisation of large international exhibitions, embarking on enormous projects, writing books and acquiring a considerable art collection, which formed the core of the Silkeborg Art Museum collection. He himself is well represented in collections abroad.

The Experimental Art School, Art Education – and Women

One of the main focuses of contemporary Danish art has been the experimental art school which was established in 1961 in protest against the stiff educational system within the Royal Academy. The initiative was taken by one artist, Poul Gernes, and one art historian, Troels Andersen. They established a school, a printing shop and exhibition facilities under the one umbrella of The Experimental Art School and, as a follow-up to the material accummulations of Neo-realism, they collectively organised campaigns, happenings and all sorts of challenges to the 'Establishment'. A whole

Asger Jorn's "Law of the Eagle", 1950, 123 x 123 cm. Jorn was the central figure in the international COBRA collaboration. Nordjyllands Kunstmuseum, Aalborg.

Bjørn Nørgaard uses elements from the whole history of art in his compilations. "The Human Wall" (1982), is located on a site in front of Statens Museum for Kunst in Copenhagen.

generation of young artists grew up under the influence of this exuberance, including the multi-artists Bjørn Nørgaard, Lene Adler and Per Kirkeby. The latter developed as both a writer, film producer and painter. His pictures contain so many levels of reality that one can never tire of looking at them.

Bjørn Nørgaard has developed a style in which he uses any number of elements from art history, as though he wants to say: the world is large, the possibilities are endless, choose for yourself!

The protest of the Experimental Art School against the Royal Academy was not the first of its kind. Action and reaction have been the driving forces in the continual development of the Royal Academy. It was often the teachers, themselves still almost unknown artists, who have had a decisive influence on a whole generation of artists. But even the basic academic nature of the teaching is constantly the subject of debate, both the method of

teaching as well as its quality and range.

Alternative courses of study have also been offered by other art colleges and evening classes, but for all aspiring artists the recognised entrance ticket to the profession has been acceptance at the official annual exhibitions.

When an artist has been accepted at five exhibitions, where the hanging committee consists of established artists, he/she is then entitled to call himself a "state-authorised artist" regardless of whether he/she is self-taught or has been to art school; the artist is then also invited to become a member of the Society of Artists, the professional association of the Royal Academy of Art. But membership does not of course provide any guarantees for art sales or a reasonable livelihood, which is why art subsidies are necessary.

You need to have a tough nature to be a creative artist and market your work yourself.

From a historical perspective the artist Sonja Ferlev Mancoba must be considered one of the most outstanding women in Danish art. She belonged to the pre-war movement and to COBRA. She was primarily inspired by surrealism and later by African art, when she came across the famous Kjærsmeyer collection of African art, now at the National Museum in Copenhagen. This influence was reinforced by her marriage to the African artist Ernest Mancoba. She spent the war years in Paris and in her correspondence she described how she worked out her sorrows and anxieties in the large *Sculpture* (1941-46, Silkeborg Art Museum). Sonja Ferlov's sculptures embody forms of lasting value.

In recent years female artists have been making an ever increasing impact. The sculptor Eva Sørensen and the painter Margrethe Sørensen are two artists who each add a new dimension to Danish art. Perhaps it is equality of the sexes which is finally making itself felt, or perhaps women are ceasing to set limits for themselves. Their incredibly sensitive interpretation of our age, their lack of compromise, and their courageous breaking down of barriers gives other women courage and faith in their own abilities.

Exhibition Venues

In addition to art museums and galleries there are of course the exhibition venues for the official annual exhibitions mentioned above and exhibitions organised by artists' associations. In Copenhagen the two most important of these are Charlottenborg, the exhibition venue of the Royal Academy at Kongens Nytorv, and Den Frie's hall at Østerport. This venue was established by an association of artists formed in protest against the policies of the Academy.

The artists associations, providing the framework for joint exhibitions and working activities, play an important role in Denmark, where cooperative ideals have been strong.

In this country of clubs, societies and associations, art lovers get together to form societies, which organise exhibitions, art purchases, and lectures, and often take the initiative to set up a local art museum. There is an art society in nearly all large business enterprises, arranging exhibitions in the staff canteen and lotter-

Many female artists have recently made names for themselves, including the sculptor Eva Sørensen. Granite sculpture, now located on the square in front of the railway station in Herning.

149

ies for the disposal of art purchases. What a good excuse to have a work of modern art on your wall at home - "I won it in a lottery"...

Museums and our Collective Heritage

Denmark is one of the countries with the highest number of museums in relation to its population. We have already noted that the local art associations have been the source of initiative for the establishment of numerous museums. In recent years there has been a myriad of new museums, a development which has met with a mixed reception by the authorities, For regardless of how good the intentions or efficient the organisation of the initiative is, at some point or other the state will be called upon to give financial support.

The reason why every single small town has to have its own museum is probably that the existing museums are full to the brim. People do not want to see the objects which they donate to museums just disappear into storage and never be put on display. So a museum society is formed, with specialist or local heritage interests, and a new "grass-roots museum" emerges, with the help of amateur enthusiasts devoting their leisure time or retirement years to work with the past. Museum professionals are used as advisors and it has sometimes been possible to establish a fruitful collaboration with a large museum in the area.

It is obvious that an age of change with the collapse of established norms and a widespread sense of rootlessness evokes a clear need in people to learn about their history, and to handle artefacts which can provide an answer to questions such as: "Who am I? What is my cultural identity?"

And this is where the Danes have a special advantage. This small country,

with few natural resources - but strategically located at the entrance to the Baltic, has had a very homogenous population throughout its 1000 year history. Just flick through Danish art and cultural history with this in mind, and you will be sure to notice how this homogeneity has left its mark.

The Royal Danish Kunstkammer

In singling out just a few Danish museums which distinguish themselves from museums abroad, we must start with the Kunstkammer (Cabinet of Curiosities). Other countries have had their cabinets of curiosities, but whereas they have been wound up and the collections dispersed, the Danish 17th and 18th century collection is still intact and preserved in a number of Copenhagen museums. The National Museum, which is the country's principal historical museum, houses some of the collection, and the rest is preserved in the State Museum of Art, the Natural History Museums and the Royal Collections in Rosenborg Castle.

Two Modern Museums

Louisiana, the Museum of Modern Art, which is situated north of Copenhagen, and the Women's Museum in Århus, are two outstanding contemporary museums which play a significant cultural role, also beyond our own national boundaries.

Louisiana is located in beautiful grounds overlooking the Øresund and with a splendid vista across to Sweden. It was created largely due to the strong will and incredible enthusiasm of one single man, Knud W. Jensen, who is a great art lover and who wished to share its pleasures with other people. He has invested all his energies and fortune into building

The Louisiana Museum in Humlebæk north of Copenhagen enjoys a beautiful location in a park overlooking the Øresund. Stairs and mobile by Calder, adjacent to the cafeteria. Photo: Poul Buchard.

up a museum of modern, in the first instance Danish, and later also international art.

Over the last 30 years the main building, the original house called Louisiana, has been extended with a number of pavilions set in the grounds and linked by glass-fronted passageways, as well as a concert hall. In addition to its permanent collection which reflects the trends in modern art, the museum acts as an important venue for major international exhibitions and other cultural events. Louisiana attracts visitors from all over the world, as well as Denmark and neighbouring Sweden. The beautiful natural setting of

the museum has also been a contributory factor in the development of a large new museum public.

The Danish Women's Museum is located in Århus, Denmark's second largest town. The motivation for the establishment of this museum was quite different.

Most museums, regardless of whether these are art or historical museums, focus on the male role. They depict the history of a town, district or country, and demonstrate the achievements of men, largely overlooking the contributions made by women. In recent years various attempts have been made to rectify this imbalance by establishing museums about women.

151

This museum in Århus was started in 1982 by a women's group as the outcome of a number of job creation projects. It is devoted entirely to the history of women and provides a venue for exhibitions by female artists.

The museum has now gained official status, which has ensured a measure of economic stability. The aim of the museum is to be socially pro-active. The documentation of the past which is collected, processed and exhibited, can act as a stimulus for the revision of our attitudes and behaviour, and reveal alternatives for the present and the future. History looks different from whatever angle it is interpreted, whether this is based on class, geographical region or marital status, and it needs to be researched from each of these angles.

The museum has gained a reputation for its untraditional, strongly emotive exhibitions. The first one, in 1984, dealt with housework and unmarried mothers, and established the museum's pattern of writing unrecorded history, of giving a voice to the unspoken and of challenging the hitherto unquestioned.

Many rich experiences await the museum-goer in Denmark, especially after 1992, when the National Museum fully reopens after an extensive programme of rebuilding, modernisation and computerisation, and with new displays of its collections both in the Prinsens Palais in the centre of Copenhagen, and in the Brede Museum, north of town, and close to the Open Air Museum.

Cultural life in Denmark is becoming more intense. Faith in the future has been preserved.

Music
in Denmark

by Flemming Madsen

MUSIC FESTIVAL IN ROSKILDE. PHOTO: MICHAEL ANDERSSON/BILLEDHUSET

Riches and Variety

Danish music is probably not pouring out of your loudspeakers just now, regardless of where in the world you happen to be. Even though Carl Nielsen, Per Nørgård, Niels-Henning Ørsted Pedersen and D.A.D. have fans all over the world, Danish music does not constitute a daily part of the global cultural menu.

On the other hand, Danish music is alive and doing well as part of Scandinavian culture and art. And musical life in Denmark is rich and full of variety.

200,000 children take music lessons in the country's 240 music schools. 150,000 adults are also active musicians, participating in folk high school and evening class courses. Denmark is buzzing with music: there are the music associations, festivals, concerts and activities in schools. This variety is a Danish hallmark.

Let the Polar Bears Dance…

If we assembled all the Danish composers and players who are visible on the cultural map of the world, they would form a kind of ice-berg; the under-water part, the "folkekultur" or community-based culture would constitute over 90% of the total. Danish cultural policy is democratic and broadly based, and promotes such activities. And this policy definitely benefits musical life in general.

However, this democratic, varied and community-based art and culture also harbours a certain self-satisfaction and laziness. It is not an absolute necessity for Danish art to tear itself away from its safe and cosy fireside and venture forth into the big wide world. Perhaps it is also a question of the passion and emotions in our northern souls, which is colder and more deliberate than those of our southern neighbours…

But a new awareness is emerging in Danish music, which is venturing forth into the new Europe and the world.

In this article I would like to invite you on a trip to the tip of "Musical Denmark's" ice-berg, where the polar bears have woken up and are beginning to dance…

Jazz and the Bass

In 1961 Niels-Henning Ørsted Pedersen, or NHØP as he is simply known both in Denmark and overseas, was voted "the best bass jazz player in the world" by the critics of the music magazine Down Beat. He was only 15 years old at the time, but had already started his international career at the jazz club "Montmartre" in Copenhagen, where he supported international stars such as Bud Powell, Dexter Gordon and Ben Webster with his virtuoso 'classical' double bass playing.

His technique is legendary. His speed, clarity and creativity is incomparable. But of course it is not only his technique which has made NHØP such a popular artist, with more than 400 recordings since 1960. He has developed his talents to encompass composing, conducting and arranging. A slightly melancholic Danish and Scandinavian tone and harmonisation can often be detected in his music, as for instance on the record of his duet "Hommage" made with his colleague Palle Mikkelborg, which also includes the choir "Ars Nova" in a fabulous version of Jacob Gade's famous piece "Tango Jalousie".

In 1991 NHØP was the first player, and the first jazz musician ever, to be awarded the Nordic Council's Music Prize, along with the sum of D.kr. 150,000. He is currently working on his most ambitious project to date: a record featuring the choir Ars Nova, the Norwegian saxophonist Jan Garbarek and the pianist Michel Petrucciani. The record is being produced by his fellow bass player Steve Swallow.

Danish jazz music enjoyed a great revival during the 1980s. Pierre Dørge's New Jungle Orchestra is a dadaist and provocative miniature big band, which has been a big hit all over the world and which is regarded as the international rejuvenator of big band music. The pianist and composer Jan Kaspersen, who was influenced by Thelonious Monk, has recorded the piano music of the French minimalist composer Erik Satie, and has thus been partially responsible for breaking down some of the barriers between the different musical genres. The saxophonist Fredrik Lundin, the quartet Page One and the pianists Jørgen Emborg and Kim Kristensen belong to the large young group of Danish jazz musicians and composers of international standing and popularity.

Nielsen and other Great Danes

In the autumn of 1883, at the age of eighteen, Carl Nielsen (1865-1931) left his home town of Odense to seek his fortune in Copenhagen, just as his famous compatriot, the fairy-tale writer Hans Christian Andersen had done half a century earlier. Even though Nielsen did not achieve the same monumental literary world fame as Andersen, he made his mark on the symphonic genre in Danish 20th century music, and is now regarded as our most famous national composer of international standing. Denmark and Nielsen are mentioned in the same breath when the topic of music is discussed overseas. He was a violinist, conductor and composer, and possessed an apparently inexhaustible supply of energy and creativity, which enabled him to work as a professional musician and teacher all his life as well as composing over 100 works, which included operas, symphonies as well as works for smaller ensembles. The best and most famous recordings of Carl

The conductor Ole Schmidt during a rehearsal. Photo: Marianne Grøndahl.

Nielsen's music include Bernstein's legendary interpretation of Symphony no.3, "Espansiva" with the Royal Danish Orchestra, and Ole Schmidt's version of Symphony no.5 with the London Symphony Orchestra.

Delving further back in the history of Danish music we encounter the organist and composer Diderik Buxtehude (1637-1707), whose German roots and musical expression were evident in the genius and originality of his organ compositions, which are now enjoying increasing recognition the world over.

Niels W. Gade (1817-1890) and J.P.E. Hartmann (1805-1900) were the main figures in the 19th century Danish Romantic period. Gade's "Efterklange af Ossian" (The Ossian Ouverture) is considered a masterpiece, and this work, as well as his cantata "Elverskud" (Elf-Shot) and his symphonies, will live on in Danish musical history. Hartmann's qualities have become more apparent as his works are revived, as in the opera "Liden Kirsten" (Young Kirsten): the musical idiom, rhythm and harmony merge into a spiritual communication which is interpreted by many as unmistakeably Danish and Scandinavian in nature.

The New Generation

One of the serious Danish composers one is most likely to come across overseas is Poul Ruders (born 1949). His international stature is demonstrated by the fact that the BBC commissioned a symphony from him for performance at the Promenade Concert Series in London in 1990. This was the first time for many years that a non-British composer had been honoured in this way. The symphony, entitled "Himmelhoch jauchzend - zum Tode betrübt" was later awarded the Royal Philharmonic Society's prestigious Charles Heidsieck Prize. Ruders has now very symbolically taken up residence in London, where he is a living example of the international confession and aesthetics of this generation of Danish composers. His music is expressive and full of images whilst being neither particularly Danish nor even Nordic in nature.

Danish composition today is characterised by its wide variety. There is a tremendous difference between the music of composers such as Bo Holten, Bent Sørensen, Ole Buck and Hans Abrahamsen. If it is nevertheless possible to postulate the existence of a common "Danish" trait, then this can only be justified by retracing our steps some 25 years to find the explanation.

The young composers of the 1960s, including Ib Nørholm, Per Nørgård and Pelle Gudmundsen-Holmgreen, were initially totally fascinated and then promptly shocked by the central European avantgarde when they first encountered the movement around 1960.

This led to a break with 'serial' music and the rest of international modernism, which they felt had progressed into the absurd. Many composers had lost touch with reality. In this vacuum they set about creating a peculiarly Danish phenomenon, which was to be called "den ny enkelhed" (The New Simplicity). Simplicity and clarity became the supreme goals. From this common 'minimalist' point of departure the composers soon developed their own individual styles, but retained this jointly achieved innovation as the value base for future development, which was gradually also influenced by new international currents. But "The New Simplicity" and its values left traces which can still be identified as peculiarly "Danish". This may also be due to the fact that Nørholm, Nørgård and Gudmundsen-Holmgreen, who are now all around sixty, have had a tremendous influence on the subsequent generations of composers.

Only one of the prominent composers of the previous generation, Niels Viggo Bentzon (born 1919), allowed himself to become temporarily involved in the turbulence of the 1960s movement. Together with Vagn Holmboe (born 1909) and Herman D. Koppel (born 1908) he represents a musical style which was established in the inter-war years. This music has the flavour of Carl Nielsen, as well as Hindemith and Stravinsky. Holmboe has written 12 symphonies and is regarded as the natural successor to Nielsen. The national record company DaCapo is currently preparing a recording of Holmboe's choral works and string quartets.

International Names on the Concert Stages

Foreign audiences are however more likely to encounter Danish musicians than music. The recorder player Michala Petri has become an international star, largely due to her numerous recordings. And most recently a number of singers have made names for themselves on the major opera circuits. These include Aage Haugland, Poul Elming, Eva Johansson, and Lisbeth Balslev. The conductor Michael Schønwandt, who is now resident conductor of the Berlin Symphony Orchestra, has also been famous for several years.

Cut'N Move, the surprise hit of 1992. Photo: Medley Records.

Yasmin, Cut 'N Move, Soulchock and Cutfather

Typical Danish names? Typical Danish music? No, these soloists and groups belong to the anglo-saxon generation of music which is currently breaking through in Denmark. They sing in English, with their antennae tuned to the international music market, and with their feet planted in Harlem, London, Africa and Copenhagen, all at the same time.

Cut 'N Move was the biggest surprise in 1992, when their melodic rhythmic hip-hop-rap-soul-funk dance music wore out the Disco turntables with hits like "Get Serious". Dr Baker, Soulchock and Cutfather are some of the latest hybrid artists, who have stuck their noses deep down into the musicology of the world and have come up with new music as well as oldies, mixed and remixed to the current musical flavour: rhythm and the physical. They produce rap and hiphop on a line with the best on the international music scene, which schedules and steers musical taste in Hongkong, Chicago, Istanbul and Århus.

Mature Women and Young Men

In 1992 Hanne Boel released "My Kindred Spirit", which, without chasing either youth or success, added another original and fascinating dimension to her mature, soul-blues personality. With her latest song "Where blue Begins", Sanne Salomonsen has reaffirmed that a large and lively part of her heart beats for the tradition of the Deep South, where blues, rock, soul and Bourbon on the rocks in a warm summer night merge into an almost languid caress of life.

In the world of pop music "Michael Learns to Rock" was fast on the heels of groups such as Toto and Europe. Their song "the Actor" put them in the international charts, and both their songwriting talents and musical skills are definitely on a par with international standards.

D.A.D. have signed a contract worth

157

millions of kroner with Warner Music, providing them with a large budget for an international launch. Even without this they are doing well in many parts of Europe, with concert halls full of fans, who appreciate these 'cowhorns' from Denmark. Their own peculiar energy-laden and heavy country style hits out at middle-class discreet charm like a fist in the face. Their record "Bad Craziness" is more about physicality and liberation of energy rather than any concrete message.

These are four names in current pop and rock music, which would cause a stir on a warm summer day on the beach anywhere in the world. Not necessarily because they are Danish, but because they are good. So perhaps you have heard Danish music before after all.

See you again!

Even though Danish polar bears are beginning to dance and to stir onto the world scene, the best way to experience the musical variety of Denmark is still to visit the country. Especially if you want to make acquaintance with the educational opportunities and active community-based culture. But regardless of where you are, you can always get more information, either by writing or by computer link-up, from the various specialised institutions and organisations, listed at the back of the book, which will be happy to assist you in finding the music which you are interested in.

See you again!

Ballet and Contemporary Dance

by Birthe Johansen

The Tradition

For centuries Danish ballet has been synonymous with ballet at the Royal Danish Theatre. This institution has been in existence so long, that its dance and drama, both under the same roof, as well as different sides of the same coin, have become one of Denmark's hallmarks.

This tradition can be traced back to the first Danish language theatre, the theatre in Copenhagen's Lille Grønnegade. Shortly after its opening in 1722 it was billing ballet alongside the new Danish comedies of Ludvig Holberg. The theatre's first ballet master was the Frenchman Jean-Baptiste Landé, who was hired in the summer of 1726 to provide entertainment in the intermissions, using short dances and acrobatic numbers. This form of entertainment soon became so popular that Holberg's comedies were adapted to include interludes of song and dance acts.

Despite their difference in form and expression, there were no great clashes between the silent and the verbal arts at that time. Landé drew from the same sources as Holberg in the production of his short numbers inspired by the commedia dell'arte. Both dealt with the same world of comedy - but the words of the writer were to have the most lasting impact on Danish culture.

When the first Royal Theatre opened in 1747 on the Kongens Nytorv site, after almost 20 years of pietist prohibition against any form of theatre, Jean-Baptiste Landé had long since earned his place in European ballet history as one of the founders of the imperial Russian ballet school in St Petersburg. But Holberg continued to write his Danish comedies and employed a succession of German, Italian and French ballet masters to produce the intermission pieces.

Danish Dancers Make their Entrance

Ballet at the Royal Theatre gradually developed into more than just entertainment for the intermissions. The theatre's management decided to train a Danish corps de ballet to replace the constant succession of foreign dancers. The ballet school, which was to form the backbone of the Royal Ballet, was founded in 1771. Four years later the Italian dancer and choreographer Vincenzo Galeotti was brought to Copenhagen to head the fledgeling ballet company. And he stayed with the company as ballet master until his death in 1816 at the age of 83.

The repertoire which Galeotti brought to Copenhagen was strongly influenced by his own teachers, the Frenchman Noverre and the Italian Angiolini, who had been the great reformers of their age and who had had similar ideas about a ballet d'action. In contrast to earlier pieces, the role of dancers in these new action ballets was more than a simple impersonation of various nationalities, professions or allegorical figures. Using the special 'language' of pantomime, they were to enact great dramatic sequences. Classical tragedy was an ideal subject. It had admittedly never been very popular amongst the Danish theatre-going public, apart from in parody form, as evidenced by Johan Herman Wessel's tragic-comic ballad opera "Love without Stockings" written in 1772. But Galeotti did more to convert the Danes than is immediately apparent from the fact that he is remembered for only one ballet, the 'old-fashioned' opening ballet "The Whims of Cupid and the Ballet Master", written in 1786. This cannot of course detract from the fact that it is the world's oldest ballet still danced in its original form.

At an advanced age Galeotti even managed to introduce Shakespeare to Denmark in the shape of the ballets "Romeo and Giulietta" (1811) and "Macbeth" (1816), but his main contribution to Danish cultural life were a number of Nordic ballets, most notably "Lagertha", composed in 1801.

The Danish Pictures of Romanticism

"Lagertha" was based on Saxo's tale of the mythical king Regnar Lodbrog and his love for the beautiful shieldmaiden Lagertha. It had its origins in the awakening Danish romantic nationalism, interpreted by a foreigner who was acutely sensitive to Nordic specificities, and whose huge success ensured its retention in the repertoire of the Royal Theatre for decades.

August Bournonville's first stage appearance at the age of 8 in 1813 was in a production of "Lagertha", playing the role of one of Regnar Lodbrog's two sons. Less than twenty years later he himself was to become the director of the Royal Ballet.

August Bournonville was a man of the new age in every respect. He had received his basic training from Galeotti and his own father, the elegant, French born dancer Antoine Bournonville, but totally new dimensions and influences were added during the years he spent training in Paris in the 1820s.

The graceful, effortless and joyful French dance style which he had learned in his youth was the ideal which he retained throughout his life. He even staged "the school" as part of the ballet "The Conservatoire" (1849). As he noted in his so-called Choreographic Creed: "With the addition of music, dance can reach poetic heights, just as it can be reduced to buffoonery with too much gymnastics." But for Bournonville ballet was above all a dramatic art.

Apart from a few interruptions, Bournonville stayed in his post as director of the Royal Ballet until 1877, and during his reign he was both the writer and producer, as well as the choreographer of more than 50 ballets as well as numerous dance divertissements for inclusion in operas and plays. He was one of the few Danish theatrical figures of the 19th century who always knew what was going on in the rest of Europe. He embarked on long theatre tours nearly every year, but back home he still preferred to pursue his own style.

Bournonville did not sympathise with the most emotional expression of romanticism, nor with much of its dual attitude towards women . His 1836 Danish version of the French masterpiece "La Sylphide" attempts to create a discreet distance to the winged forest creature. In

Drawing of Lucile Grahn, who danced Bournonville's "Sylphide" in the 1830s.

In Bournonville ballets, pure dance scenes are usually performed within the framework of some festivity. Edvard Lehmann's drawing of the 1851 première of "Kermess in Bruges". The Royal Theatre.

his dramatic scheme of world it is interaction and harmony which feature strongly, not the solo 'gymnastics' of supernatural female creatures, which gradually came to dominate the ballets of other countries in the 19th century.

Without giving his ballets realism, Bournonville nevertheless expressed himself both more freely and more 'naturally' than either his predecessor Galeotti or his contemporaries in Europe. As he was also the creative spirit behind the stories which his ballets were designed to relate, he found it difficult to come to terms with the limitations of the traditional pantomime language of ballet. His choreography expanded this language with the addition of many expressive gestures and movements. Pure dance scenes always required the framework of some form of festivity. He came closest to his ideals in scenes such as the dance provoked by magic in "Kermess in Bruges" (1851) and the elf-maidens' dance in "A Folk Tale" (1854), where the dance itself has a dramatic function - and which coincides with modern thinking on the dramaturgy of ballet.

Like his predecessor Galeotti, Bournonville started delving into the realm of the Nordic myths in the latter part of his career. Gods and heroes were in fashion again. Whilst Richard Wagner was working on his epic mythological operas, the Danish Ballet master created "The Valkyrie" in 1861 and "The Agony of Thrym" in 1868. But these master-pieces have not stood the test of time as well as the folklore of "Napoli" (1842), the oriental fantasy in "Abdullah" (1855) and the simple everyday idyll of "Far from Denmark" (1860) or "The King's Volunteers on Amager" (1871).

Tradition and Renewal

The Royal Ballet was a much quieter place in the years following Bournon-ville's death. It has often been said that his ballets were only kept alive because there were no great choreographic talents amongst his successors. They were content to cherish the past, especially Hans Beck, who codified exercises and sequences of steps from the ballets and arranged them into a series of Bournonville Schools. These daily training pro-grammes, with one School for each day of the week, served as the sole technical foundation for the Royal Ballet in the ensuing 30 to 40 years. But the tradition was also self-reinforcing in other ways.

The Royal Theatre was closed to any new ideas until well into this century. Gone was the age when the theatre, with its magical ability to show life as it was elsewhere, commanded a position not unlike TV today. Popular entertainment had shifted over to the new cinemas. But the national theatre was prepared to spearhead the avant-garde arts.

Drama, which was supposed to push back the barriers of the naturalistic living-room scene in which the age had become enclosed, was also a long time coming.

The first time the leading 20th century dramatist Kjeld Abell had his work staged was as the scriptwriter for the ballet "The Widow in the Mirror" (1934) choreo-graphed by Børge Ralov.

The preparatory work which paved the way for this little expressionist dance dra-ma was done by Harald Lander, who became ballet master in 1932. First he had changed the format of the daily training sessions. Russian Schools were now intro-duced on a equal footing with the tradi-tional French Schools of Bournonville. These Schools created the prerequisites for radical modifications to the repertoire of the Royal Ballet, which culminated in 1948 with the production of Harald Lander's own "Etudes", which gave him his international breakthrough.

Silia Schandorff and Sorella Englund in Bournonville's "A Folk Tale", from a performance in the autumn of 1991, with stage design by H.M. Queen Margrethe.

This abstract choreographic fantasy on the dancers' daily practice sessions is only partially representative of the multi-facetted choreographic talents which Harld Lander demonstrated for the Royal Theatre right up to 1951. Whereas his contemporaries like Børge Ralov and Nini Theilade concentrated mainly on abstract, symphonic ballets, Lander preferred to work with the dramatic elements of ballet. Like his greatest predecessor, he was first and foremost a man of the theatre.

Contemporary Dance

Since the history of dance in Denmark has always been linked with the history of the theatre, the 1960s' group theatre movement provided opportunities for a new kind of dance, unrelated to classical ballet.

Its emergence followed a struggle against the established institutions. One of the chief exponents was Eske Holm, who in 1975 resigned from his secure

164 *Harald Lander's "Études", first performed in 1948, is an abstract choreographic fantasy on the dancers' daily practice sessions. Drawing by Hans Bendix from one of the many performances at the Royal Theatre.*

Scene from Flemming Flindt's Ionesco ballet "The Triumph of Death", performed at the Royal Theatre in 1971.

"civil service" position as a solo dancer with the Royal Ballet to give 'barefoot' performances in a warehouse in the harbour district of Copenhagen. Prior to this, his ballets "Tropism" (1964), "Agon" (1967) and "Cicatricis" (1969), demonstrated to the audiences of the Royal Theatre that ballet could be more than tutus and pink ballet shoes - which was completely in line with the ideas that Flemming Flindt, ballet master since 1963, had for the Royal Ballet. Flindt actually went much further, with naked dancers performing in the Ionesco ballet "The Triumph of Death" (1971). But for the enthusiasts of the new dance form it was important to create spatial art which was totally liberated from the gilt frame of the traditional proscenium theatre.

The fact that Eske Holm was both a man and a Dane made him an exception in the world of the contemporary dance groups which sprouted up in the space of a few years, each centring around American, or U.S. trained dancers, all women. The first group, Living Movement, was formed in 1972 around the Norwegian-born Randi Patterson, the Italian-born Graziella Hsu and the Dane Jytte Kjøbæk. Then the movement and the pace of immigration really took off. There always seemed to be room for one more. In 1976 Cher Geurtze came to Copenhagen from Boston, a year later Ann Crosset from New York, followed in 1981 by Rhea Leman and in 1982 by the Swede Nanna Nilsson. These are just a few of the most prominent names which dominated the alternative dance scene in Denmark in the 1980s.

Language has followed these choreographers, teachers and directors. Even though in recent years contemporary Danish dance has received a considerable injection of Danish dancers, it mostly 'talks' English with an American accent. That also goes for Danish rock music. The technical foundations of this contemporary dance were also created by Americans, including Martha Graham and Merce Cunningham. But let us not forget that the language of classical ballet has always been French, which did not prevent choreographers such as Galeotti, Bournonville and Lander from making the ballet very Danish.

Danish themes are already quite often being used in contemporary dance productions. The choreographers Warren Spears and Anette Abildgaard of New

Danish Dance Theatre have done much with their "A Dream of the Gods" (1984) based on Nordic mythology, "But the Dance Goes on" (1991) based on folk songs, and "Skagen" based on themes from the artists' colony in the North Jutland fishing village of Skagen in the 1890s.

In the last few years contemporary dance has also adopted more traditionally dramatic modes of expression. Unfortunately, some will say. But you can only create spatial art in an open space if you have the space. And the contemporary dance groups still lack stages which have been designed to meet their needs. Stages which provide the space for the hallmark of a new century.

Theatre and Film

by Jens Kistrup

The Changing Cultural Scene

The Danes have always been slightly crazy about the theatre - perhaps slightly more in the past than now, where the cultural scene is in a process of change.

This change is due to several factors. Firstly, the middle classes no longer constitute the kind of core audience, on which, until recently, the theatre has always been able to rely. Then the new media situation - with numerous additional television channels - has created a

The Royal Theatre's first outstanding era, during the latter half of the 18th century, was dominated by the comedies of Holberg. Scene from "Jacob von Tyboe or the Bombastic Soldier", showing the title figure and Jesper Snyltegæst. 19th century drawing by Wilhelm Marstrand.

spread, even a fragmentation, in the interests of the theatre audience base, which the theatre has had difficulty in adjusting to. Who are the theatre audiences anyway?

Television Drama

For over two hundred years the nation maintained a common interest in the theatre. And this communality of interest continued after the advent of cinema, the radio and even television. Television drama, and particularly the works of the leading playwright Leif Panduro (1923-77), created an enormous interest, the like and intensity of which had never before been experienced in Denmark. When they watched Leif Panduro's TV plays, the Danish viewers felt that they were learning the *truth* about the Danes. And Leif Panduro's unique position as a TV dramatist - as well as psychoanalyst, provocateur and documentary maker - was somehow consolidated in the long-running folk comedy series "Matador", which was based on a synopsis by Lise Nørgaard and directed by Erik Balling and included most of the most popular Danish actors in the cast. The series ran for several years, and followed the historical development of a medium-sized Danish provincial town from about 1930 to about 1970. It was not until TV Theatre's Danish repertoire was reduced to the minimum that the Danes realised that the position of 'real' theatre had also been diminished. Did we actually know what we wanted from it?

The Royal Danish Theatre and Tradition

It is not possible to understand the position of the theatre in Denmark without looking at the period from around the middle of the 18th century until the

The Royal Theatre enjoyed a period of outstanding success in the 1930s and 1940s when a lot new Danish drama was produced, including plays by Kaj Munk. Scene from a 1938 performance of "An Idealist", with Poul Reumert as Herod and Bodil Ipsen as Cleopatra. Photo: Rigmor Mydtskov/Steen Rønne.

middle of the 20th century, when the theatre, and here this means first and foremost the Royal Theatre in Copenhagen, was regarded as, and for long periods actually *was*, the artistic focus of the nation, the centre of most of its secular intellectual life. The Royal Theatre was the place to which Danish writers aspired, to make their names and achieve success. The bourgeois middle classes regarded it as the centre of entertainment and family theatre, which it certainly was, with all three dramatic arts forms under one roof; drama, opera and ballet, and the country's leading orchestra - The Royal Orchestra, in the orchestra pit.

There have been four outstanding eras in the history of the Royal Theatre, on which its reputation still rests. The first was the second half of the 18th century, which was dominated by the comedies written by Ludvig Holberg (1684-1754) - the Danish counterpart to Molière - which still feature on the repertoire today. The second was the High Romantic and Biedermeier era, as exemplified by the writer of tragedies, Adam Oehlenschläger (1779-1850) as well as the writer of comedies, Johan Ludvig Heiberg (1791-1860), and the ballet master and choreographer August Bournonville (1805-79) as the most prominent names.

The third era was Naturalism, which lasted from the last decade of the 19th

169

century until well into the 20th century. The Royal Theatre was responsible for staging Henrik Ibsen's most famous play "Et dukkehjem" (A Doll's House). For a long time the naturalist style of acting was the one most favoured by the theatre's artistic team. Henri Nathansen's play "Indenfor murene"(Within the Walls, 1912), which dealt with the conflict between Jews and gentiles in a middle-class Copenhagen environment, was the most vigorous product of the naturalist style in Denmark. The last outstanding period for the Royal Theatre was in the 1930s and 1940s, which was partially due to another new wave of Danish dramatists ; Kaj Munk, Kjeld Abell, Soya and Knud Sønderby, and which culminated in 1948 with a three-week theatrical calvacade to celebrate the 200th anniversary of the theatre.

Of course all this is history now. But without knowledge of this theatrical past it would be impossible to understand the existence of such an intense and tenacious interest in the theatre in Denmark, at least amongst the older generation. This interest in the theatre, which is often criticised for its conservatism, provides much of the core market for the considerable activity of the regional theatres.

The Regional Theatres

In addition to the Royal Theatre in Copenhagen, the Århus and Aalborg Theatres in Jutland, the Odense Theatre on Funen, and the touring company "Det Danske Teater", all seek to maintain a fruitful balance between the classical and modern and between the popular and the avant-garde.

The Royal Theatre and the three regional theatres are the only theatres in Denmark which can afford a large resident company, whilst the other theatres, especially those which belong to "Den Storkøbenhavnske Landsdelsscene" (The

Greater Copenhagen Group of Theatres), hire their actors for each individual production. Their tight budgets mean that they can only afford a small cast, and this naturally influences the choice of repertoire. In Copenhagen an exception is made in the case of musicals, for which special grants may be sought, whilst the provincial theatres have a freer rein to stage musicals. Odense Theatre had a big hit with its production of "Les Misérables" and Aalborg Theatre likewise with "Into the Woods" by Stephen Sondheim. The Danish classic, "Within the Walls" has also been turned into a musical, called "Esther". It was first performed at the Royal Theatre, and has since been produced by Aalborg Theatre.

Total-theatre Productions

The 'small' productions have thus become the norm, whilst the 'mega' productions have found their own special venues. Of special note are the producer Kaspar Rostrup's total-theatre productions at Gladsaxe Theatre, and Morten Grunwald's musical theatre productions at Østre Gasværk. Kaspar Rostrup has staged an impressive number of total-theatre productions, which have all been tremendous popular successes. These include "Niels Klim", "Faust", "Frændeløs"(Alone in the World), "Toms eventyr"(Tom's Adventures), and "Odysséen"(The Odyssey). Peter Langdal has recently developed this type of production even further with his own very personal interpretations.

And Morten Grunwald is the artistic director who has managed to make the most of the difficult conditions which the budgetary constraints imposed on the theatre. But after many years as the director of the Bristol Theatre and then the Betty Nansen Theatre (formerly the Allé Scenen), he is now devoting his efforts entirely to the large theatre at Østre Gasværk. This was the venue for Peter

Musicals tend to be produced by the regional theatres. The Odense Theatre's production of "Les Miserables" was a great success.

Brook's touring productions of "Carmen" and "Mahabharata". Peter Langdal staged Shakepeare's "A Midsummer Night's Dream" here and Morten Grunwald put on Stephen Sondheim's "Sweeny Todd". These productions indicate the depth and breadth of the repertoire, with which this large venue has already demonstrated its theatrical potential.

The Theatrical Spectrum in the 1990s

It is undeniable that the picture of Danish theatre in the early 1990s is both confused and heterogeneous. There are many reasons for this. One of the problems, as already mentioned, is the fact that the theatre can no longer count on its audience. Another problem is the uncertain economy - inadequate grants necessitate constant cut-backs. A third problem, related to the last one, are the difficulties encountered by individual theatres in creating an image, which their audiences can accept. An example of this is the Nørrebro Theatre - how much can you change a theatre, which is regarded as a popular theatre (operettas etc) by the public? The Aveny Theatre has also had difficulties in motivating the audience for its "avant-garde" work, whilst including many of the older and more recent classics.

It has also become increasingly difficult for The Royal Theatre to accommodate three theatrical art forms under a single directorship and in two theatres, including the drama theatre, which is now unsuitable for this purpose. The theatre cannot give value for the vast sums it costs to run without a new theatre building.

Nevertheless, new and viable initiatives have been taken in many of the theatres. One example is the "Privat Teatret", which does not receive central government subsidies, which stages productions in Copenhagen and then tours the country with them. The director of this theatre, Niels Bo Valbro, in partnership with the director, producer and actor Bent Mejding, is planning the refurbishment of Copenhagen's second largest theatre "Det Ny Teater", which has been closed due to lack of additional public funds.

In view of this uncertain situation the amount of life in the theatre in Denmark is both remarkable and admirable. Group theatre and children's theatre, which flourished in the 1960s and 1970s, have been forced to make serious reassessments, but have nevertheless managed to adjust to the new political and economic conditions. The three 'open' Copenhagen theatres: Københavneren, Café Teatret and Rialto, have improved their potential despite their fluid borderline between amateurs and professionals. And even though the roles in the established theatre companies are often filled on the star system - new and unknown actors usually have to wait a long time to get into the limelight - the best of the younger producers have been able to herald the regeneration which often only hesitatingly and half-heartedly finds a platform.

It is difficult to say where the regeneration will come from. But the combination of theatre director-producer has often proved to be the right one, and now, at a time where a new generation of theatre directors is moving into the Copenhagen theatres the system is still basically the same: Peter Langdal is at the Betty Nansen Theatre, Lars Knutzon is at the ABC Theatre, the theatre group Dr Dante is directed by the producer-writer Nikolaj Cederholm at the Aveny Theatre. And the regenerative attempts which we have seen so far, have largely stemmed from the producers. A good example is Staffan Valdemar Holm, also a playwright, who has staged a total of three Strindberg productions, all of them revolutionary.

This does not mean that the producers have totally taken over the theatres at the expense of the playwrights. The partnership of Klaus Hoffmeyer (producer) and Jess Ørnbo (playwright) has produced some of the most original productions in the last two to three decades of theatre, the latest of which was "De Forkerte" (The Wrong Ones) at the Royal Theatre. This is also true of the cooperation between Emmet Feigenberg (producer) and Erling Jepsen (playwright), with their latest product "Elskende i et fodgængerfelt" (Lovers on a pedestrian crossing) at the Hippodrome. Finally, ever since his breakthrough with the musical "Teenager Love" at the Royal Theatre in 1962, Ernst Bruun Olsen has proved to be one of our best playwrights, and also one of our best producers, often staging his own plays.

The Talent

There is no doubt, that as far as the amount of talent is concerned, Denmark is a very rich theatrical country. And that also goes for the actors. All the most important role types are well catered for. For instance it is remarkable that even though Danish theatre is primarily comedy oriented, the last few years have seen the emergence of a number of great tragic actresses: Ghita Nørby, Kirsten Olesen, Benedikte Hansen. The latter two reached a climax in their careers starring in Eugene O'Neill's "Mourning becomes Electra" at the Royal Theatre. And Ghita Nørby has consolidated her position as Denmark's current leading actress even further in her recent roles in Edward Albee's "Who is afraid of Virginia Woolf", in which she co-starred with Frits Helmuth; in Per Olov Enquist's "The Night of the Tribades" and in

Ghita Nørby has given brilliant performances in partnership with Frits Helmuth. Scene from Strindberg's "Dance with Death" at the Privatteatret in Copenhagen. Photo: Morten Jensen/Polfoto.

Strindberg's "The Dance of Death". It is notable that the Danish actors command both the tragic as well as the comic roles. This is also true of the greatest male talents of the older generation: Jørgen Reenberg and Henning Moritzen.

And it is not only within drama that Danish theatre is demonstrating its vitality. Interest in opera has never been greater, whether it is performed by the Royal Theatre Company or by the touring Jutland Opera. This company has made a name for itself with major Wagner productions, first the whole of the "Ring" cycle and then "Parsifal", all produced by Klaus Hoffmeyer. The same interest has been evident in ballet, or rather dance, where The Royal Theatre has staged a new production of Bournonville's "Et folkesagn" (A Folk Tale), with the set and

costumes designed by H.M. Queen Margrethe. In addition, the Nyt Dansk Danseteater (New Danish Dance Theatre) has provided a valuable complement to the largely classical repertoire of the Royal Theatre.

The dramatic arts in Denmark are multifarious, and cannot be uniformly defined. When the theatres shut for the summer - most of them for three, four or five months, it is time for the Summer Revues, of which some 20 to 30 are put on all over the country. Some of Denmark's brightest comic artists have found, and still find most scope for their talents performing in the revues. But the summer season is not exclusively revues. For the last ten years the Grønnegård Theatre has staged a Holberg play in the open-air courtyard theatre of the Museum of Arts **173** and Crafts. For the last three years this company has extended its activities further with autumn productions staged in the "Ridehuset" (Riding School) at Christiansborg Castle. New plays with Danish historical themes by Danish playwrights (Svend Åge Madsen, Ebbe Kløvedal Reich, Dorrit Willumsen) have been performed. These also constitute attempts at rousing the public's interest via increased theatrical activity.

The pursuit of theatre as theatre - different from all the other art forms - has proved to be highly significant for the development of the branch of Danish theatre which is looking to the future. This development has been inspired by Peter Brook and Dario Fo, and is led by the producers Peter Langdal, Kaspar Rostrup, Klaus Hoffmeyer, Søren Iversen, Staffan Valdemar Holm and Madeleine Røn Juul, who have all made major contributions to this theatricalisation of the theatre. But they are not the only ones. Continuity in the theatre owes a great debt to producer Sam Besekow, now over 80, who has actively inspired and injected new life into the theatre for over 50 years, as a creative artist in practically all the theatrical arts. And many new, young names are appearing on the scene.

The traditional and the innovative live all too peacefully alongside each other - this has been a drawback, but also a strength. It cannot be said that the essential updating of theatre and drama has

Scene from Bille August's award-winning film "Pelle the Conqueror", with Pelle Hvengaard and Max von Sydow. Photo: Per Holst Film.

Scene from Morten Arnfred's film "Heaven and Hell", with Karina Skands and Erik Mørk. The film is based on a novel by Kirsten Thorup. Photo: Vibeke Vinding/Warner & Metronome.

been achieved to a satisfacory degree. Compromise and its policy of adjustment have been the order of the day in all too many places.

On the other hand Eugenio Barba has pursued a totally uncomprosing artistic policy in his theatre cum theatre laboratory, the Odin Theatre in Holstebro, bringing him closer to the secrets of life and the secrets of the theatre than any other Danish theatrical personality.

A Few Words on the Film Industry

The Theatre and Cinema don't really have much in common, even though many actors perform in both art forms, and even though some producers work in both genres. For instance Kaspar Rostrup scored a major popular hit with his film "Dansen med Regitze" (Waltzing Regitze), a lighthearted everyday tragedy based on a novel by Martha Christensen, and featuring the Danish theatre's star 'couple', Ghita Nørby and Frits Helmuth in the main roles. And Helle Ryslinge, who usually works in the film medium, has produced the play "Samme tid, næste år" (Same time, next year) for the theatre. In the film "Flamberede hjerter" (Coeur Flambé) starring Kirsten Lehfeldt as the girl Henry, she produced a wonderfully funny and moving picture of the confusion of our times in a rather anti-social youth environment. Her next picture, "Sirup" was somewhat weaker, a peculiarly unloving revelation of the deceptions of life and the commercial art world.

Danish Cinema is dominated by a few great directors, with a lot of lesser names who usually only get to demonstrate their talent in one or two films. The most interesting and innovative director is Lars von Trier, whose two most ambitious films "Forbrydelsens element" (Element of Crime) and "Europa" both reveal and create the myth of the western world at one and the same time. Bille August has attracted a much wider audience, especially with his award-winning masterpiece, the filmatisation of the first volume of Martin Andersen Nexø's proletarian novel "Pelle Erobreren" (Pelle the Conqueror). And Nils Malmros has had a number of hits with his films based on the exploration of his own childhood and his own professional world ("Århus by Night"), but has created works of greater artistic merit when, in films such as "Kundskabens træ" (The Tree of Knowledge) and "Skønheden og udyret" (Beauty and the Beast), he has managed to distance himself from his own life and world.

Other younger directors of note include Søren Kragh-Jacobsen, whose films "Har du set min smukke navle?" (Wanna see my beautiful navel?) and "Drengene fra Sankt Petri" (The Boys from St.Petri) are films designed for boys, and the latter is set during the occupation. Morten Arnfred has made a film of Kirsten Thorup's novel "Himmel og Helvede" (Heaven and Hell). He is also known for his film "Der er et yndigt land" (Land of Plenty), one of the best ever Danish films about farming life. This does not mean that the public have forgotten the veterans of Danish cinema . These include Palle Kjærulff-Schmidt and his film "Peter von Scholten", about the Danish colonial rule in the West Indies, and Henning Carlsen, whose film based on Knut Hamsun's novel "Sult" (Hunger) ranks as a modern classic, as well as Astrid Henning-Jensen, who filmatised Dea Trier Mørch's novel "Vinterbørn" (Winter's Child) and then made the Tove Ditlevsen film "Barndommens gade" (Early Childhood).

Life and Death

- Crisis and Redemption:
The Great Questions of Existence as Illustrated in Danish Literature

by Sven Hakon Rossel

Demonic Nature and a Longing for Paradise

Hans Christian Andersen's fairytale "Skyggen"(The Shadow), written in 1847, that is, the middle of the last century, marks the turning point where the idealistic-religious view of life was replaced by modern phenomena such as materialism, anarchy and nihilism - and from then on attention focused on human irresolution, loneliness and destruction. Prior to this time, and in harmony with romantic philosophy, it was accepted as indisputable that man was either completely good - a lucky fellow, an Aladdin type as we find in *Arabian Nights* or in Adam Oehlenschläger's romantic dramatic masterpiece written in 1805, *Aladdin eller den forunderlige Lampe* (Aladdin or the Wonderful Lamp) - or completely evil, as Aladdin's opponent, the sorcerer Noureddin. In "The Shadow" however the moral concepts become relative. The learned man only wishes to write about the good, the beautiful and the truth, but nobody takes any notice of him. The hero of the tale does therefore not win his princess and half the kingdom in the traditional manner, but on the contrary, he is conquered

and finally executed by his own shadow, which has disengaged itself from its master, that is by something beyond his control and without substance. There is no escape into either the realm of metaphysics or the world of fantasy or the arts. Even though the ever optimistic flax in Andersen's tale "Hørren" (1849; The Flax) can joyfully exclaim: "The song is never over! That is the best of everything", the tragic refrain "It's over! Past! It's all over! And that's how it is with all stories" was already resounding in "Grantræet" (1845; The Fir Tree). Death triumphs, and significantly, there is no life beyond beckoning - not even a memory or "the judgement on each and every death" as extolled so emphatically by Odin in the Old Norse poem *Hávámal* (The Words of the High One).

The belief in death as the final full stop was in accordance with both the ancient and modern man's non-Christian, materialistic philosophy of life. And long after the introduction of Christianity to Scandinavia mediaeval man still regarded death as a destructive force, the threat of which was anthropomorphically projected out onto the unknown and frightening natural environment, which was inhabited by demonic mythical beings: trolls, mermaids, elf-maiden and giants.

Thus one of the earliest ballads, of which Denmark has a treasure unequalled by other countries, known as *Elveskud* (The Elf-Shot) written before 1200, relates how Sir Oluf rides forth to invite guests to his wedding. The Elf-king's daughter attempts to entice him into the dance and even though he resists, his fate is sealed:

"And wilst thou not tread the dance with me,
plague and sickness shall follow thee."
She smote him then across the back,
never was he harder struck.

Drawing by Vihelm Pedersen from H.C.Andersen's fairy-tale "The Shadow".

Poeple in the Middle Ages projected the threat of death into nature, which harboured dangerous forces. Fresco from a church in Tune, around 1550.

And now catastrophe strikes blindly - and the anonymous poet concludes stoically:

Early that morning when sun came out,
the bride arrived with the wedding crowd.
(...)
She raised the cover so red,
there was Sir Oluf, and he was dead.
Early that morning when sun came out,
three bodies there were in Sir Oluf's
house .
Sir Oluf and his beloved maid,
his mother, too, from sorrow dead.
(trans. Henry Meyer)

In the ballad of *Dronning Dagmars Død* (Queen Dagmar's Death) written some 50 years later, the Catholic philosophy of the late Middle Ages has penetrated com-pletely. Even though the main character is also unable to avoid death, she is able to return to life briefly in order to give her husband, the king, some good advice about the future. On her deathbed she expresses no fear of final extinction but rather, with a finely portrayed humanity, her fear of purgatory and lastly her con-viction about the glory of heaven.

Whilst it was in complete harmony with late mediaeval theology to enjoy life to the full as a foretaste of the pleasures of eternity, the attitude of the baroque peri-od, largely due to the bloodiness of the Thirty Years War of 1618-48, tended to regard life on earth as merely a station on the terrestrial pilgrimage, a voyage between two harbours, the first being the cradle and the second the grave - as

179

expressed in one of the favourite metaphors of the baroque period. Thomas Kingo expressed this total dualism very powerfully in his hymns, and perhaps most thoroughly and perfectly in "Sorrig og Glæde de vandre til Hobe" (Sorrow and Joy They Wander Together) written in 1681:

Sorrow and Joy they wander together
fortune and misfortune along the way
prosperity and adversity beckon to each other
sunshine and showers take their turn
our earthly gold
is the rich soil
and heaven alone is rich in salvation.

Kingo always speaks on behalf of his contemporaries, for whom the right choice is never in question, and thus in another hymn of the same year he can exclaim with conviction, "Fare World, Farewell, I am tired of being your slave", with a refrain taken from the Ecclesiastes: "Vanity, vanity".

The Struggle between Mind and Matter

It is this dualism between this world and the next, matter and mind, life and mortality, which is reconciled by the Christian creed of atonement and immortality which dominated Danish literature until the time of Hans Christian Andersen. In the second half of the 18th century this dualism is evoked in the pietist hymns of Johannes Ewald as a personal and existential experience. Here the fall from grace is equated with death, but God's mercy is ever beckoning as a possible salvation, offering eternal life. In the 19th century this dualism is represented by the poet-priest N.F.S. Grundtvig and the philosopher Søren Kierkegaard. Grundtvig returned to Old Norse mythology and legend, in-

geniously using their world of ideas and symbols to explain his own interpretation of Christianity. Thus his sombre and visionary poem *Nyaars-Morgen* (1824; New Year's Morning), is deliberately structured in the manner of the Old Norse *Vølvens Spådom* (Voluspa). The dramatic and philosophical climax is reached in the scene where the soothsayer wrenches the head off a cockerel and throws it over the wall of ice, which divides life from death:

Then was to be heard
the strangest chorus.-
On the far side of the wall
as loud as the lur
the cock beat his wings and crowed!

This poem is one of the most powerful and original expressions of Christian faith in eternity ever written. It was also a proclamation of Grundtvig's faith in a spiritual awakening in Scandinavia, which for his part resulted in the so-called "mageløse opdagelse" (matchless discovery) that it is not the written word of the Bible, but rather the *living* word, which we receive through baptism and holy communion, which confirms God's pact with mankind. Grundtvig's dynamic interpretation of Christianity was embodied both into his 1400 hymns and in his educational ideas for "a school for life" which developed into the Folk High School movement.

The other intellectual giant in Danish spiritual life in the middle of the 19th century, Søren Kierkegaard, also participated energetically in the spiritual debate of the time, and with the same polemic passion as Grundtvig. And as both Grundtvig and Hans Christian Andersen, Kierkegaard's universality points far beyond Romanticism into the 20th century. Kierkegaard's radicalism is expressed in his main work *Enten-Eller* (1843; Either-

Or) in his insistence on the Imitation of Christ rather than an aesthetic or ethical philosophy of life as the only way to human salvation. Kierkegaard failed to find this commitment in the Danish State Church, which led to his bitter and violent battle against the Church, especially in the controversial pamphlet, *Øieblikket* (1855; The Moment). It is through such an existential choice that man reaches an understanding of his own ego. Kierkegaard demands a profoundly personal and passionate attitude to life, which man is solely responsible for. He was thus the forerunner of modern existentialism and had a significant influence on writers such as Henrik Ibsen, Strindberg, Dostoyevsky, Kafka, Faulkner, Camus and Sartre. But in his own lifetime Kierkegaard was not only ignored, but even stifled into silence by public opinion. True Christianity could thus not be realised and Kierkegaard must be regarded as one of the *last* great Christian thinkers of the world.

In "Niels Lyhne", the author J.P. Jacobsen settles up with religion. Section of a wood engraving after a painting by Ernst Josephson. Nordstjernen 1882.

Metaphysical Collapse

Grundtvig also had premonitions of the crisis of Christianity. Even though the Folk High School movement spread victoriously across the globe, the poem New Year's Morning nevertheless ends with the despondent prophecy, that the coming summer will end with the winter of doom. The reconciliation of the dualism through faith is not tenable. It is as though Grundtvig, and Kierkegaard, anticipated those question marks which the advent of naturalism around 1870 posed to the whole of religion, and which, after frontal attacks by German radical Bible critics, by Darwinism and Marxism, led to its collapse; towards the end of the century Nietzsche could thus proclaim: God is dead! Thus too, one of the greatest naturalist writers, J.P. Jacobsen, could permit

Niels Lyhne, the title figure of the novel of the same name written in 1880, to die triumphantly without a priest at his side. But he still had to add: "And then finally he died his death, that difficult death". With a simple flick of the wrist Andersen permitted the learned man to be obliterated in a universe without a merciful God, without love; and thus both in "The Shadow" and "The Fir Tree" he centred on man's existential solitude. Nevertheless, a number of other tales, such as "Den Lille Havfrue" (1837; The Little Mermaid) and "Hørren" (The Flax) and latterly "Hvad gamle Johanne fortalte"

181

(1872; What Old Johanne Told) demonstrate that Andersen could not live with the prospect of obliteration after all, but tries to conjure up that immortality which he personally found indispensable. Jacobsen, however, has accepted man's lot, but here too the old religious Adam shows resistance and thus Niels Lyhne becomes a tragic hero.

A much more modern approach was employed by the other great prose writer of this period, Herman Bang, to incorporate death in life. The title figure of his masterly story *Irene Holm* (1890) leaves the scene accompanied by the following comments: " *There* she went - to continue *that* which we call life", which for her - and Bang - was nothing other than death. For Andersen as well as Jacobsen and Bang, death is a reality, frightening because it is inevitable and impossible to harmonise with life. However both Andersen and Jacobsen strive in a romantic fashion towards a reconciliation, one on eternal, the other on temporal terms. It is as though they both are struggling, albeit along diametrically opposite lines, against the disintegration and fragmentation of modernity, which Bang however accepts.

A last attempt to retain a whole view of man, in his confrontation with death, may be found around the turn of the century in the work of Johannes V. Jensen; the Darwinist who strove all his life to find the eternal dimension in earthly life and the harbinger of modern technology, who worshipped reality

but who was himself a dreamer. Jensen's writing encompasses the totality of both his firm belief in the ecstasy of the moment and a boundless longing for eternity, which is symbolically expressed in the myth, which transcends all dimensions of time and place. Thus his most outstanding work, the novel *Kongens Fald* (1900-01; The Fall of the King) is not only one of the finest historical novels ever

written but also a myth about life and death, about man who is subjected to the law of "the fall", which is death itself; and it is not until he stands face to face with obliteration that he is able to find the meaning of life.

Disillusion and Chaos

The outbreak of the First World War sparked off an explosive revaluation of all values which in turn led to disillusion and chaos. The expressionist poet Tom Kristensen could thus defiantly burst out "Our youth, our might, our wild ideas are as beautiful as a railway station bombed to smithereens." The awareness of being left outside the scene of battle because of Denmark's neutrality led to a sense of impotence and meaninglessness amongst Danish writers, of a wasted opportunity to stand face to face with death and thereby experience and test one's own identity. In their desperation they form a pendant to the international "Lost Generation", associated with the likes of Gabriele D'Annunzio, Erich Maria Remarque, André Malraux and Ernest Hemingway.

It was also Tom Kristensen who gave the most convincing artistic expression to this crisis and an attempt at a solution, in his semi-autobiographical novel *Hærværk* (1930, Havoc). In the main character of this work, the literary critic Ole Jastrau, the sense of life's absurdity arouses a feeling of fear, which he tries to overcome by denying any sense of responsibility to his fellow man and by systematic self-destruction through alcohol. But at the same time Jastrau's vandalism is also an attempt to reach the core of his own personality: the self and the soul. His stubborn search for the truth bears the impression of the Kierkegaardian existential search, a search which he shares with the characters of James Joyce's novel *Ulysses* (1922) and Aldous Huxley's *Point Counter*

Illustration by Sikker Hansen for the 1944 edition of Johs.V. Jensen's "The Fall of the King".

Point (1928). But whether Jastrau manages to define his own identity and thus create a new system of values is a question which is left unanswered at the close of the book. It is precisely this ambiguity which establishes the modernity of the work.

Whilst for Kristensen the existential crisis is a personally experienced battle between life and death, Karen Blixen (pseud. Isak Dinesen) removes this issue from both historic and photographic reality and into the realm of mythology. Indeed reality itself becomes a myth about a certain world order, to which we must submit, a myth about the roles which people have been allocated by God, the divine theatre director, and which they have to play regardless of whether they are tragic or comic. Blixen's detached view of man's life and death as a single completed work of art is expressed no-

where better than in the story "Sorg-Agre" (1942; Sorrow Acres), a brilliant adaptation of an old Danish legend. A nobleman gives permission for the penalty of harsh punishment sentenced on a young man to be paid by his old mother, with her life staked in settlement. She is made to reap a field of rye from morning to evening, after which she collapses dead from exhaustion. But the nobleman, who has to defend his tyrannical idea to his young nephew, is only exerting, albeit to his own disadvantage, the responsibility given to him by God (that which Jastrau tried to escape from); and *he* too has a role to play, in that he has to enforce the moral code of the aristocracy. But nevertheless it is his suffering, as well as that of the mother, which provides both of their lives with real meaning.

This sophisticated justificational theol- **183**

The feeling of fragmentation and disintegration which dominated the period between the wars is also reflected in the visual arts of the time. "Young man and woman reading a book at a round table in a garden". Painting by Wilhelm Freddie, 1930s.

ogy, which probably tended more towards the creation of a metaphysics of art, was light years away from the other ideological discussions of the period, which focused on man's relations to a crisis-ridden social and political reality. The years between the wars were characterised by insecurity and fear and increasing scepticism regarding the feasibility of any firm philosophical position in life. With the next catastrophe of this century, the outbreak of the Second World War, this contemporary fragmented view of the world became generally accepted. At best it produced a realisation of the relativity of all things and at worst it produced terms of existence based on total alienation and disintegration.

Disintegration and Alienation

After the war a group of poets emerged clustered around the periodical *Heretica* (1948-53), who identified the cause of this crisis as the absence of a unified culture, as was prevalent in the Middle Ages. Modern civilisation is a "wasteland", as previously described by one of the most important sources of inspiration for these poets, T.S. Eliot. Ole Sarvig discovers the city as the place where the fate of modern man is decided:

Late afternoon.
People stand
as though they were listening.

But it is a stony desert inhabited by the living dead. However in other poems by Sarvig there is a hint of love as the saving grace, and the other "Hereticans", Ole Wivel and Thorkild Bjørnvig, express a Messianic longing and - in the sense used by Karen Blixen - a faith in the redemptive force of art.

In the next generation of modernists who appeared around 1960 there is an overriding acceptance of the status quo, of a material world without any supreme order or principles: "Empty, empty, empty the world is blissfully empty of all but things" was the jubilant cry of the lyrical standard-bearer Klaus Rifbjerg in 1960. But nevertheless the observing ego cannot maintain its objective distance, which has both an outward and inward orientation. Just one year later, in the collection of poems entitled *Camouflage* (1961), this ego embarks on a journey through the subconscious into a personal past, to the realm of myths and memories, to reconquer reality, to grasp at life and to overcome man's isolation from himself and the world around him.

The process of liberation from traumatic blockages and/or the meaninglessness of existence is expressed in different ways by two of the greatest prose writers of the post-war period, Villy Sørensen and Peter Seeberg. Sørensen's diagnosis of modern man's alienation and impotence in the short story "I fremmed land" (In Strange Country) in the collection *Formynderfortællinger* (1964; Tutelary Tales), takes on frightening dimensions. An anonymous stranger arrives in a mysterious, Kafkaesque country to kill its dictator. But it turns out that his only means of communication, language, is no good to him. Nobody can or wants to understand him and gradually he becomes a pawn in a game which he can no longer control - and from which there is no escape; he becomes trapped in a role which differs little from that of the dictator - or for that matter the nobleman in Blixen's "Sorrow Acres", apart from the

fact that no metaphysical reference can be used as an explanation. There is no solution to the stranger's absurd situation, and consequently no release. The end result is the samme as in the "Elf-Shot" ballad and in Andersen's tale "The Shadow", but with the significant difference that Sørensen's stranger has *not* freely chosen his destiny as Sir Oluf and the learned man, but in the final count he is a slave of his own impotence and lack of liberty. Sørensen identifies the root of this bondage in man's wanting ability to identify and accept all sides of his personality, including the negative side, which is repressed and thus traumatised. The tone in *Tutelary Tales*, which focuses on man's use and abuse of power, is overwhelmingly pessimistic and resigned. Although in the last story in the collection, "En fremtidshistorie" (A Tale of the Future), which

Karen Blixen's view of human life as a work of art also manifests itself in the story "Babette's Feast". Scene from Gabriel Axel's 1987 award-winning film version of the story. On the right, Stephane Audran as Babette. Photo: Phate-Nordisk.

is a variation on the Oedipus theme, Sørensen does include a hint of hope. Filius,
the son of the dictatorial president of the
country, wins his freedom when he both
spites the oracles which predict that he
will kill his own father and decides to
break down the totalitarian government.
He relinquishes the role of guardian for
others and chooses himself, in a Kierkegaardian sense, with all his positive and
negative aspects and thus he chooses life
and a future rather than brutal subjection
and destruction.

In his fantastic tales and legends
Sørensen projects the problem of alienation and meaninglessness from a metaphysical onto a psychological plane, since
he locates its cause in the split between
our instinctive and our intellectual lives.
When this split has been healed, man will
once more be a whole! Peter Seeberg
works on another tangent, which invokes
the reader to turn meaninglessness inside
out, since we have to use it to find meaning in our existence and thus a release
from absurdity. In the story "Braget"
(The Crash) Seeberg talks about an inexplicable crash which is heard in a block of
flats:

"Pietro was having an after-dinner nap
when he heard the sudden crash, which
sounded as though a section of staircase
had fallen down through the stairwell; he
jumped up, grabbed his jacket and ran
into the kitchen, where his wife was
standing, her face as white as a sheet.
"Did you hear that?" he shouted, "the
staircase has collapsed". They went out
together. Their neighbours were standing
in their doorway and stared at them in
fright. They could see the other residents
on the floors below, standing two by two,
peering up and then down, Pietro cried
out to ask where it was. There was
nothing to be seen was the answer from
below. Someone suggested a balcony had
collapsed".

But this was not the case either, and
soon all the residents join in the search
for an explanation. But, as so often in
Seeberg's searches - one of his favourite
themes and the title of the collection of
stories which include "The Crash",
Eftersøgningen og andre noveller (1962; The
Search and other Stories) - this search is
also initiated without any real enthusiasm.
The crash is just a nuisance or weird. Of
course the residents are interested in finding an explanation, but only to rid themselves of the crash. Gradually however
they realise that the crash has become
part of their reality, that this search has
provided them with *the real* content in
their lives, which they have hitherto been
lacking. Seeberg's inspiration for this
story was Andersen's tale "Klokken"
(1845; The Bell), which is also about the
search for the source of an inexplicable
sound. But unlike Andersen's tale,
Seeberg's story is not about a metaphysical meaning *outside* the human
realm. Seeberg's searches always end with
the discovery of reality in a deeper sense
as a regained meaningfulness. The
perspective is extended inwards, but definitely *not* towards a realisation of the
absurdity of all things. For Seeberg, the
importance of the search lies not in what
one finds, but in the continuation of the
search.

The future, and this also means hope,
thus exists for both Sørensen and Seeberg
and even though the latter would appear
to belong to Beckett's and Ionesco's
School of the Absurd, they are both
eminent representatives of an occidental
humanistic tradition, which indefatigably
persists in the search for an answer to the
emptiness and rootlessness of modern
man.

These kinds of complex existential
issues are the ones which, in many
different disguises, dominate Danish literature of the post war era, even though it is

For the characters portrayed by Peter Seeberg, the search becomes a goal in itself. "The road to town". Woodcut by Palle Nielsen. 1954.

also possible to identify a thread running from the early naturalism in the young Henrik Pontoppidan and the social criticism in the great proletarian writer Martin Andersen Nexø right up to the present day. For even Pontoppidan and Nexø could not completely restrict themselves to pure and simple descriptive realism. Pontoppidan's stories from the 1880s portray the impoverished rural proletariat with unprecedented stark realism. But the descriptions are drawn with detached objectivity and primarily act as a background for a penetrating psychological analysis of human greed and vindictiveness. As the years went by Pontoppidan's realism was transformed into an existential discourse of compelling symbolic intensity. The hero of the novel *Lykke-Per* (1898-1904; Lucky Per) characteristically overcomes his paralysing Lebensangst by finally opting for absolute self-denial and

thus true reality and life itself in its spiritual dimension. But the main character in *De Dødes Rige* (1912-16; The Realm of the Dead) is not even able to cope with a choice of this kind. This sort of commitment, which both Sørensen and Seeberg regard as the only solution to the existential crisis, is impossible because of the main character's inability to love. When the young woman, Jytte, hears of the death of her childhood sweetheart, Torben, she considers him to have been lucky: "Now he had battled his last in life's wicked struggle. He was released from this terrible world, where everything was deception except disappointment, all a delusion except loss and sorrow." And when she too dies the following year she cries out: "Yes, now I die (...) And yet I have never lived!". With the profoundest pessimism Pontoppidan puts any psychological explanation behind him in favour of an extension of the metaphysical horizon, when he allows this statement to embrace Torben as well as the whole of mankind.

The Social Perspective

In contrast to Pontoppidan, Nexø was an optimistic writer passionately involved in social issues. But even in his two novels, *Pelle Erobreren* (1906-10; Pelle the Conqueror), the film version of which won an Oscar in 1989, and *Ditte Menneskebarn* (1917-21; Ditte, Child of Man), the goal is not solely to disclose the social misery of the rural workers or the inhuman living conditions sustained by the proletariat in the slums of Copenhagen. Nexø's writing also attains its true validity on a symbolic level so that his description of "the worker's heavy stride across the earth on his endless, semi-conscious journey towards the light" expands to a general vision of the indomitable, ambitious man. In *Ditte, Child of Man* the political agitation no longer has any part to play. Ditte rises above the everyday struggle to survive and become the epitomy of the commandment of love. In death - she works herself to death by the age of 25 - she is resurrected as an immortal symbol of life!

After the Second World War writers working in the realistic tradition turned their attention in particular to the welfare state and the affluent society. From the 1960s on, Christian Kampmann's and Anders Bodelsen's novels have been characterised by critical analyses of the middle-class fight for material wealth at the expenses of personal integrity and identity - the role play is made permanent but in contrast to Blixen it is limited to a purely social context - and with a negative outcome. Marriages collapse and families are torn to pieces in the dance around the golden calf and death lurks everywhere but nobody will acknowledge it. In a

number of gripping novels, which exploit the science fiction, thriller and detective story genres, Bodelsen uses the crime itself to symbolise the destructive forces, in a demonstration of death as totally uncontrollable. This gravitation beyond purely realistic description towards an ethical even metaphysical complex of issues is evident in the science fiction novel *Frysepunktet* (1969; Freezing Point). The main characters are frozen and then defrosted again several times, first to experience the future, then to escape from it and finally to find death. Nevertheless death can never be more than a deep sleep and thus a symbol of, but also a protest (admittedly futile!) against the rootlessness of the individual in the "brave new world".

Thorkild Hansen also uses the realistic genre as a basis for a purely existential complex of problems. This he does in a number of documentary novels, a genre which invites a discussion in principle on whether it is at all possible to describe reality objectively. Thus the theme of Hansen's principal work, his trilogy on the Danish slave trade (1967-70), is not only the slave trade between the Gold Coast of Africa and the West Indies but also just as much a focusing on the ethical issue of right and wrong and a discussion of man's relation to the recognition of truth; and in this it reaches far beyond the actual epic plot.

Ideology and Women's Writing

But on the whole the realistic genre of the 1960s and 1970s was oriented towards topical issues, sometimes with militant and dogmatically socialist tendencies, which found a spirited opposition in the novels of Ole Hyltoft, whose cutting satire spikes those he has dubbed "the monastic marxists" and their opportunist fellow travellers. The Vietnam War left its mark but that aside, it was the feminist movement which dominated. A number of reportage books were published, as for instance *Kvinder på fabrik* (1971; Women in Factories) or *Kvindernes bog* (1972; Women's Book) but also here there was a movement towards a more personal, subjective stance. Grete Stenbæk Jensen's novel *Konen og æggene* (1973; The Woman and the Eggs) is about women, but not written exclusively *for* women , and Suzanne Brøgger's writing is an excellent example of how feminist literature matured into a more general discussion of gender roles and the use of different genres from the semi-documentary style of *Crème Fraîche* (1978; Sour Cream) to pure fiction with the epic poem about *Tone* (1981).

A renewed interest in historic material in the 1980s led to a large number of bio-graphical accounts. These are mostly por-traits of Danish historical or literary fig-ures, but for instance Dorrit Willumsen, in her internationally acclaimed novel *Marie* (1983), has chosen a more widely known person, Madame Tussaud, and written a work which is far from a tradi-tional biography. As in Willumsen's other books, this one is an analysis of *modern* man's feelings of loneliness and empti-ness, which persists in forcing us to don masks and swap roles - and here again we are reminded of Blixen - but Willumsen does not share the latter's spiritual exposi-tional model at all.

Kirsten Thorup began her cross-sec-tion of Danish society with her novel *Lille Jonna* (1977; Little Jonna), which is dis-tinguished by its scenes from the Danish provinces and Copenhagen described with the utmost attention to detail. How-ever, the following three volumes in the series demonstrate Thorup's amazing ability to transpose pure description into a mythical landscape, where the characters and their destinies are transformed into

symbolic expression of man's incessant urge to create a different and better life for himself. This is not so much a social but a psychological discussion about man sus-pended between *Himmel og Helvede* (Heav-en and Hell) - the title of the third volume in 1982. In this book Thorup reaches back to Martin Andersen Nexø, the author of *Ditte, Child of Man*. And when in 1976 Dea Trier Mørch wrote her best-selling novel *Vinterbørn* (Winter's Child) about the des-tinies of women in the maternity ward of the National Hospital, it was not primarily designed as a criticism of society but as a tribute to community and empathy, to life ever victorious.

Thus it is once more the great eternal questions which preoccupy the writers of today - not for nothing are they working in Søren Kierkegaard's homeland. In the 1970s Henrik Stangerup wrote a number of satirical novels about the welfare society, which for him means the deprivation of the individual's self-determination leading to destructive crises of identity. In his three-volume work (1981-91), the most convincing intellectual achievement in modern Danish literature, Stangerup em-ployed the Kierkegaardian philosophy of aesthetic, ethical and religious stages. Stan-gerup selected the documentary novel as the genre, just like Thorkild Hansen. The common link in the three volumes are three historical figures, whose fate Stan-gerup describes through their battle with foreign environments. The subjects of the first two volumes, a rationalist natural scientist, and a romantic bel-esprit, divided between idea and reality, are both unable to find a modus vivendi. The last volume, *Broder Jacob* (1991; Brother Jacob), which is about a Danish prince from the Renais-sance who ended his life as a charismatic Franciscan munk and missionary in Mexico, concludes with an assertion of a spiritual and cosmopolitan philosophy of life as the deliverance from the crisis and

Dea Trier Mørch's "Winter's Child" is homage to the fellowship experienced in a maternity ward. Original illustration by the author.

chaos which always haunt those deprived of identity and self-determination. This is a philosophy which Stangerup cannot find in his homeland but rather in a metaphysical system, which alone is able to unite the physical world, art and longing in a universal utopia.

Language and Existence

Inger Christensen and Sven Åge Madsen's work are characterised by pure philosophical speculation coupled with linguistic experiments. They both made their literary debuts in the 1960s, strongly influenced by what is called systemic or concrete poetry, the purpose of which was to establish structures or "systems" of linguistic material as the background for our cognitive process. Christensen's poetry and prose deal with the same main theme: because of his fear of the unknown, man seeks escape into fixed roles, which can either be self-selected or imposed by society. As in Dorrit Willumsen, but not Blixen, these roles are seen as restrictive in our relations to the world and thus only serve to heighten man's identity crisis. Only language, the process of writing, can liberate our imagination and return our freedom; it is language which has the power to bring new life to dead reality. Christensen has described this process in the principal poetic work of the 1960s, the epos *Det* (1969; It), which describes how it is only the creative self which is able to overcome the fatal schism between language and experience and thus facilitate the awareness of an otherwise elusive world and consequently the nature of the human self.

For Svend Åge Madsen - particularly in his early writing - the problem of identity was also of central importance. But in the novel *Lad tiden gå* (1986; Let Time Pass) the view is enlarged to include a more universal existential discussion. Madsen focuses on the concept of time and warns against experiments with time, for these would also eliminate death, which together with art is one of the two providers of meaning in life. Madsen's work is exceedingly demanding. He is the modern Scandinavian literary master in linguistic juggling, turning our conceptual world upside down and creating puns. His novels are impregnated with intellectual perspicacity and their main function is to involve the reader in an artistic and therefore existential experience. Whilst in

Madsen's early novels the world was nothing more than a fictive creation, i.e. an illusion, it is now the work of art which not only establishes our identity but also provides the background for the cognitive process, which can assist us in answering those questions about faith, art and eternity, which will always be posed.

Mythology and Ecology

With the relative stability in world politics in the wake of the Vietnam War, writers increasingly dropped out of direct involvement with politics. When Denmark joined the European Economic Community in 1972, political literature enjoyed a brief renaissance, but this interlude aside, it altered direction and joined in the ecological debate. Thus in her collection of poems *Alfabet* (1981; Alphabet) Inger Christensen introduces a clear ecological perspective in the attempt to expose the negative forces of modern civilisation. Her texts revolve around the theme of destruction and ruin in a world, where not even love can be considered a source of redemption.

It is in the work of women writers that there has been most evidence of conscious attempts to present alternative values to the rationalist and technological norms which preside today. This has been accomplished by placing more emphasis on emotional life and emotional experiences and by organising grass roots movements to fight pollution and the destruction of the environment. Another interesting trait of the 1970s was a dramatic rise in interest in mythology - not the Old Norse mythology as in the romantic period but in mythology with an international perspective, mostly in connection with the ecological issues. Vagn Lundbye's prose works thus express a strong fascination for those primitive cultures who treat their environment with far greater respect than western industrial societies; the Lapps, Eskimos and Indians. These latter, their culture and mythology, constituted the central themes of Lundbye's books in the 1970s, whilst later on he emerged as spokesman for the whales in Alaska with *Fra Verdens begyndelse* (1982; From the Beginning of the World) and the arctic peoples in *Mytologisk rejse i et grønlandsk landskab* (1985; Mythological Journey in a Greenland Landscape). The young Ib Michael's sphere of interest was similar to Lundbye's. After a brief flirtation with the mythology of flower power in his first book produced in 1970, he published a number of travel books about the Mexican indians in which reality and mythology have fused completely. Michael's bestselling novel *Kilroy Kilroy* (1989), is a mythological account of a person with amnesia who journeys forth in a world unknown to him in search of his identity - a journey from emptiness to rebirth.

Departures and Renewal

Interest in the near "self" as well as the farflung exotic or unknown lands went hand in hand with the general neo-romantic, largely lyrical trend of the 1980s, anticipated by the lyricist Henrik Nordbrandt, who made his debut as early as 1966. His texts mix the concrete with the mystical, Asia Minor with Europe, the past with the present, sometimes in the form of profound philosophical speculations, sometimes as precise registrations of the external world. His many travel poems are symbolic expressions of the poet's sense of displacement and his worship of beauty is nothing other than a cover for his attraction towards the omnipresence of suffering and death. The sense of absence, yearning and elusiveness surfaces everywhere: "Wherever we travel, we always arrive too late/ to whatever we set out to find". And love is no longer, as in Nordbrandt's earli- 191 er poems, able to provide redemption through devotion to another person.

more than yourself, my love
I loved your eyes
and more than your eyes, their lashes
and the weight of your eyelids
I have since grown to love
my own being in love. (...)

With each new collection of poetry Nordbrandt has further consolidated his position as the most outstanding lyricist of his generation, a classic in his own time!

In one of Nordbrandt's most important works, *Guds hus* (1977; God's House), a metaphysical tone surfaces, anticipating another characteristic trend of the 1980s.

The new literary departures of the 1980s were mainly centred on poetry. Poetry Day at Louisiana in North Zealand. Photo: Louisiana 1981.

Klaus Høeck's collection of poetry, *Hjem* (1985; Home), runs to 608 pages, and is an ambitious attempt to encompass God, and titles such as *Requiem & messe* (1981; Requiem and Mass) by Bo Green Jensen, and *Requiem* (1985) by Peer Hultberg also point to the religious trend of that decade. Hultberg's 537 lyrical prose monologues constitute in sum one of the major works of the 1980s, a diagnosis and thus also the beginnings of an orientation in the emptiness of our chaotic times but also its wealth, schisms as well as its cohesive elements - yet another product of the continuing humanist tradition in Danish literature. The eclectic structure of this opus is, however, a typical reflection of the cacophony of attitudes, possible solutions and forms of expression in a postmodernist age.

Even though Søren Ulrik Thomsen has tried to formulate the poetry of his generation in his essay *Mit lys brænder* (1985; My Candle Burns), on the whole the young poets of the 1980s, all born in the 1950s, are distinctly individualistic, who do not easily fall into any definite "school", but only share a clear rejection of sociological or ideological analyses. Some employ an extremely fine sensitivity to register their own personal collision with the world of the media, technology and pop culture and the ensuing disorientation as demonstrated by Michael Strunge, the almost cult-like frontrunner of this generation. Others seek refuge in a self-created lyrical universe, like the linguistic equilibrist F.P. Jac. In contrast to the 19th century romantics, but like Ole Sarvig, the great poet of the post-war crisis, attention is focused on the big city, as in Thomsen's collection *City slang* (1982) or in the somewhat chaotic and anarchist writing of the multi-talented Dan Turèll, which includes over 100 provocative but also entertaining books from poetry to crime stories. Literary tradition is redis-

Nature, the body and love are central themes in the poetry of the 1980s. Engraving by Jes Fomsgaard, 1989.

covered, not only the Romantics but also the early modernists Baudelaire, Mallarmé, Rimbaud, Eliot and Pound, an influence which is blended with elements of rock and punk music, such as that of Bob Dylan and David Bowie.

The more contemplative, speculative line drawn by Nordbrandt is followed up by poets such as Bo Green Jensen, whose poetry cycle in seven volumes, *Rosens veje* (The Roads of the Rose), completed in 1986, is a major attempt to create coherence in a splintered post-modernist world, and Niels Frank, whose collection *Genfortryllelsen* (1988; The Reenchantment) consists of a journey through loneliness but also through the regenerative sphere of memories and love. Since her debut in 1981, Pia Tafdrup has consistently sought to unite erotic experiences, impressions of nature and an awareness of the necessity to capture the full scope life,

described in images of exquisite sensual beauty. *Transformationer* (Transformations) is the indicative title of the anthology, with which she presented her generation's poetry in 1985. Contemporary Danish literature is in a constant process of new departures and change. The potential subjects seem endless: physical and spiritual love, myths of rebirth and visions of the Day of Judgement, pop-culture and tradition, big city and country idyll, exotic lands and mystical utopia.

The direction of Danish literature in the 1990s is unpredictable - and thank the lord for that. It will continue to be dynamic and renewing. The variety will continue. But one thing is certain: the talent is there and it will always be the ever-topical existential issues which will preoccupy writers: questions about life and death, loneliness and togetherness, emptiness and love, crisis and redemption.

193

As Others See Us

Three Approaches to a Character Sketch of the Danes

Denmark -
a Declaration of Love

by Julian Isherwood

It is 8 o'clock in the morning. The smell of coffee and freshly baked rolls wafts slowly and irresistably into the living room. The morning chorus of the birds in the birch trees outside seems to amplify the silence, and the early heat of the sun evaporates the light rain that has fallen overnight outside in the sparkling garden. Summerhouse. Holidays. Relaxation. Can there be anything better than the Danish summer, in a Danish summerhouse, together with one's Danish family? Of course not. At least not for Danes and for her adoptive children who nurture nothing but love for our foster-mother Denmark.

15 years after first setting my feet on Danish soil, I have finally realised that I am beginning to nourish those same provincial, semi-nationalistic feelings for Denmark which I so vehemently accused my first Danish girlfriend of having. This country is infectious, and one should not be afraid of recognising this as a foreigner.

Looking at Denmark from within, one's opinions are coloured by the strong bonds which must exist between the foreigner who has lived here for a long time, and who, because of work, family and home, has an obligation to interest himself in local society, and that headstrong country which has provided the framework, with relatively open arms, for a secure life. If one then begins to criticise, it is out of love.

196   *Can there be anything more wonderful than the Danish summer? Photo: Geert Mørk.*

Life, and Denmark, are a complicated interaction of positive and negative aspects which combine to produce an overall impression which one either likes or dislikes. If one dislikes the totality then one turns to something else. If one likes it, one must not be uncritically positive - or negative - but reflect the multiplicity which prevails in Denmark, despite its modest size.

And there is plenty to discuss.

Education

Some years ago an English journalist came to Denmark with his two children. He debated, as I had also done, whether his children should go to an English speaking school. We both decided against this. His 8 year-old son had already completed two years of school in England, was bright and able. It came as a surprise that he was to be placed in the second form, but this was accepted in view of the fact that he had to learn the language before he could make further progress. He learned to speak Danish fluently in six months but the school refused to move him up to a class which corresponded to his skill level. The last words which this journalist said to me before he left Copenhagen were "I can't do this to my children. We live in a competitive world. They won't be prepared for it here". I did not understand him.

Now, with my own children in the Folkeskole, I understand him a little better.

The Folkeskole

The decision to opt for the Folkeskole was a difficult one for me. To a product of the English private boarding school system, where silence and obedience (and liberal doses of the cane) were the order of the day, the discipline of the Folkeskole seemed, understandably enough, to be less effective, if not non-existent. And to put things into true perspective I actually loved my schooldays, but would never dream of giving my own children such a strict and tough childhood.

But the lack of discipline in the Folkeskole, the lack of homework, the fact that one is not allowed to teach children to read or write in the Infant classes, the total lack of foreign language teaching in the Junior forms, as well as certain educational trends which were clearly demonstrated at the first parents' meetings, all made this a difficult choice. And it has not become easier now that I have a daughter in the 3rd Grade and a son in the Infants' Class. The class is clearly lagging behind when compared to what my children's cousins are doing overseas - and that is in spite of the fact that my two are fortunate in being bilingual and coming from a home where books and the written word are very important.

Having said that, there are also positive sides to the Folkeskole, which count in favour of keeping the children there.

A high priority is given to the development of social behaviour, play and freedom are central parts of the daily routine, and above all, children they were with in the crèche and kindergarten are now in the same class. The advantage of having the same friends right through childhood and adolescence is irreplaceable.

But there is all too little preparation of children for the difficult task of participating in a world which is neither slowing down nor becoming less competitive.

Janteloven

The educational structure may have been influenced by the most unfortunate of Danish character traits - the one which is released via the deeply rooted "Jantelov" (Jante's ten commandments). This is a system which rewards mediocrity, punishes promotion and is instrumental in reducing the Danish impact in the international markets. For in spite of some notable scoops, Denmark has not achieved the volume of overseas market coverage that it should have. The image which Denmark has created is inadequate - the Little Mermaid, free sex, Tivoli and other trivial and mistaken role models.

What is missing is the existence of aggressive businessmen and politicians who dare to stand out, to lead the way, to rise above society as a whole and demonstrate leadership - qualities which most Danes seem to detest.

The Jantelov is entirely based on excessive envy. It is a kind of self-destructive drive which ensures that nobody is allowed to have a greater *opportunity* than anyone else to either earn more, to become a leader or gain respect in society. No wonder then that many promising young people leave as soon as they get the chance.

Equality

It is often suggested that the commandments of the Jantelov stem from a political desire for equality for everyone. This is untrue. The Jantelov is based on envy and embittered inadequacy.

In fact the equality established by law and in Danish society is as positive as the Jantelov is negative, and this equality is something which the rest of the world would do well to aspire to.

The Queen walks down the main shopping street and feels safe. Women go to pubs by themselves and need fear no-one. The peasant, the prostitute and the Prime Minister all have the same rights, and are not afraid of fighting for them. The company director and the check-out lady play in the same badminton club. At the same time Danish society is fortunately unfettered by the sort of super-bureaucratic,

omnipotent, oppressive and powerful prohibitive system which the Swedes have to live with. Things will change on the other side of the Sound, but - just as in the former Soviet Union - it will be difficult to acknowledge so many years of mistaken policies. There is no such problem in Denmark.

Deprivation of liberty

An off-shoot of Janteloven, which those people who have been through it have had to experience at their own cost, this is the only real blemish in an otherwise highly revered judicial system.

Every civilised legal system is based on the theory of innocence. That is the sound philosophy which states that an accused cannot be found guilty before society - and this is in most cases the police - can prove his guilt.

Of course the police need time to collect evidence. But it is only an uncivilised society which locks people away in isolation for months on end - and sometimes even over a year - because the police have not got around to admitting that they cannot find sufficient evidence, or what is even worse, because they have not had time to deal with the case.

There can be no doubt about it. Long-term prison isolation is equivalent to publicly sanctioned torture, which is something that Denmark is the first to protest against in other countries.

Foreigners

"L'accent du pays où l'on est né demeure dans l'esprit et dans le coeur comme dans le langage"

Duc de la Rochefoucauld

In these unsettled times all over the world, there has been much talk about how foreigners are treated in Denmark.

Subjectively speaking, one single attack on one single foreigner amounts to racism. But there is no racism in Denmark. Believe me. There are political opportunists who stir up a small amount of xenophobia. There are groups in society who are either afraid of foreigners or who do not like them. That is the price of a highly developed democracy.

But on the whole the general public is relatively well disposed to foreigners - regardless of colour, religion or political inclinations. The attacks on and antipathies towards foreigners in Denmark stem from situations which we foreigners can alleviate by recognising Danish society as an equally valuable society, whose norms and values we can accept and into which we can make the effort to integrate. There is no doubt that an inadequate knowledge of the language is the main cause of misunderstandings and difficulties. If two years after arrival one is still unable to communicate with the host society, then this is a sign of disrespectful contempt. And this makes it difficult to expect kindness and acceptance by society and respect for one's own way of life.

There is time to play and relax in the Danish Folkeskole, but too little discipline for the demands of modern life. Photo: Lars Bahl/2.maj.

A Declaration of Love

Respect is not something one gets without having earned it. And despite what could almost be regarded as a list of problematic national characteristics, after 15 years in a country which I have actively chosen to live in, I now cherish a deep respect and love for Denmark. For the Danish flag, for the environment, for peace, for the Danes, the national anthem "There is a lovely Land", for handball, the Great Belt Bridge and - yes even for Danish politics.

But I shall knock out the next person who asks me in amazement why on earth I have not adopted Danish nationality. For one cannot be something one isn't. And I am quite proud of what I am.

Denmark – Living together, Getting together

by Esther Edelsten

"There is a lovely Land".... is how simply and beautifully the Danish national anthem begins, and as a foreigner, who has lived in Denmark for many years, one can only nod in recognition and agree with every word. Denmark, that little Nordic country, which is affectionately called the kingdom of the Vikings, is more than just a lovely land. Denmark is a fairy-tale adventure in its own special way, which is unknown to the majority of tourists. Denmark does not boast many large tourist attractions; it has neither gigantic castles, ravishing fjords nor spellbinding mountains. But the greatest attraction of this small northern country is its people and its peaceful and exquisite countryside. Fairy-tale groves with beech trees and running streams, whose murmuring mingles with the whispering of the wind. Here the eye is delighted by the light green plains, and one can feel the wide open spaces and the blue skies. One is dazed by the lights and colours and lush countryside, in the company of birds, whose song and twittering at daybreak sound like some mysterious flute.

Targets of their own Irony

Denmark's best tourist attraction is its people. Friendliness, politeness and restraint - not to be confused with naivety - have justifiably become the hallmarks of the Dane. The Danes are a relaxed , common-sense people. They are not snobbish, but rather modest and with a high tolerance threshold.

The ability to laugh at themselves and their good humour separate them from their Scandinavian brothers. The Danes are fun-loving, and their ability not to take themselves seriously is one of their greatest qualities. Nobody can make fun of himself and hit the nail on the head like a Dane. One could compare Danish humour with fire. Sometimes we enjoy its warmth and at other times we get burnt by it. This humour is everywhere. In the streets, in the squares, the parks and in the green forests. It gets at rich folk and poor alike, "Upstairs and downstairs". It affects and strikes at all aspects of life, even the subject of sex.

The Danes created their smoothly run little society themselves, and they guard its law and order as well as they can. Denmark has a solidly based society with rich traditions, whose people have enjoyed an uncomplicated identity for a thousand years. The average Dane has enough surplus energy to help the needy in difficult times.

The Danes detest authority, and any politician who takes himself too seriously or uses strong charismatic language will only attract derision. There is no other place is the world which can boast such a positive and easy relationship between the people and the authorities. There is no bowing and scraping to anyone in Denmark.

The Danes know that they live in one of the richest countries of the world, in a welfare state, with a very high standard of living. They share with others, if not gladly, then from a sense of moral obligation. The country has justifiably gained a reputation for being a smooth-running constitutional democracy, and despite its small size, Denmark enjoys great respect overseas.

Tendency to Sleep

The Danes, both the people at large as
well as the authorities, are puzzled by
outsiders' very limited knowledge of little
Denmark, which is often confused with
Sweden or Holland. People are surprised
by the difficulties encountered when promoting Danish culture overseas. Why is
Denmark associated with pastry, alcohol-
ism, pornography and free love; and who
created the myth of the "incredibly boring Dane"?

Perhaps the answer lies in the Danish
tendency to sleep and dream as far as
their image is concerned; they muse con-
tentedly and confidently on old illusions.
When it comes to innovation in relation
to competitive developments in the world,
they tend to cling to old successes and the
"take-it-easy policy". Many Danes believe
that Denmark still serves as a model to
the rest of the world in the sphere of sexual equality, in the labour market, or in
policies for women. They still believe that
Denmark is hitting the world headlines
on the subject of pornography and sex.

It is difficult to be a Dane with ambi-
tions in a society where mediocrity is
often accepted as the norm; where the
commandment "You shall not believe that
you are better than the others", is allowed
to rule and stifle bright initiatives in an
otherwise common-sense society. The
Danes console themselves with a friendly
slap on the back and "it'll all work out in
the end"; regardless of hospital waiting
lists, housing shortages for young people
etc.

Malicious Mentality

A typically Danish phenomenon is the
concept based on "Tordenskjolds sol-
dater." Tordenskjold was a Danish-Nor-
wegian naval hero (Peter Wessel, 1690-
1720) who distinguished himself several

*Denmark is a fairy-tale. St.Hans (Midsummer) bonfire on
the meadow by the Skovsøen in Odense. Photo: Geert Mørk.*

times during the Great Northern War
with a trick whereby he used the same few
soldiers over and over again to rush out of
the front door, go round the house and
come in again at the back door, until the
Swedish enemy became frightened by the
'size' of his battalion. This same principle
flourishes in Danish cultural circles,
where the same few familiar faces appear
everywhere. Perhaps it is Denmark's
small size, which has allowed the development of a kind of intellectual corruption
in what almost resembles a 'cultural
mafia'. At the same time it must be pointed out that the isolated world of literary 201

criticism is characterised by democratic integrity and anti-nepotism.

Another typical phenomenon which is observed in the Danes is the "malicious mentality", which one of Denmark's greatest writers described so well in a novelle entitled "It happens in Denmark".

The writer, Carl Erik Soya (1896 - 1983) comments ironically on the little envy which normally thrives amongst Danes. But what is peculiar to the Danish form of malice, in contrast to perhaps that of other nations is that, after the joy of seeing a successful person fall, this joy is transformed into compassion, sympathy and pity. The good natured Danish heart can now demonstrate all its endearing greatness.

Creative Queen

Simplicity is a national heritage, and one which has been an inspiration to the Danish Royal family, or maybe vice versa. The gap between the people and the Royal House is indeterminate. In Denmark a minister will ride around on a bicycle and the Queen will shop in town unattended. Queen Margrethe II enjoys enormous popularity, which one must admit is well deserved. She is admired and loved, not because of her position, but because of her personality and many talents.

The Danish Queen is surely the only living monarch who, besides fulfilling her formal role, also expresses herself creatively as an artist. Queen Margrethe II is a translator of literary works, an illustrator of books, a painter, designer of stamps, talented embroiderer and successful set designer for Danish theatre and TV productions.

Cultural Riches

The Danes are relatively modest and reserved, which makes many foreigners consider them to be a boring nation. But they are far from being a boring people. They are good listeners, and they jump for joy if one is able to utter just a few words of their impossible language. They become really enthusiastic if foreigners display a knowledge of and interest in the history and culture of the country. For Danish culture must be their sore spot. The rest of the world is too unfamiliar with the great cultural wealth of Denmark. I have had the pleasure of translating some of Denmark's best prose writers, whose literary works definitely deserve a better position on the literary map of the world.

Danish culture comprises far more than even the Danes can perceive, and more than they themselves realise. Perhaps it would be worth investing resources and energy in the promotion of the cultural riches of Denmark first of all to the Danes themselves.

The new literary centre, "The Danish Literature Information Centre", which was recently established as an additional booster to increase the dissemination of Danish literature overseas, can help to change the picture and also to look after the interests of Faroese and Greenland culture. The Danes show too little interest in the Faroes and Greenland in respect of these independent and distinctive cultures. Denmark cannot but be enriched by demonstrating more interest and respect for the numerous cultural qualities and values which constitute a natural part of identities of these two self-governing Nordic societies.

Denmark is a Garden of Eden when it comes to free "folkelig" cultural activities of a very high standard. There is a wide range of functions on offer, including literary readings and lectures, concerts of classical music, open-air opera performances, international jazz or rock concerts and numerous experimental and amateur theatre groups.

Hygge

A wonderful Danish phenomenon is en-
capsulated in the miracle word "hygge"
(cosiness). It not only constitutes a lifestyle, but is the country's trademark. The
Danes love to be cosy, and they create
this cosiness as often as possible, where-
ever they are. "hygge" is a Danish cultural
phenomenon, which cannot be exported,
and cannot be copied. It requires a specifically luxuriant atmosphere, as well as the
ability to view life on a Danish scale; to
prioritise small pleasures, to appreciate a
get-together with soft lighting and
candles, the smell of freshly baked pastries
and a beautifully laid table with lots of
superb food, or just herring, beer and
aquavit.

"Hygge" means forgetting the problems of the world for a moment and
enjoying the sun, the blooming flora,
the ecstasy of nature, and the feeling of
deep three-dimensional horizons. The
Danes also call it "Hip Hip Hurray", a
mood which has been described and
painted by many Danish artists, including
P.S. Krøyer (1851-1909), in his famous
painting from the close of the century.
This picture also inspired a Danish film.

The Danes can be very nationalistic,
although they are not fanatical. Their
declaration of love to their country is
either extremely ironic or very solemn.
They will either sing "There is something
wrong with Denmark, Dybbøl Mill is
grinding quite awfully" or "as a beautiful
tune touches my heart, the brisk Danish
shore with wild swans' nest, I love you,
Denmark my fatherland".

To live with the Danes is to be with
interesting people, who teach one to

*"Hip, hip, Hurray!" Section of P.S.Krøyer's famous paint-
ing, 1888. Gøteborgs Kunstmuseum.*

express spontaneous joy at small and
simple things; for instance when the sun
shines after a long and cold winter. There
is nothing to compare with a sunny
Spring day, when the lawns and parks are
bursting at the seams with happy Danes,
armed with a bottle of beer in one hand
and a "nice cup of coffee" in the other.

An easy overview, simplicity, idyllic
nature and earnest human qualities; that is
what makes Denmark, for better or
worse, a little fairy-tale.

Culture, Climate and State Support

by María Camino Sánchez

When the Viking expeditions through Europe reached the Galician fiords or even as far as Guadalquivir, there was nobody who even considered that they were spreading Nordic culture. But as a result of these expeditions, Viking artefacts, ruins and remains have been found all over the Continent.

Contemporary Denmark has a more pleasant way of conquering Europe. Practical items of furniture, beautifully designed household goods, and buildings which have become symbols, like the Opera House in Sydney or the Triumphal Arch in Paris, are all products of the bloodless expeditions of contemporary Vikings.

The foreigner comes to Denmark with a preconception of the Danes as an art-loving, somewhat philosophical people with a world-famous ballet company.

They are therefore not unduly surprised to witness a music lover spending hours, even days, standing in a queue for tickets for a Placido Domingo or a Prince concert.

However Danes will display the same enthusiasm for queuing at say a photographic shop sale, waiting outside to buy a camera for next to nothing. This reminds the foreigner living in Denmark, that man is of both the spirit and the flesh, and that the Danes appear to actually enjoy queuing. The term "køkultur" (queue culture) actually features in the Danish vocabulary describing the duty to respect "somebody else's turn". However it is not always a case of first come, first served.

One example of an innovation which has been a great success are the cafés, which were quite unknown in this country until about 10 years ago. The Danes' numerous holiday trips to destinations collectively called "The South", have given them a taste for bars with an unmistakably 'southern' atmosphere, and which are popping up on every other street corner. These venues, originally the haunts of students discussing economics lectures, are now also frequented by the businessman, allowing himself the odd "cappucino", and the solitary visitor, reading a newspaper whilst polishing off a cake. The shelves are adorned with bottles of all colours, but the price of a standard two decilitre measure of alcohol is still prohibitive, thanks to the formidable duties on alcohol and tobacco, which the politicians are so fond of, and which are designed to prevent addiction and conserve the health of the taxpayers.

Going for a walk in Copenhagen, one sometimes gets the feeling of being in a previous century and it is not necessary to visit the well appointed museums in order to sense history all around. The house facades, lovingly restored; the small courtyards, where one surprises upon century-old trees and oak beams spiting the poor weather conditions, that is what the passer-by meets on his way through the maze of streets which start around the university and stretch down towards the canals surrounding Christiansborg, the seat of the parliament.

Careful restoration of the buildings has ensured the preservation of the patrician style; 18th century warehouses have been restored to their former glory, and a house, which was the leading brothel in town some two hundred years ago, has been restored and now houses a wine importing company.

In this country, with an annual consumption of 500 million litres of beer, the foreign wine lover is at no loss to find wine connoisseurs, who as well as recog-

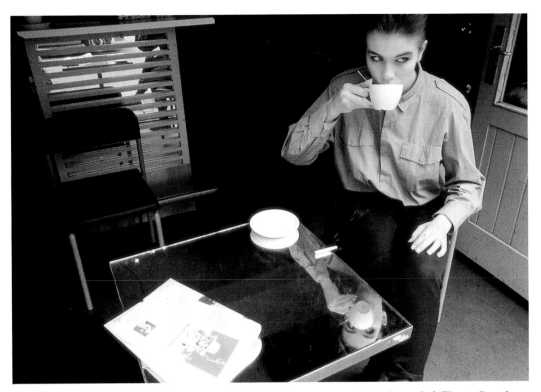

The numerous cafés have been inspired by all those holidays trips to more southerly climes. Café Floss in Copenhagen. Photo: Michael Daugaard/2.maj.

nising a good wine, are also able to expound on its origin, its amber or ruby-red colouring and its aftertaste.

However not all is left to the learned. One of the greatest pleasures in Copenhagen is to watch the peaceful citizens, sitting enjoying one of those rare sunny days down by the old harbour or in the quiet parks, and always with a beer for company.

The impression of peace is perfect, even when, to the amazement of the foreigner, the silence of a summer day is broken by the sounds of a Dutch band, playing a very Spanish pasodoble in the middle of the peaceful square of the Franciscan monks, the name of which, Gråbrødre Torv, is quite impossible to pronounce.

The Danes don't have to wait for the opera season or the Royal Ballet to enjoy a cultural experience; culture comes to everyone, just by going for a walk in town. The annual jazz festival offers as many free outdoor concerts as ticketed indoor events, and at venues such as "Kanonhallen", an erstwhile arsenal which has been converted into a theatre, it is possible to see the weirdest experimental theatre.

Regardless of how well one understands the language, as a foreigner one will never be able to understand the popular theatrical revues, where highlights of the social and political events of the last year are interlaced with songs. Their rather unusual humour leaves the foreigner cold, whilst the rest of the audience is

205

convulsed with laughter. But one cannot help feeling a certain admiration for the fact that not even Queen Margrethe is spared, but is often the target of caricature in these revues.

The theatre has lots to offer and the ticket prices are reasonable, thanks to state subsidies; in 1991 theatrical subsidies amounted to some 414 million kroner.

A monologue in French on life in the Gallic province can attract just as big an audience as the classical Skakespeare tragedy of Hamlet, when it is performed in the original language at Kronborg Castle.

The theatre has lots to offer and the ticket prices are reasonable. The Royal Theatre in Copenhagen.
Photo: Marianne Grøndahl.

It is standard practice for Danes to learn foreign languages, and English is a compulsory subject in schools. It could be said that they have no choice, as Danish has such a limited area, and they can hardly even be understood by their neighbours in Sweden and Norway. But the modern Viking is a practical being. He knows that if he wants to negotiate business overseas, he has to speak the language of his customers.

Denmark has a complex about its very small size, and politicians and businessmen alike refer to its smallness all the time. Nevertheless, or maybe because of this, Denmark has a public library system which is the envy of many other nations.

The 275 municipal public libraries are anything but bureaucratic mausolea. They are meeting places, where children and adults can borrow books, as well as brail books, records and tapes and sometimes also graphic works, posters and videos.

The Danes borrow approx. 80 million books a year (16 books per inhabitant), and 10 million records and tapes. Children account for more than half the loans.

In 1946 an act of legislation ensured Danish authors a royalty fee for each book purchased by the public and school libraries. This means that the State pays approx. 125 million kroner annually to 9000 Danish authors as a compensation for the use of their books.

With a tax rate of over 50% , there are sufficient funds available to support the fine arts. The official vehicle for state support to Art, Statens Kunstfond, which was established in 1965, spent 29 million kroner in 1991 on grants, the purchase of works of arts and commissions for the decoration of buildings and public places.

This institution also nominates those artists whom they consider merit the award of a life-long annuity, which will allow them to concentrate on their creative work without having to worry about

Danish children are keen library users. Hørsholm Library. Photo: Sonja Iskov/2.maj.

economic realities. In 1991 the state budget allocated 9.7 million kroner for life annuities, shared by 209 artists, as an expression of official gratitude for their contribution to culture in Denmark.

Even though more and more Danes are connecting up to satellite TV stations, they still enjoy going to the cinema. The national output is quite limited, and Danish films do not always meet with international acclaim as was the case with Bille August's "Pelle the Conqueror" or "Babette's Feast", which was directed by Gabriel Axel and based on a novelle by Karen Blixen. But an annual ticket sale of over 10 million certainly justifies the existence of the numerous multi-cinema complexes, where the repertoire, always in the original version with Danish subtitles, will cover anything from any edition of "The Godfather", to "Dances with Wolves", and other four-legged creatures,

as well as Pedro Almodovar's latest pirouettes .

However life is not confined to indoor activities. Recent surveys show that 67% of the population enjoy walking or bicycling, and 43% engage in sport on a regular basis.

It is not unusual to see people going for a walk along the beach or in the parks, even though they risk being blown away by the wind, and expose themselves to climatic conditions which in more southerly latitudes would chase people indoors, and camping has a considerable number of devotees.

This love of fresh air is very conspicuous in everyday life. To a foreigner it seems most peculiar to leave a pram out in the street in the middle of winter, when it is freezing cold, so that the baby, well tucked in under its duvet, can get some fresh air.

207

Somebody once said that the culture and character of a people are influenced by the climate they live in, and there are few places where the climatic influences are so obvious as in the Scandinavian countries.

A "sunshine story" is an optimistic tale, and "sunshine" is the most beautiful nickname one can give a loved one, apart from the rather dubious term "skat"(treasure) which means both 'precious' and tax.

One of the songs which has been extremely popular for decades and is sung by the brilliant Danish rock star Kim Larsen, runs as follows: "go out and buy hyacinths, and forget that it was winter, for today it is a sunny day".

The newspapers may devote their front pages to a picture of the first flower peeping through the snow, or the early buds on the beech trees; too much rain makes the headlines, as does lack of the same, and there is always lots of good advice on how to cope with either a heatwave or a cold spell.

One thing for sure; the Danes have learned to adapt their cultural activities and their nature to climatic conditions which are not always optimal.

But gradually the foreigner living in Denmark begins to understand why so many civilisations both in the past and the present have been sun worshippers.

The Future of Denmark

Two Political Views

What will the Danes Live on in 20 -25 Years?

by Henning Dyremose
Minister of Finance, the Conservative
People's Party

It is a thankless task to attempt to foretell the future. You always run the risk of being wrong.

Forecasts which relate to population and economic trends are however based on a sounder foundation than other types of prognoses.

In this article I will discuss what the Danes will live on in the next millenium. How Denmark will fare in the 'new Europe' - and in relation to the other Scandinavian countries.

I would like to start by highlighting three trends which will influence Danish society well into the next millenium.

Firstly, we will experience an ever increasing European integration both in depth as well as breadth. By this I mean that more and more areas which affect the everyday lives of the Danes will be determined and regulated in cooperation with the other EC countries. We will also witness a marked expansion of the EC. The other Scandinavian countries, a number of central European countries and many of the Eastern European countries, will seek some form of association with the EC.

Secondly, we will witness a dramatic change in the composition of the Danish population. There will be far more elderly people. If we look at the latest population estimates we note that by the year 2030 there will be 25% more elderly and 25% fewer young people than today. This development will obviously have consequences for Danish society.

Thirdly we will witness a radical change in the economic structure of the country. Denmark has a long tradition as an agricultural country and agriculture has always played an important role. For the last fifty years the food and manufacturing industries have constituted the driving forces of Danish society. But a new sector has grown up alongside these two - the service sector. If we look at the trend in occupational sectors then it emerges that by far the greatest increase has been in the service sector.

I believe that this trend will continue. The growth areas for new jobs - and we will have to create hundreds of thousands of these in the 1990s - will largely be limited to those which fall into a category which we may loosely define as private service industries.

In addition to these three trends the current state of Danish society and the Danish economy is also a significant determinant for the potential development of our society and our economy over the next 20 to 25 years.

The following Facts are Significant

The Danish economy is currently very strong. We are in the process of solving the problem of our foreign debt. After 27 years of deficit on our balance of payments, Denmark is now enjoying a healthy surplus. This means that we can now gradually pay off our foreign debt. For many years the burden of foreign debt has imposed a considerable restraint on our economic freedom of action.

Another factor is the rate of inflation, which at around 2% per annum is one of the lowest in the world. Denmark currently enjoys very stable prices. Furthermore, Danish society is characterised by a relatively high level of education and a very high female labour market participation.

So we are aware of several factors

which will influence the future development of Denmark. But we are also aware of the problems which may affect Danish society in the years to come.

The main structural problems in the Danish economy are related to the size and organisation of the public sector, the system of taxation, the conditions for savings and investments as well as an inflexible labour market. In addition there is the high rate of unemployment. An unemployment rate of 10 to 11% of the labour force is unacceptable, both from a social as well as an economic point of view.

I have now outlined some of the actual factors which will influence Danish society in the coming 20 to 25 years and some of the problems which we will face.

The main objective of the government is to bring down unemployment in the 1990s. No other problem has such a high priority. This requires the implementation of policies aimed at a dramatic reduction of unemployment. Above all we have to create a healthy growth in the Danish economy. And a healthy growth is synonymous with growth in the export sector.

In the long term - when the unemployment which is determined by recessional trends has been reduced - growth will be inhibited by the structural problems mentioned above. There will be bottle necks on the labour market and the cycle of price and wage increases will take off again. This will diminish our competitiveness, which in turn will result in a balance of payments deficit and another rise in unemployment.

If the most significant structural problems are resolved there will gradually be more scope to manoeuvre and to steer economic policy towards a focus on growth and employment problems.

If we are to achieve these objectives, then measures must be introduced which:
* Reduce the public sector and increase its efficiency;

Denmark will experience an increasing integration with Europe. Drawing by Peter Lautro.

* Create better conditions for industry by improving the infra-structure, more provision for research and development and greater opportunities for our predominantly small and medium-sized enterprises to compete on the world market;
* Reorganise the ressourcing structure of the unemployment benefit system so that the major players in the labour market have to adopt greater economic responsibility for employment developments;
* Reorganise the payment structure for unemployment benefits and develop the opportunities for further training and education in close cooperation with the labour market partners;
* Adjust the Danish tax and excise system to harmonise with the new circumstances of a customs-free economic cooperation.

211

We can expect an incease in building activity. Photograph in the 1983 Gutenberghus Yearbook.

An aggressive structural policy of this nature will obviously create a new kind of Denmark, and in particular a new climate of employment.

Let us look at where the increases and reductions in employment are likely to take place.

Since one of Denmark's greatest structural problems is the disproportionately large size of the public sector in relation to the private sector, it follows that growth in employment and all the new jobs to be created over the next 10 to 20 years must be created in the private sector.

A large number of the functions currently under public administration will be put out to private tender for independent administration, subject to certain economic limitations. The public institutional society which we know today will be replaced by a society run according to the individual decisions of its members.

An increased application of market mechanisms in the public sector by privatisations and tenders will lead to radical shift of jobs from the public to the private sector.

Of course it is impossible to give a clear or accurate estimate of the employment pattern of the Danes in 20 to 25 years. It can be no more than a guess - based on the facts which I have already enumerated.

Historically there is a relatively steady correlation between economic growth and employment trends, and it has also been shown that a relatively constant proportion of increased wealth is ploughed into consumption and investments. However there are far greater variations in the benefits of increased wealth enjoyed by the specific sectors of industry.

There has however been a noticeable trend over the last 30 years which demonstrated that new jobs in the private sector have largely been created in the service

This will mean a reduction of certain taxes, lower top rates of income tax and increased social security contributions, which must be introduced gradually to ensure continued competitiveness;
* Encourage savings, so that the surplus on the balance of payments is maintained;
* Implement essential improvements to the infra-structure to ensure that Copenhagen becomes an economic, financial and cultural centre in Northern Europe.

These reforms and initiatives should provide the basis for economic growth capable of creating 100,000 new jobs in the private sector by the year 1996.

industries. This trend is hardly likely to change over the next few years, but it is difficult to apply historic criteria to pinpoint the specific sectors where employment is likely to benefit from overall growth .

In the light of past experience it is estimated that the majority of the new jobs in the private sector are likely to be created in the service industries. It is also likely that the manufacturing industries will experience a modest growth, and the construction industry will also experience some growth compared with the current very high level. A growing demand for repair and maintenance work can be expected;

work which is fairly labour intensive.

A continuing growth in the Danish economy will only be possible if the private sector expands, and the public sector constitutes a correspondingly smaller share of the economy.

It is therefore my estimate that over the next 20 to 25 years we will witness a constant increase of employment in the private sector, for both men and women. And that these jobs will largely evolve in the service sector. Consulting work, computer development, system export etc. The leisure and tourist industries will also be responsible for the creation of many new jobs.

Denmark must Concentrate on Know-how and Become a major Supplier of Environmental Technology

by Jes Lunde
Member of Parliament, Socialist People's Party

Danish society lives off the accumulated know-how of several generations. A favourite Danish cliché is the claim that our most important raw material is people - and there is more than a grain of truth in that statement.

Denmark is not rich in natural resources. North Sea oil and gas have only recently assumed a significant role - and we have always been used to having to import all the raw materials for industrial production.

Given these limitations it is only possible to survive by being extremely good at processing the raw materials, which requires highly skilled workers, and Denmark was one of the first countries to recognise this necessity.

Denmark is one of the nations which, together with Norway, Sweden, Finland and Iceland, comprise the "Scandinavian Model", where for decades the taxpayers have been prepared to pay relatively high rates of tax. This has provided the foundations for an efficient public sector. It has been possible to create an elaborate infra-structure (roads, telecommunications etc.) as well as a highly developed educational system. Denmark was one of the first countries to introduce compulsory basic education, and in the middle of the 19th century this initiative was supplemented by the work of the folk high school movement. This movement, which included N.F.S. Grundtvig amongst its founders, produced a surge in educational readiness amongst the population at large, creating the basis for further education of both a general as well as a qualifying nature.

In international commercial circles Denmark has a reputation for paying relatively high wages - but Danish workers deserve these high rates. The obvious economic rationale of this is our positive balance of payments. But foreign entrepreneurs have also had occasion to see for themselves why this should be so at first hand. One of Denmark's industrial leaders told me recently how, during a visit by one of his European colleagues, they went to a construction site together where they saw a group of workers standing discussing a technical drawing. The foreign colleague had assumed that these workers were all engineers, since they appeared to understand the drawings. The Danish director was able to identify them as unskilled workers, but they had all been on courses run by the school for unskilled workers.

This highly qualified labour force has not been so easy to achieve. It is the result of many sacrifices - and the very high level of taxation, for which we are not envied by the rest of the world.

I believe that the future prospects for Denmark over the next 20 to 25 years will depend on whether we can continue to be one step ahead of our competitors in the education of our labour force. This position is currently under threat, and if we do not start allocating more resources to this sector again there will be grounds for serious concern about Denmark's economic stability.

This need should be pretty obvious in Denmark (and several other countries) just now. The current average unemployment rate is more than 10% of the labour force, and more than 25% for many categories of unskilled workers.

Unemployment is of course a curse for the individual. It is accompanied by a large reduction in income, a loss of self-esteem, of colleagues and opportunities to make a contribution to society. I believe that it is basic human need to be useful - and this need is frustrated when one is made redundant.

But unemployment can also be regarded as an enormous social challenge. We are presented with a considerable amount of spare time - time which people are offering for the use of their skills - and this is time which we must aim at using constructively in the coming years.

We can achieve this by tackling tasks which lie outwith the remit of the industrial market (i.e. in the public sector) or by using all this spare time to educate the labour force. We have to educate the unemployed better, so that they stand a chance of getting another job - but we must also remove some of those currently in employment for periods of further education - thus providing temporary work placements for the unemployed.

This is basic logic. But it has not yet been sufficiently implemented in Denmark.

Those sectors which will dominate the market in Denmark in 20 to 25 years will include some of the current leaders - but also a number of new ones.

I am convinced that the global development in the coming decades will be characterised by a dramatic rise in environmental awareness. The ecological threats are becoming so great that they are matters of serious concern in more and more countries. The EC is planning to adopt measures for even closer cooperation on environmental issues. Many countries are lobbying for the adoption of uniform compulsory minimum norms - and on a global level the UN organisation is gradually becoming more involved in environmental policy.

The future of Denmark depends on even better education of the workforce. Apprentices at the Technical School in Hillerød. Photo: Stig Stasig/2.maj.

The Greenhouse effect, the hole in the ozone layer, the pollution of drinking water, have all become problems concerning all countries - and if we look ahead 20 to 25 years from now, it is certain that a much more stringent environmental policy will be in force on a global level. If some countries intend to avoid this then they will run the risk of being subjected to international boycotts in line with those currently imposed on countries which practise racism or constitute a military threat to their neighbours. Environmental policy will gradually be accepted as a matter of common concern, and the pollution of common resources by individual nations will not be tolerated.

This means that there will be a tremendous increase in the international demand for environmentally friendly forms of production. There will be considerable opportunities for those countries who are the first to change course. Their industrial enterprises will be accustomed to having to meet more stringent environmental requirements - and they will have developed technological solutions to many evironmental problems.

I believe that Denmark stands a chance of being one of these countries. In the course of the 1980s we have introduced stricter industrial requirements than several other countries in Western Europe - and far more than in Eastern Europe or the Third World. Danish enterprises have of course complained a lot about this legislation, but they are now beginning to reap the benefits. Denmark is currently exporting environmental technology equipment to the tune of some 3 to 4 million kroner per annum. We are particularly strong in the fields of renewable energy, cleaning of smoke emissions and measuring equipment.

One of Denmark's better traditions is that of assessing technology and setting standards for the social implications of the applications of technology. For instance in the field of bio-technology this has led to both one of the world's strictest sets of required standards as well as one of the world's strongest industries.

If we continue to concentrate our efforts then in 20 to 25 years time Denmark will possess a very significant environmental industry, which will be able to specialise in the supply of technology for the conversion of world's industrial production apparatus to an ecologically sound system.

Denmark's established industrial sectors will also need to focus on environ-mental issues to ensure continued success. Agriculture will move towards sounder ecological practices, both because of the need to preserve drinking water resources in Denmark, and the growing external market interests in forms of production. At present Denmark gives a certain amount of state subsidy to projects involving conversion to ecological farming methods. In 20 to 25 years time similar schemes will be well established within the EC.

As for the food industry, I believe that world market requirements, for better or worse, will continue to focus on increasingly highly processed goods. It would be nice to think that the increased environmental awareness might lead away from a focus on economic growth - and thus point to a less stressful existence. But I doubt whether this will come about in the near future. This would require a total change of attitude in the western world. And if it does not occur then we will witness an increasing demand for highly processed goods, which Denmark will be in a strong position to supply. If however it does occur, it will lead to even more stringent consumer demands for methods of production based on environmentally and ethically acceptable standards. In my opinion Denmark should welcome this development as a contributive measure towards the survival of the planet.

International developments in general in the coming decades will lead to a dismantling of trade barriers - especially in relation to the developing countries. In the long run the wealthy industrialised countries will not be able keep the developing countries out of their own markets - and an impending new international world order will afford the Third World nations greater opportunities to hold their own in global competition. This means that it will be even more impossible for Denmark to compete in the field of long

Environmental policy will be accepted as a matter of common concern, and the pollution of common resources will not be tolerated. Aktion Nordsø. Photo: Sonja Iskov/2.maj.

runs of standardised mass-produced goods. The large nations already have a far better background for this, and with the entrance of the developing world and the Eastern European countries the competition will become even more intense.

Denmark can survive by concentrating on specialised products and on advanced technology and design. For instance we should no longer compete so much in the field of traditional shipbuilding, but rather concentrate on the development of technologically advanced ships which are already in production in our shipyards. The same principle goes for design: the existence of a textile industry in Denmark is largely due to the great emphasis placed on the development of design. And this also applies to furniture and hi-fi equipment. Denmark's ability to sell radios and televisions to Japan indicates that there will always be a market for this kind of high price products. But how large a market? This depends largely on economic development, since these design-based products do not exactly constitute basic necessities. They form a product category which is at the bottom of the list of priorities, and which is endangered in times of economic recession.

Another important sector in Denmark is the construction industry. A combination of good supplies of raw materials for construction (clay and chalk) and a progressive housing policy has produced a strong building sector. It established itself 217 on a strong domestic market, but as the average living area per person gradually increased there has been a certain corresponding saturation and the sector has experienced a dramatic down-turn. Whether it will be able to survive in 20 to 25 years time will entirely depend on its ability to penetrate export markets. The need for reconstruction in Eastern Europe may be enormous, but there will be intense competition for this market because of course it has been identified by all the players, and the development will take many decades because the citizens of Eastern Europe will have difficulty in raising enough hard currency, regardless of how much credit Western Europe is willing to give.

Finally it will be interesting to see how Denmark fares in the tertiary sector (the service industries). We would have a fairly good handicap in the race for public sector related services. As the standard of Danish public health system is very high, there are ample opportunities for export of medical technology. This is a good example of the interplay between a successful public sector and private industry. Denmark has a large share of the world market for hearing aids. This is due to the fact that Denmark was probably the first country to provide grants for hearing aids under its public health care system, thus enabling Danish producers to develop and sell the product on the domestic market - which subsequently provided a basis for commanding a strong position on the world market as the demand grew overseas.

Denmark would do well to be more aware of these links and effects in the future. There is little tradition for collaboration between the public sector and private industry - and we have much to learn from the example of other countries. If we can exploit the potential inherent in the public sector there will be numerous opportunities for development, including the export of systems for total solutions in the social, educational and especially in the environmental sector.

On the whole, Denmark's international prospects look rosy. But success will depend on whether we can play the right political role *both* in the international context *and* at home. Denmark will need to focus even more on environmental problems and the need to create space for human development if she is to play a constructive role on the world stage.

The Writing Team

HELLE ASKGAARD, born 1942. MA in History and Geography from the University of Copenhagen. Awarded the University's Gold Medal for Geography in 1969. Senior teacher at Øregård Gymnasium since 1982. Geography editor for the publishers 'forlaget systime' since 1982.

Has specialised in industrial history and development in Denmark, and published papers and textbooks for the Gymnasium and the Higher Preparatory Course on these subjects. Writes for a number of journals.

HENNING DYREMOSE, born 1945. Took his first degree in Civil Engineering (chemistry) in 1969, and then HD (B.Com.), (Organisation), in 1972. Employed by NOVO Industri A/S from 1973-86, latterly as the Marketing Director for the Enzyme Division. Committee member of Conservative Party youth organisation and local constituency group from 1966, as well as several terms on the Conservative Central Committee. Board member of several international companies 1983-86. Conservative Member of the Folketing since 1979, Minister of Labour 1986-89, Minister of Finance since 1989.

Co-author of party political programmes for the Conservative People's Party.

ESTHER EDELSTEN, born in Israel. Teacher-training in Israel. Resident in Denmark since 1965, married to a Dane. Studied Jewish Literature at the University of Copenhagen. Scandinavian correspondent for the Israeli daily "Ma'ariv" since 1975.

In Israel she has published Faroese and Danish anthologies in Hebrew and in Denmark "Israeli Poetry", "Women in the Bible" and "Five Israeli Authors" translated into Danish.

TORBEN FRIDBERG, born 1946. Senior Research Associate. Masters degree in Social Sciences. Employed at the Danish National Institute of Social Research in Copenhagen since 1976.

Has researched and published reports on social policy, the welfare state, social problems and the social assistance apparatus, as well as a number of subjects relating to living conditions in Denmark such as the family, work, leisure-time and cultural activities.

TORBEN HANSGAARD, born 1942. MA in History and Geography from the   219

University of Copenhagen. Senior master at Aalborghus Gymnasium. Has published papers and textbooks on the recent history of agriculture in Denmark, from the Agrarian Reforms to the First World War. Board member of the Association of History Teachers in the Gymnasium and the Higher Preparatory Courses from 1979-1985, as well as of the Agricultural Historical Society since 1978.

Is also a writer and critic for a number of scientific and educational journals.

HARRY HAUE. Born 1941. Masters degree in History from Århus University. Master at Nordfyns Gymnasium and part-time lecturer at Odense University since 1980, teaching history and cultural dissemination. Has written a number of textbooks, has worked on documentary publications for the upper secondary courses and published the results of educational research. From 1983-88 history editor of the publishers 'forlaget systime' and since 1988 on the editorial team of the Journal "Uddannelseshistorie" (The history of education).

JULIAN ISHERWOOD, born 1953. British journalist with the newspaper Politiken from 1975-79. Radio Denmark's Radio News in English since 1979. Chief Scandinavian correspondent for The Daily Telegraph, Time Magazine and UPI, as well as BBC correspondent for Denmark and Norway 1979-92. Since 1989 also chief editor for UPI in Europe, the Middle East and Africa. Special interest: Scandinavian-Baltic defence and security policies.

BIRGIT JEPPESEN. Architect, member of the Academic Association of Architects. Has been editor of the architectural journal "Blød By" for a number of years, in addition to working with and teaching graphic design. Author of numerous articles as well as a number of books ; "Andelsboligen" (Cooperative Housing), "Dansk design historie - fra Kirke til Café" (The History of Danish Design - from Church to Café) (co-author), and "New York- en kulturguide" (New York, A Cultural Guide).

BIRTHE JOHANSEN. Journalist and Masters degree in the Dramatic Arts from Copenhagen University. Drama and ballet critic for several Danish dailies. Danish correspondent for several foreign ballet magazines including "Ballet International". Has written articles about the theatre and ballet for a number of publications, including the Royal Theatre programmes as well as the anthologies "Perspektiv på Bournonville" (Perspective on Bournonville), "Gulnares Hus" and contemporary dance in "Dance in Denmark" as well as "Bournonvilliana".

JENS KISTRUP, born 1925. Masters degree in Literary History, 1949. Free-lance film critic for Berlingske Tidende from 1946 and employed as drama and literary critic for this newspaper since 1950. Editor of the feature column 1956-64. Several periods as drama critic for the journal "Perspektiv". Chairman of the Literature Committee of the State Endowment Fund for the Arts, 1984-86.

Has written several books on literary subjects. Awarded the Publicist Prize in 1983.

JØRGEN KOCK, born 1924. Degree in Law from Copenhagen University, 1948. Civil servant in ministries of Employment and Social Services. Director of the National Rehabilitation Centre in Vejle 1961-71. Director of the Health and Social Services Department, Municipality of Århus, 1971-86, whilst also external reader in Social Legislation and Social Administration at the University of Århus. Co-author of books on social policy, social legislation and social administration.

INGERLISE KOEFOED, born 1922. Libraries Adviser. Diploma in librarianship from The Danish School of Librarianship, 1961. Librarian with Lyngby-Tårbæk municipal libraries, then Libraries Consultant with the Danish Libraries' Association and the State Inspectorate of Public Libraries (Ministry of Culture) from 1976.

Member of the Folketing 1979-91 (Socialist People's Party). Chairperson of the Folketing's Cultural Committee 1982-91. Member of a number of boards and committees in the library sector, in the Ministry of Culture, the Writers' Association, and the Folk High School Secretariat. Since 1991 Chairperson of the Board of the Danish Cultural Institute.

Literary critic for children's books for Politiken since 1973. Has written and translated a number of books for children and young people.

KAI LEMBERG. Degree in Political Science from the University of Copenhagen, 1945. Professor of Social Planning at the Geographic Institute of Roskilde University Centre. Chief Planning Officer for the Municipality of Copenhagen 1967-87, Asst.Professor at RUC since 1986. 1988-89 also Professor at Nordisk Institut för Samhällsplanering in Stockholm. From 1971-90 represented the Ministry of Environment Planning Agency at OECD meetings on urban issues.

Author and co-author of several works on planning, democracy, economics and the environment.

JES LUNDE, born 1956. Degree in Economics from Aalborg University Center 1980, and employed as an economist at the Center from 1979-84. Served on a number of committees. Chairman of several committees in the Socialist People's Party, Financial Policy Spokesman for the Party since 1984. Member of the Folketing since 1984. Member of Danmarks Nationalbank General Council since 1986.

Has written several publications on economic policy as well as the provocative "Vision og ansvar" (Vision and Responsibility), on the economy in the 90s.

FLEMMING MADSEN, born 1953. Head of the Danish Music Information Centre from 1992. Has had a career in folk and rock music. In 1977 he founded the Rhythmic Evening School, now the largest in Scandinavia in the field of Jazz, Rock and Folk music. Member of the State Music Council 1983-91 and the Nordic Music Committee, 1988 -92. Editor of Danish Music Yearbook.

Has written articles for specialist magazines and publications on rhythmic music in Denmark and is active in the musical debate.

221

ANDERS MONRAD MØLLER, born 1942. MA in History and music, 1972, and PhD in 1981. Historical consultant with the Customs and Excise Agency since 1985. Editor of ZISE, the Customs and Excise historical journal since 1985, and of the Historisk Tidsskrift (the Historical Journal) since 1989.

Has written books and articles on recent Danish history with special emphasis on shipping, industry, customs and the postal service.

SVEND HAKON ROSSEL, Masters degree in Comparative Literature and Scandinavian Literature, University of Copenhagen, 1968. Professor of Scandinavian Languages and Literature and Comparative Literature at the University of Washington, Seattle, since 1974. Chairman of the Scandinavian Dept., 1981-90. Visiting Professor at the University of Vienna in 1987 and 1991.

Has lectured at universities in the USA, Denmark, Great Britain, Germany and Austria. He serves on several editorial boards and is consultant for a number of university presses. Has published 17 books on Danish authors, literary history etc.

MARÍA CAMINO SÁNCHEZ, born 1944 in Spain. Head of the news agency Agencia EFE in Copenhagen. During her 20 year career in journalism in Denmark, the author has experienced Denmark's integration into Europe without losing its distinctively Scandininavian character and without losing its ability to surprise foreigners. She has also translated several chapters of "Discover Denmark" into Spanish.

LISE H. SKJØTH, born 1939. Masters degree in Art History. Consultant in FOLKEVIRKE (socio-cultural-political educational organisation). Has taught at various Danish folk high schools and at the Institute of Art History, Århus University. Has been employed in the Art Museums in Herning and Århus. Editor of Århus County Museums' Report and on the editorial committee of the UNESCO journal "Museum".

Has organised a number of Danish, Scandinavian and international museum conferences.

The translator:

VIVIEN ANDERSEN, born 1946 in London. BA in German and Psychology from Birmingham University,1967. Merkonom (Diploma in Business Studies) Grenaa, 1980; MBA from Edinburgh University, 1989. Spent ten years in tourism marketing, first for British Tourist Authority and then as a tourist officer in Denmark, where she lived from 1973-85. Has taught English in Denmark and Danish in Scotland. Has also taught Marketing for new and small businesses and cultural services organisations.

Free-lance translator and writer, professional since 1991. Publications include "Highlights of Copenhagen", "Udvekslingsrejser in Europe" (Exchange Travel in Europe), "Insight Guide to Denmark", The Danish Literary Magazine and several catalogues for major exhibitions at Aarhus Art Museum.

Bibliography

by Hanne Bing, librarian

Denmark and the Danes

A geography of Norden : Denmark, Fin-land, Iceland, Norway, Sweden. Editor Axel Sømme. Rev. edition. Oslo, København, Stockholm, Helsingfors. Cappelen. 1961. 363 p. ill. (Scandinavian University Books).

Korst, Mogens: Industrial life in Denmark, the Faroe Islands and Greenland : a survey of economic development and production. Copenhagen. The Foundation for International Understanding. 1987. 316 p. ill.

Lauring, Palle: A history of Denmark. Translated from the Danish by David Hohnen. 7. edition. Copenhagen. Høst & Søn. 1986. 274 p. ill.

Molesworth, Robert: An account of Denmark as it was in the year 1692. Copenhagen. Rosenkilde og Bagger. 1976. 271 p. ill.

Norden - man and environment. Edited by Uuno Varjo and Wolf Tietze. Berlin. Borntraeger. 1987. 535 p. ill.

Nye, David E.: Denmark and the Danes - a short description for foreign visitors. Copenhagen. Foreningen til Unge Handelsmænds Uddannelse. 1991. 43 p. ill.

Rying, Bent: Danish in the south and the north. Translation Reginald Spink. Copenhagen. Royal Danish Ministry of Foreign Affairs. 1981-1988. 2 volumes. ill.
Volume 1: Denmark : introduction : prehistory. 1981. 111 p.
Volume 2: Denmark : history. 1988. 416 p.

Seidelin Jacobsen, Helge: An outline history of Denmark. København. Høst & Søn. 1986. 120 p. ill.

Simonsen, Kjartan; Stahlschmidt, Nils: GO-Denmark. Editor Troels Tunebjerg. Translation Vincent Murphy. 2. edition. Brenderup. Geografforlaget. 1991. 31 p. ill.

Stubkjær, Jens: Facts about Denmark. Translation Michael Metcalfe. Copenhagen. Ministry of Foreign Affairs of Denmark, Press and Cultural Department in cooperation with Aktuelle Bøger. 1991. 112 p. ill.

Shipping - a Historical Cross-section

Hornby, Ove: „With constant care"...". A.P. Møller : shipowner 1876-1965. Copenhagen. Schultz. 1988. 325 p. ill.

Johansen, Hans Christian: Shipping and trade between the Baltic area and Western Europe. Odense. Odense University Press. 1983. 139 p.

6000 Years of Danish Agriculture

Agriculture in Denmark 1991 : statistics on Danish agriculture 1991 : tables and summarized text of landøkonomisk oversigt 1991. Copenhagen. De Danske Landboforeninger = Danish Farmers' Union. 1991. 96 p.

Bjørn, Claus: Co-operation in Denmark. Translated by Kurt Ravnkilde. 2. edition. Copenhagen. Danske Andelsselskaber. 1990. 47 p. ill.

Christensen, Jens: Rural Denmark 1750-1980. Translated from Danish by Else Buchwald Christensen; with a preface by Martin Nielsen. Edited by Claus Bjørn. Copenhagen. The Central Co-operative Committee of Denmark. 1983. 187 p. ill.

Ravnkilde, Kurt: From fettered to free. The farmer in Denmark's history. Hurst. Danish Language Services. 1989. 128 p. ill.

Environmental and Physical Planning

The green wedges of the capital : the story of the green areas of Greater Copenhagen. Copenhagen. The Ministry of the Environment, the Planning Department; the Greater Copenhagen Council. 1984. 56 p. ill.

Lemberg, Kai: National, regional and local planning. In : Nordic Democracy. Ideas, issues and institutions in politics, economy, education, social and cultural affairs of Denmark, Finland, Iceland, Norway and Sweden. Editor Folmer Wisti. Copenhagen. Det danske Selskab. 1981.

Lemberg, Kai: The need for autonomy : improving local democracy. In : Cities in a Global Society. Editors Richard V. Knight and Gary Gappert. London. Sage Publications. 1989.

The overall Danish physical planning system and planning for the sectors of land use and natural resources : international conference paper 1981 by Niels Østergaard. Copenhagen. Ministry of the Environment. Denmark. 1981. 14 p.

Rasmussen, Steen Eiler: Greater Copenhagen planning. Status. Summary in English. Copenhagen. Munksgaard. 1952. 76 p. ill.

Regional planning in the Greater Copenhagen Region 1945-1978. Copenhagen. Hovedstadsrådet. 1978. 15 p. ill. (English summary; no. 2).

Svensson, Ole: Dansk byplan-guide = Danish town planning guide. Copenhagen. Miljøministeriet, Planstyrelsen; Dansk Byplanlaboratorium. 1981. 116 p. ill.

Learning in Denmark

Publications available from the Danish Ministry of Education:
*The Ministry of Education's International Relations Division
**The Ministry of Education's Publishing Office
***Department of Primary and Lower Secondary Education
****Publications available from Statens Informationstjeneste (The Danish State Information Service)

General:
Education in Denmark. A brief outline. 1992.**

Educational statistics. Factsheet. 1991. 4 p.**

Preschool education:
Early childhood and pre-school education in Denmark. 1989. 15 p.*

Folkeskole (primary and lower secondary education):
Executive order on the teaching of non-Danish-speaking pupils in the Folkeskole. 1988. 8 p.*
Innovation programme for the Folkeskole and the school as a community centre. 1989. 4 p.*
Regulations pertaining to school libraries in the Folkeskole. 1987. 4 p.*

Upper secondary education:
The Danish Gymnasium. General rules. 1991. 54 p.****
The Danish higher preparatory examination. General rules. 1991. 45 p.****

Vocational education and training:
Introduction to the Danish vocational education and training system. 1991. 6 p.*
The vocational education and training in the field of agriculture. 1991. 25 p.*

Higher education:
An open market for higher education. Report to the Parliament. 1992.**
Teacher education and training in Denmark. 1985. 16 p.*

Education of special categories of pupils:
The development of the Danish Folkeskole towards a school for all. Integration of handicapped pupils in the mainstream school system. 1990. 12 p.***
Handicapped students in the Danish education system. 1991. 23 p.***

Borish, Steven M.: The land of the living : the Danish folk high schools and Denmark's non-violent path to modernization. Nevada City, Calif. Blue Dolphin. Cop. 1991. - xxiii, 488 p. ill.
Dahllöf, Urban: Comprehensive schooling at the lower secondary level : joint review of the experience in four countries : review of Denmark. Organisation for Economic Co-operation and Development. Paris. Directorate for Social Affairs, Manpower and Education. 1985. 39 p. ill.
The Danish Folk High School to-day : a description of residential adult education in Denmark. Edited by Arne Andresén. Translation Ann Andresén. 2. edition. Foreningen for Folkehøjskoler i Danmark. København. Højskolernes Sekretariat. 1985. 40 p. ill.
The Folk High School 1970-1990 : development and conditions. Edited by Ebbe Lundgaard. Translation Mogens Frølund, Jonell Kristensen. Copenhagen. The Association of Folk High Schools in Denmark. 1991. 91 p.
Grundtvig's ideas in North America. Influences and parallels. Copenhagen. Det danske Selskab. 1983. 173 p.
N.F.S. Grundtvig. Tradition and renewal. Grundtvig's vision of man and people, education and the church, in relation to world issues today. Edited by Christian Thodberg and Anders Pontoppidan Thyssen. Copenhagen. Det danske Selskab. 1983. 428 p. ill.

Work and Leisure Time

Strategies : studies in modern cultural policy. Edited by Jørn Langsted. Aar-

225

hus. Aarhus University Press. Cop. 1990. 84 p. ill.

Time and consumption : time use and consumption in Denmark in recent decades. Edited by Gunnar Viby Mogensen. Copenhagen. Danmarks Statistik. 1990. 440 p. ill.

Yearbook of Nordic statistics = Nordisk statistisk årsbok. Edited by the Nordic Statistical Secretariat. = Nordisk Statistiska Sekretariatet.
Vol. 1 (1962)-. Copenhagen. Nordic Council of Ministers; Nordic Statistical Secretariat. 1963 - . 1991 (vol. 29). 1991. 431 p. ill. (Nord, 1991:1).

The Living and Working Environment

Bernsen, Jens: Design : the problem comes first. 3. edition. Copenhagen. Danish Design Council. 1986. 118 p.

Byg og Bo 88 Odense : fremtidens boligbyggeri i Danmark = future housing in Denmark. Edited by Jørgen Steen Knudsen et al. English translation John Warbrick, Gerda Hvidberg Henriksen. Odense. Odense Kommune, Magistratens 2. afdeling, Byplan-/arkitektafdelingen. 1988. 162 p. ill. Danish and English text.

Danish building design. Edited by Jens Bernsen, Susanne Schenstrøm. Copenhagen. Danish Design Council. 1984. 72 p. ill. English, German and French text.

Dansk møbelkunst gennem 40 år = 40 years of Danish furniture design : the Copenhagen Cabinet-makers' Guild exhibitions 1927-1966. Compiled and edited by Grethe Jalk. Tåstrup. Teknologisk Instituts Forlag. 1987. 4 vols. ill.
Volume 1: 1927-1936.
Volume 2: 1937-1946.
Volume 3: 1947-1956.
Volume 4: 1957-1966.

Den designbaserede virksomhed = Design-based enterprise = La empresa basada en el diseno. Edited by Jens Bernsen and Kirsten Lerstrøm. Copenhagen. Danish Design Centre. 1988. 146 p. ill. Danish, English and Spanish text.

100 + 3 great Danish industrial designs : ID-prisen 1965-85. Editors Jens Bernsen and Susanne Schenstrøm. Copenhagen. Danish Design Council. 1985. 179 p. ill. Danish and English text.

Henning Larsen. Special issue. ARKITEKTUR DK; 2. 1989. Copenhagen. Arkitektens Forlag. ill. Danish, English and German text.

Hiort, Esbjørn: Finn Juhl : furniture, architecture, applied art. Translated by Martha Gaber Abrahamsen. Copenhagen. Arkitektens Forlag. 1990. 144 p. ill.

Johan Otto von Spreckelsen. Special issue. ARKITEKTUR DK; 1/2. 1990. Copenhagen. Arkitektens Forlag. ill. Danish, English and German text.

Kastholm, Jørgen: Arne Jacobsen. Copenhagen. Høst & Søn's Forlag. 4.edition. 1968. 88 p. ill. Danish, English, German and French text.

Mollerup, Per: Virksomhedens designprogram = The corporate design programme = El programa de diseno corporativo. Copenhagen. Danish Design Council. 1980. 84 s. ill. Danish, English and Spanish text.

Objects one : an account of Danish arts and crafts 1985/86. Editors ... The Objects Group; Nils Fagerholt et al. Frederiksberg. The Objects Group. 1986. 117 p. ill.

På dansk - dansk byggeri i udlandet = The Danish way - Danish building abroad. Edited by Steen Heide and Kim Dirckink-Holmfeld. Copenhagen. Dansk Arkitekturcenter; Arkitektens Forlag. Cop. 1986. 80 p. ill. Danish and English text.

Scandinavian modern design 1880-1980. Editor David Revere McFadden. New York. Harry N. Abrams Inc. 1982. 287 p. ill.

Sestoft, Jørgen; Hegner Christiansen, Jørgen: Guide to Danish architecture I. Translation Peter Avondoglio. Copenhagen. Arkitektens Forlag. 1991-. 2 vols. ill.
Volume I: 1000-1960. 1991. 271 p.

Women in Danish architecture. Editor Helle Bay et al. English translation Gerda Hvidberg Henriksen. Copenhagen. Arkitektens Forlag. 1991. 82 p. ill.

Aarhus City Hall. Edited by Erik Møller and Kjeld Vindum. Copenhagen. Arkitektens Forlag. 1991. 92 p. ill.

The Citizen and the Social System

Contact with Denmark 1989 (no.3) : The elderly in Denmark. Copenhagen. The Danish Cultural Institute. Cop. 1989. 47 p. ill.

Rold Andersen, Bent: Rationality and irrationality of the Nordic welfare state. In : Norden - the passion for equality. Edited by Stephen R. Graubard. Oslo. Universitetsforlaget. Cop. 1986. 323 p. (Scandinavian Library).

Welfare administration in Denmark. Edited by Tim Knudsen. Copenhagen. University of Copenhagen; Institute of Political Science. 1991. 391 p.

Danish Cultural Policy

Act on the allocation of financial support to „folkeoplysning". Copen-

hagen. Danish Ministry of Cultural Affairs. Department of Folkeoplysning. 1991. 31 p.

A model for culture Holstebro. A study of cultural policy in a Danish town. By Ingvar Holm, Viveka Hagnell and Jane Rasch. Stockholm. Almqvist & Wiksell. 1985. 224 p.

Folkeoplysning : popular enlightenment and educational opportunities for adults in Denmark. Danish text Jette Kammer Jensen. Edited by Jens Clausager. Translation Gitte and Norman Shine. Copenhagen. Det Danske Kulturinstitut. 1991. 23 p. ill.

Langsted, Jørn: Double strategies in a modern cultural policy. In : The Journal of Arts Management and Law. Vol. 19; no 4. Washington D.C. 1990.

Participation in cultural life in Europe : current trends and future strategies : the situation in Denmark. Copenhagen. Ministry of Cultural Affairs. 1991. 6 p.

Public expenditure on cultural activities in 1991. Copenhagen. Ministry of Cultural Affairs. 1991. (30 p.).

Report on Danish cultural policy and programme of ideas : presented to the Folketing by Ole Vig Jensen, Minister of Cultural Affairs on 16 March 1989. Copenhagen. Ministry of Cultural Affairs. 8 June 1989. 20 p. (Information from the Ministry of Cultural Affairs April 1989).

Strategies : studies in modern cultural policy. Edited by Jørn Langsted. Aarhus. Aarhus University Press. Cop. 1990. 84 p. ill.

Art and „folkelig" Culture

Birtwistle, Graham: Living art : Asger Jorn's comprehensive theory of art

227

between Helhesten and Cobra (1946-1949). Utrecht. Reflex. 1986. -VIII, 258 p. ill.

Gundestrup, Bente: Det Kongelige danske Kunstkammer 1737 = The Royal Danish Kunstkammer 1737. Translation Kirsten Ravel Solstad et al. Copenhagen. Nationalmuseet; Nyt Nordisk Forlag. 1991. 2 vols. ill. Danish and English text.
Volume 1: - XXXIX, 417 p.
Volume 2: - VII, 477 p.

Monrad, Kasper: Danish painting : the Golden Age : a loan exhibition from the Statens Museum for Kunst, Copenhagen. Edited by Alistair Smith and Diana Davies. Translated by Jan Bredsdorff. London. The National Gallery. Cop. 1984. 272 p. ill.

Poulsen, Vagn: Danish painting and sculpture. Translated by Sigurd Mammen. 2. edition. Revised by H.E. Nørregaard-Nielsen. Copenhagen. Det danske Selskab. 1976. 234 p. ill.

Saabye, Marianne: Thorvaldsen. Guide book for young people. Translation Susanne Lindgren. København. Thorvaldsens Museum. 1972. 40 p. ill.

Stokvis, Willemijn: Cobra : an international movement in art after the Second World War. Translated from the Dutch by Jacob C. T. Voorthuis. New York. Rizzoli. 1988. 128 p. ill.

Sørensen, Eva: Sculptures/drawings = Sculture/disegni. Editor Vanni Scheiwiller. Copenhagen. Danish Ministry of Cultural Affairs. 1982. 32 p. ill. English and Italian text. (Danish pavilion. The Venice Biennale 1982).

Varnedoe, Kirk: Northern light : Nordic art at the turn of the century. New Haven. Yale University Press.

1988. 285 p. ill.

Voss, Knud: The painters of Skagen. English translation and bibliography by Peter Shield. 1. edition. Tølløse. Stok-Art. 1990. 260 p. ill.

Wivel, Ole: Anna Ancher 1859-1935. English translation Peter Ditlevsen; German translation Lisa Lundø. Lyngby. Herluf Stokholm. Cop. 1987. 63 p. ill. (Skagen monografier; 1). Danish, English and German text.

Music in Denmark

Music in Denmark. Edited by Knud Ketting. Translated by Michael Chessnutt. Copenhagen. Det danske Selskab. Cop. 1987. 111 p. ill.

Musical Denmark. Published jointly by The Danish Cultural Institute and the Danish Music Information Centre. Copenhagen. 1952- . Periodical. 2 issues a year.

The New Grove Dictionary of Music and Musicians. Volume V p. 366-373. "Denmark" : and various individual composers. With bibliographies. London. Macmillan. 1980. ill.

Nordic Sounds. Published for NOMUS by The Danish Music Information Centre. Copenhagen. 1982- . Periodical. 2 issues a year.

Ballet and Contemporary Dance

Bournonvilleana. Edited by Marianne Hallar og Alette Scavenius. Translation Gaye Kynoch. Copenhagen. The Royal Theatre and Rhodos. (International Science and Art Publishers). 1992. 256 p. ill.

Dance in Denmark. Editors Erik Aschengreen, Ebbe Mørk, Ole Kjær Madsen (editor-in-chief). Translation Paula Hostrup-Jessen. Copenhagen.

Royal Danish Ministry of Foreign Affairs, Press Secretariat. 1991. 41 p. ill.

Jürgensen, Knud Arne: The Bournonville ballets. A photographic record 1844-1933. London. Dance Books. 1987. 179 p. ill.

Jürgensen, Knud Arne: The Bournonville heritage : a choreographic record 1829-1875 : twenty-four unknown dances in labanotation. Reconstructed by Knud Arne Jürgensen. Notated by Ann Hutchinson Guest, ass. by Marion Bastien. London. Dance Books. 1990. 186 p. ill.

Theatre and Film

Theatre:

Barba, Eugenio: Beyond the floating islands/with a postscript by Ferdinand Taviani. Translation by Judy Barba et al. New York. PAJ Publications. Cop. 1986. 274 p. ill.

Barba, Eugenio: The floating islands : reflections with Odin Teatret. Edited by Ferdinando Taviani. Translation by Judy Barba et al. Gråsten. Drama. 1979. 199 p. ill.

Grotowski, Jerzy: Towards a poor theatre. Odin Teatret. Holstebro. Denmark. Edited by Eugenio Barba. London. Methuen. 1984. 218 p. ill.

Teater i Danmark = Theatre in Denmark. Danish Centre of the ITI. No. 15 (1979/80) - No. 21 (1985/86). Ballerup. Bibliotekscentralen. Danish and English text.

Teater i Danmark. ITI Årbog. No. 25 (1989/90). København. Fiskers Forlag. 1991. 119 s. ill. Danish and English text.
No. 26 (1990/91). København. Dansk ITI & Teaterunion. 1992. Danish and English text.

Film:

Bordwell, David: The films of Carl-Theodor Dreyer. Berkeley. University of California Press. 1981. 251 p. ill.

Carney, Raymond: Speaking the language of desire. The films of Carl Th. Dreyer. Cambridge. Cambridge University Press. 1989. 363 p. ill.

Danish films 1966-. København. Filmfonden/ The Danish Film Institute. 1966 - . ill. Published annually.
1968-70: Danish film.
1971-72: Danish film news.

Engberg, Marguerite: Danish films - through the years : a survey of films, directors, cinemas, companies etc, in Denmark 1896-1985. Edited by Helge Strunk. Translated by Per Calum. København. The Danish Film Institute. 1990. 32 p. ill.

Mottram, Ron: The Danish cinema before Dreyer. Metuchen, N.J. Scarecrow Press. 1988. -v, 310 p.

Life and Death in Danish Literature

Borum, Poul: Danish literature : a short critical survey. Copenhagen. Det danske Selskab. 1979. 141 p. ill.

A history of Danish literature. Editor Sven H. Rossel. Lincoln, Nebraska. University of Nebraska Press. 1992.

Mitchell, P.M.: A history of Danish literature. 2. edition. New York. Kraus-Thomson. 1971. 339 p. ill.

Rossel, Sven H.: A history of Scandinavian literature 1870-1980. Minneapolis, Minn. University of Minnesota Press. 1982. 492 p.

As Others See Us

Dronningen, hyrdinden og skorstensfejeren = The queen, the shepherdess

229

and the chimney-sweeper/eventyret = the fairytale Hans Christian Andersen. Commentary Hans Chr. Nørregaard. Copenhagen. Rhodos. Cop. 1987. 69 p. ill. Danish, English, French and German text.

Estates and manor houses in Denmark. Danish Journal. Special issue. Text Geoffrey Dodd. Copenhagen. Royal Danish Ministry of Foreign Affairs; the Danish Tourist Board. 1982. 32 p. ill.

Hans Christian Andersen. Danish Journal. Special issue commemorating the 100th anniversary of the Danish writer. Editors Anders Georg, Ole Kjær Madsen, Jørgen V. Larsen. Copenhagen. Danish Ministry of Foreign Affairs. 1975. 45 p. ill.

Insight Guides : Denmark. Edited by Doreen Taylor-Wilkie. Singapore. Höfer Press Pte. Ltd.; c. Apa Publications (HK) Ltd. 1991. 342 p. ill.

Melchior, Arne: There is something wonderful in the state of Denmark. New Jersey. Secaucus; Lyle Stuart Inc. 1987. 136 p. ill.

Nordic democracy : ideas, issues and institutions in politics, economy, education, social and cultural affairs of Denmark, Finland, Iceland, Norway and Sweden. Editor Folmer Wisti. Copenhagen. Det danske Selskab. 1981. 784 p.

Out of Denmark : Isak Dinesen/Karen Blixen 1885-1985 and Danish women writers today. Edited by Bodil Wamberg. Copenhagen. The Danish Cultural Institute. 1985. 174 p. ill.

Stubkjær, Jens: Facts about Denmark. Translation Michael Metcalfe. Copenhagen. Ministry of Foreign Affairs of Denmark, Press and Cultural Department in cooperation with Aktuelle Bøger. 1991. 112 p. ill.

The Danish Cultural Institute

The Danish Cultural Institute is a self-governing institution, whose aim is to spread information about Denmark through cultural exchange and cooperation with other countries. Activities organised to further this goal include seminars, study tours and conferences, publications, exhibitions, lectures, concerts, and Danish language teaching. The Cultural Institute has offices in a number of European countries, some of which also operate in neighbouring countries.

Head Office

Denmark

DET DANSKE KULTURINSTITUT
Kultorvet 2
DK-1175 Copenhagen K.
Tel. +45 33 13 54 48
Fax +45 33 15 10 91

Secretary-General
Per Himmelstrup

Offices Abroad

Baltic States

DANIJAS KULTURAS INSTITUTS
Kr. Barona iela 12
226011 Riga, Latvia
Tel. +7 0132 28 99 94
Mobile phone and Fax 30 24 89 98

Branch office:
TAANI KULTUURIINSTITUUT
Vana-Viru 4
200001 Tallinn, Estonia
Tel. +7 0142 44 68 36
Fax +7 0142 60 12 47

Branch office:
DANIJOS KULTUROS INSTITUTAS
Mokytoju Namai
Vilniaus 39/6, room 204
232600 Vilnius, Lithuania
Tel. +7 0122 22 24 12
Fax +7 0122 22 28 32

Benelux

DEENS CULTUREEL INSTITUUT /
INSTITUT CULTUREL DANOIS
Av. Expo Universelle 9 - Bte 15
B-1080 Bruxelles
Tel. +32 2 428 87 46
Fax +32 2 426 37 16

France

INSTITUT CULTUREL DANOIS
25, Place de la Cathédrale
F-76000 Rouen
Tel. +33 35 70 88 81
Fax +33 35 07 57 87

Italy

ISTITUTO DANESE DI CULTURA
Via Dogana 2
I-20123 Milan
Tel. +39 2 869 36 80
Fax +39 272 0236 64

Great Britain

THE DANISH CULTURAL INSTITUTE
Carlsberg House
3, Doune Terrace
GB-Edinburgh ED3 6DY
Tel. +44 31 225 71 89
Fax +44 31 220 61 62

Germany

DÄNISCHES KULTURINSTITUT
Postfach 10 09 45
Steinstrasse 48
D-4600 Dortmund 1
Tel. +49 231 81 16 82

Austria

DÄNISCHES KULTURINSTITUT
Ferstelgasse 3/4
A-1090 Vienna
Tel. +43 222 408 67 90
Fax +43 222 408 70 86

Useful Addresses

I   The State

1.
UDENRIGSMINISTERIET
(The Royal Danish Ministry of Foreign
Affairs)
Asiatisk Plads 2
DK-1448 Copenhagen K
Tel. (+45) 33 92 00 00
Fax (+45) 31 54 05 33

*The following embassies have a press-
and cultural division:*

USA

ROYAL DANISH EMBASSY
3200 Whitehaven Street
Washington DC. 20008 3683

France

AMBASSADE ROYALE DE
DANEMARK
77 Avenue Marceau
F-75116 Paris

Great Britain

ROYAL DANISH EMBASSY
55 Sloane Street
GB-London SW1X 9SR

Germany

KÖNIGLICH DÄNISCHE
BOTSCHAFT
Pfälzer Strasse 14
D-5300 Bonn 1

*Also belonging under the Ministry of
Foreign Affairs:*

DET DANSKE HUS I PARIS
(Address, see Ambassade Royale de
Danemark)

2.
UNDERVISNINGS- OG
FORSKNINGSMINISTERIET
(The Royal Danish Ministry of Educa-
tion and Research)
Frederiksholms Kanal 21-25
DK-1220 Copenhagen K
Tel. (+45) 33 92 50 00
Fax (+45) 33 92 55 47

DET INTERNATIONALE KONTOR
(International Relations Division)
Frederiksholms Kanal 25 D
DK-1220 Copenhagen K
Tel. (+45) 33 92 52 03

UDVALGET VEDR. DANSKE
LEKTORER I UDLANDET
(The Danish Committee on
Lectureships Abroad)
Frederiksholms Kanal 26
DK-1220 Copenhagen K
Tel. (+45) 33 92 54 03

DET DANSKE STUDENTERHUS
I PARIS
(The Danish Students' house in Paris)
9 Boulevard Jourdan
F-750 14 Paris
Tel. (+33) 45 89 29 47

DET DANSKE INSTITUT I ATHEN
(The Danish Institute in Athens)
 Cavallotti 5
GR-117 42 Athens
Tel. (+30) 01 92 20 789
Fax (+30) 01 92 40 769

3.
KULTURMINISTERIET
(The Royal Danish Ministry of Cultural
Affairs)
Nybrogade 2
DK-1203 Copenhagen K
Tel. (+45) 33 92 33 70

KOMITEEN FOR INTERNATIONALE
KUNSTUDSTILLINGER (KIKU)
(Committee of International Art Exhi-
bitions)
Nybrogade 2
DK-1203 Copenhagen K

DET DANSKE INSTITUT FOR
VIDENSKAB OG KUNST I ROM
(The Danish Institute of Science and
Art in Rome)
Via Omero 18
I-00197 Rome

DANSK-TYSK AKADEMI
(Danish-German Academy)
Horner Landstrasse 85
D-2000 Hamburg 74

STATENS MUSEUMSNÆVN
(Danish Council of Museums)
Nyhavn 31 E
DK-1061 Copenhagen K
Tel. (+45) 33 14 01 21
Fax (+45) 33 14 18 75

STATENS KUNSTFOND
(The Danish State Art Foundation)
SANKT ANNÆ PLADS 10 B
DK-1250 Copenhagen K
Tel. (+45) 33 11 36 01

STATENS MUSIKRÅD
(Danish Music Council)
Vesterbrogade 24, 4.
DK-1620 Copenhagen V
Tel. (+45) 31 24 61 66
Fax (+45) 31 24 22 42

TEATERRÅDET
(The Theatre Council)
Vesterbrogade 24, 4.
DK-1620 Copenhagen V
Tel. (+45) 31 24 73 04
Fax (+45) 31 24 22 42

235

II Counties and Municipalities

Denmark is administratively divided into 14 counties, which are associated in:

AMTSRÅDSFORENINGEN I
DANMARK
(The Association of County Councils in Denmark)
Landemærket 10
DK-1119 Copenhagen K
Tel. (+45) 33 91 21 61

There are 275 municipalities, which are associated in:

KOMMUNERNES LANDSFORENING
(The National Association of Local Authorities in Denmark)
Gyldenløvesgade 11
DK-1600 Copenhagen V
Tel. (+45) 33 12 27 88

VENSKABSBYSEKRETARIATET
(Twinning Secretariat)
Boulevarden 13
DK-9000 Aalborg
Tel. (+45) 98 11 22 11

Apart from these associations there are Copenhagen and Frederiksberg which are both county and municipality.

KØBENHAVNS KOMMUNE
(The Municipality of Copenhagen)
Rådhuset
DK-1599 Copenhagen V
Tel. (+45) 33 66 33 66

FREDERIKSBERG KOMMUNE
(The Municipality of Frederiksberg)
Rådhuset
DK-2000 Frederiksberg
Tel. (+45) 31 19 21 21

III Institutions, Organisations etc.

DET DANSKE KULTURINSTITUT
(The Danish Cultural Institute)
see page 232/233

DANMARKS TURISTRÅD
(The Danish Tourist Board)
Vesterbrogade 6 D
DK-1620 Copenhagen K
Tel. (+45) 33 11 14 15
Fax (+45) 33 93 14 16

The Tourist Board has offices in the following places:

Norway

DANMARKS TURISTKONTOR
Tollbugaten 27
N-0103 Oslo

Sweden

DANSKA TURISTBYRÅN
Riddargatan 7
S-114 85 Stockholm

Germany

DÄNISCHES
FREMDENVERKEHRSAMT
Glockengiesserwall 2
D-2000 Hamburg

The Netherlands

DEENS VERKEERSBUREAU
Schipholweg 96 a
NL-2316 XD Leiden

Great Britain

THE DANISH TOURIST BOARD
Sceptre House
169/173 Regent Street
GB-London W1R 8PY

Finland

DANSKA TURISTBYRÅN
P.O. Box 48
SF-02701 Grankulla

USA

THE DANISH TOURIST BOARD
655 Third Avenue, 18th floor
New York, N.Y. 10017

DANSK KIRKE I UDLANDET
(Danish Church in Foreign Countries)
Nørrevænget 43 B
Postbox 83
5100 Odense C
Tel. (+45) 66 13 95 31

There are Danish churches in the following places:

Argentine:
Buenos Aires
Necochea
Tandil

Australia:
Sydney

Austria:
Vienna

Belgium:
Bruxelles

Canada:
Calgary
Edmonton
Grimsby
Surrey
Toronto
Vancouver

France:
Nice
Paris

Germany:
Berlin
Flensborg
Husum
Rendsburg
Slesvig

Great Britain:
London
Newcastle

Israel:
Jerusalem

Italy:
Rome

237

Luxembourg:
Luxembourg

Norway:
Oslo

Spain:
Fuengirola

Sweden:
Göteborg
Lidingö
Malmö

Switzerland:
Genève
Zürich

DANSK SØMANDSKIRKE I
FREMMEDE HAVNE
(Danish Seamen's Church Abroad)
Frederiksberg allé 10 A
DK-1820 Frederiksberg C
Tel. (+45) 31 21 09 44

DANSK DESIGN CENTER
(Danish Design Centre)
Industriens Hus, Rådhuspladsen
H.C. Andersens Boulevard 18
DK-1553 Copenhagen V
Tel. (+45) 33 14 66 88
Fax (+45) 33 32 00 48

DANSK ARKITEKTURCENTER
(The Danish Centre for Architecture
and Building Exports)
Gammel Dok
Strandgade 27 B
DK-1401 Copenhagen K
Tel. (+45) 31 57 19 30
Fax (+45) 31 54 50 10

DANSK FOLKEOPLYSNINGS
SAMRÅD
(Danish Council for Adult Education)
Rømersgade 7
DK-1362 Copenhagen K
Tel. (+45) 33 15 14 66
Fax (+45) 33 15 09 83

DANMARKS RADIO/TV
(Radio Denmark)
TV-byen
DK-2860 Søborg
Tel. (+45) 31 67 12 33
Fax (+45) 39 66 10 36

TV 2
Rugårdsvej 25
DK-5000 Odense C
Tel. (+45) 65 91 12 44

DANSK LITTERATUR-
INFORMATIONSCENTER
(The Danish Literature Information
Centre)
Amaliegade 38
DK-1256 Copenhagen K
Tel. (+45) 33 32 07 25
Fax (+45) 33 91 15 45

DANSK MUSIK INFORMATIONS
CENTER (MIC)
(Danish Music Information Centre)
Gråbrødre Torv 16
DK-1154 Copenhagen K
Tel. (+45) 33 11 20 66
Fax (+45) 33 32 20 16

DET DANSKE FILMINSTITUT
(The Danish Film Institute)
Store Søndervoldstræde 4
DK-1419 Copenhagen K
Tel. (+45) 31 57 65 00

STATENS FILMCENTRAL
(National Film Board of Denmark)
Vestergade 27
DK-1016 Copenhagen K
Tel. (+45) 33 13 26 8

HØJSKOLERNES SEKRETARIAT
(Folk High School Information Office)
Farvergade 27 G
DK-1463 Copenhagen K
Tel. (+45) 33 13 98 22
Fax (+45) 33 13 98 70

UDVIKLINGSCENTER FOR
FOLKEOPLYSNING
OG VOKSENUNDERVISNING
(Danish Research and Development
Centre for Adult Education)
Tordenskjoldsgade 27
DK-1055 Copenhagen K
Tel. (+45) 33 32 55 33

DANSK IDRÆTS-FORBUND
(Danish Sport Confederation)
Brøndby Stadion 20
DK-2605 Brøndby
Tel. (+45) 42 45 55 55
Fax (+45) 42 45 62 45

DANSK UNGDOMS FÆLLESRÅD
(The Danish Youth Council)
Scherfigsvej 5
DK-2100 Copenhagen Ø
Tel. (+45) 31 29 88 88

DANSK KUNSTNERRÅD
(The Danish Artists Council)
Gl. Strand 48
DK-1202 Copenhagen K
Tel. (+45) 33 32 82 92

DANMARKS BIBLIOTEKSFORENING
(The Danish Library Association)
Trekronergade 15
DK-2500 Valby
Tel. (+45) 36 30 86 82

DET KGL. BIBLIOTEK
(The Royal Library)
Christians Brygge 8
DK-1219 Copenhagen K
Tel. (+45) 33 93 01 11

STATSBIBLIOTEKET I ÅRHUS
(The State and University Library at
Århus)
Universitetsparken
DK-8000 Århus C
Tel. (+45) 86 12 20 22

SOCIALFORSKNINGSINSTITUTTET
(The Danish National Institute of
Social Research)
Borgergade 28
DK-1300 Copenhagen K
Tel. (+45) 33 13 98 11

LANDSSEKRETARIATET FOR DANSK
AMATØRMUSIK
(National Secretariat for Danish
Amateur Music)
Rosenkrantsgade 31
Postboks 235
DK-8100 Århus C
Tel. (+45) 86 19 80 99
Fax (+45) 86 19 24 54

DANSKE FOLKEDANSERE
(Danish Folk Dancers)
Søndertoften 272
DK-2630 Tåstrup
Tel. (+45) 42 99 95 52

239

DANSK AMATØR TEATER
 SAMVIRKE
(Danish Amateur Theatre Association)
Ladegårdskov 14
DK-6300 Gråsten
Tel. (+45) 74 65 11 03

USE IT
YOUTH INFORMATION
COPENHAGEN
Rådhusstræde 13
DK-1466 Copenhagen K
Tel. (+45) 33 15 65 18
Fax (+45) 33 15 75 18

IV   Trade Organisations:

DANSK ARBEJDSGIVERFORENING
(The Danish Employers Confederation)
Vester Voldgade 113
DK-1790 Copenhagen V
Tel. (+45) 33 93 40 00
Fax (+45) 33 12 29 76

LANDBRUGSRÅDET
(The Agricultural Council
of Denmark)
Axelborg, Axeltorv 3
DK-1609 Copenhagen V
Tel. (+45) 33 14 56 72

INDUSTRIRÅDET
(Confederation of Danish Industries)
H.C. Andersens Boulevard 18
DK-1790 Copenhagen V
Tel. (+45) 33 15 22 33
Fax (+45) 33 32 32 81

LANDSORGANISATIONEN I
DANMARK (LO)
(The Danish Confederation of
Trade Unions)
Rosenørns Allé 12
DK-1634 Copenhagen V
Tel. (+45) 31 35 35 41
Fax (+45) 35 37 37 41